Ethics as a Weapon of

What role does ethics play in modern-day warfare? Is it possible for ethics and militarism to exist hand-in-hand? James Eastwood examines the Israeli military and its claim to be 'the most moral army in the world'. This claim has been strongly contested by human rights bodies and international institutions in their analysis of recent military engagements in the West Bank, Gaza, and Lebanon. Yet at the same time, many in Israel believe this claim: including the general public, military personnel, and politicians. Compiled from extensive research including interviews with soldiers, Eastwood unpacks the ethical pedagogy of the Israeli military, as well as soldier-led activism which voices a moral critique, and argues that the belief in moral warfare does not exist separately from the growing violence of Israel's occupation. This book is ideal for those interested in military ethics and Israeli politics, and provides crucial in-depth analysis for students and researchers alike. It examines theories of morality and ethics in war through a comprehensive study of the Israel Defence Forces. It will appeal to researchers and students exploring military ethics and Israeli politics, international relations, as well as those studying war and politics in the wider Middle East.

JAMES EASTWOOD is Lecturer in Politics and International Relations at Queen Mary University of London. He previously taught at SOAS, University of London, where he also completed his PhD, and has previously published in the *European Journal of International Relations*. The PhD thesis on which this book is based was awarded the 2016 Malcolm H Kerr Dissertation Award by the Middle East Studies Association and was jointly awarded the 2016 Michael Nicholson Prize by the British International Studies Association.

Ethics as a Weapon of War

Militarism and Morality in Israel

JAMES EASTWOOD
Queen Mary University of London

CAMBRIDGE
UNIVERSITY PRESS

CAMBRIDGE
UNIVERSITY PRESS

University Printing House, Cambridge CB2 8BS, United Kingdom

One Liberty Plaza, 20th Floor, New York, NY 10006, USA

477 Williamstown Road, Port Melbourne, VIC 3207, Australia

4843/24, 2nd Floor, Ansari Road, Daryaganj, Delhi – 110002, India

79 Anson Road, #06-04/06, Singapore 079906

Cambridge University Press is part of the University of Cambridge.

It furthers the University's mission by disseminating knowledge in the pursuit of
education, learning, and research at the highest international levels of excellence.

www.cambridge.org
Information on this title: www.cambridge.org/9781108415231
DOI: 10.1017/9781108231671

© James Eastwood 2017

First published 2017

Printed in the United Kingdom by Clays, St Ives plc

A catalogue record for this publication is available from the British Library.

Library of Congress Cataloging-in-Publication Data
Names: Eastwood, James, 1988– author.
Title: Ethics as a weapon of war: militarism and morality in Israel / James
    Eastwood, Queen Mary University of London.
Description: Cambridge; New York: Cambridge University Press, 2017 | Includes
    bibliographical references and index.
Identifiers: LCCN 2017035934 | ISBN 9781108415231 (hardback)
Subjects: LCSH: Military ethics. | Military ethics—Israel. | War—Moral and
    ethical aspects—Israel. | Israel. Tseva haganah le-Yiśráel—Rules and practice.
Classification: LCC U22 .E22 2018 | DDC 172/.42—DC23 LC record available at
    https://lccn.loc.gov/2017035934

ISBN 978-1-108-41523-1 Hardback

Contents

Figures

Tables

Acknowledgements

I knew that I had incurred many debts of gratitude while researching and writing this book, although I had not appreciated quite how many until I came to recount them here.

My first thanks must go to those friends who initially got me interested in Israel/Palestine, without whom I might never have had the idea to start this research – Ben Jacobs, Zach Eilon, and Rachel Cohen. I also thank Glen Rangwala for supervising the Masters dissertation which would eventually develop into the PhD which produced this book.

This research was funded by a three-year doctoral research scholarship from the Economic and Social Research Council and I am immensely grateful for this support.

My Hebrew would never have developed without the help of several amazing teachers, especially Daphna Witztum, Rachel Williams, Mazal Cohen, and above all Tamar Drukker, who also did a great deal to help shape and improve my research.

I am extremely grateful to all those colleagues and students at SOAS and Queen Mary who have given me support, participated in intellectual exchanges, and shown solidarity in struggle over the last few years. I would especially like to thank Meera Sabaratnam, Felix Berenskoetter, Matt Nelson, and Mark Laffey for their support, feedback, and advice. I also thank all those fellow PhD students from the department of politics at SOAS who participated in workshops and discussions, and particularly those who read and commented on a draft of one of my chapters. I am further grateful to participants in the SOAS Centre for Palestine Studies research seminar series for their presentations and for their questions and comments about my work.

While on fieldwork I was lucky enough to have the help and support of the wonderful staff at the Kenyon Institute in Jerusalem. My thanks go to Maida Smeir, Sami Salah, Hussein Ghaith (Abu Hani), Josephine Abu Sa'da, and especially to its endlessly good-humoured and indefatigable director, Mandy Turner. I was also fortunate to find friendship and intellectual companionship among other 'inmates' during my stay there, especially Oscar Jarzmik, George Cregan, Avi Raz, Yoni Furas, Una McGahern, Toufic Haddad, Francesca Burke, as well as Julie Trottier and her daughter Talia-Aïsha. Many pleasant hours were also spent practising Hebrew and discussing my research in the company of Ora Ardon. I thank all of these friends for making my fieldwork more enjoyable and its difficulties more bearable.

I was assisted in my fieldwork by Eitan Diamond and I received helpful advice from Edna Lomksy-Feder at the Hebrew University and Michal Givoni at Ben Gurion University. I am grateful to all those who granted interviews but especially to the activists of Breaking the Silence, who did a huge amount to facilitate my research and tolerated my presence and questions with the utmost patience. I am particularly indebted to Nadav Weiman for sharing his excellent photograph, which he generously allowed me to reproduce in this book.

A number of friends and colleagues read drafts and in other ways contributed to the development of this research. In particular, I would like to thank Hagar Kotef, Craig Jones, Leila Stockmarr, Chris Rossdale, Tarak Barkawi, Louiza Odysseos, Carl Death, Helle Malmvig, Sharri Plonski, Efrat Even-Tzur and Alasdair Churchard. The friendship, feedback, and support of Nivi Manchanda were constant features of the research process.

I would like to thank my thesis examiners, Nimer Sultany and Patricia Owens, for their extremely thoughtful comments and advice on how to prepare the manuscript for publication. I am also very grateful to the prize committees of the British International Studies Association and the Middle East Studies Association for generously recognising my thesis with awards.

I have had the privilege of working with three incredible supervisors during my studies – Laleh Khalili, Yair Wallach, and Charles Tripp. As second supervisor, Yair continuously challenged me to improve and refine my work, providing a sympathetic but critical ear which proved especially useful in the closing stages of the write-up. His detailed and thoughtful comments did much to enhance this book. Above all, Laleh has been an inexhaustible source of enthusiasm, energy, and wisdom since I first proposed this research to her. I thank her for placing trust in me, for the inspirational example she sets to young scholars, and for the innumerable improvements she has made to this project through her continuous curiosity and questions. Her hard work and support made this thesis possible, and her contributions have truly transformed it.

All these contributions notwithstanding, any errors that remain are mine alone.

I thank my parents, Haidee and Ken, and my whole family for their support during this research. Tessa Buchanan has offered companionship, support, confidence, and intellectual engagement ever since I began this project and must take enormous credit for helping me bring it to its conclusion. I thank and love her with all my heart.

This book is dedicated to the memory of my grandfather, Eric John Woods, who passed away while I was writing it. He did and gave so much to make me able to do this.

Introduction: 'The Most Moral Army in the World'

> Briefly, my aim is to examine the case of a society which has been loudly castigating itself for its hypocrisy [. . .], which speaks verbosely of its own silence, takes great pains to relate in detail the things it does not say, denounces the powers it exercises, and promises to liberate itself from the very laws that have made it function.
>
> (Michel Foucault, *The History of Sexuality, Volume 1*)

In late 2014, a story appeared in an Israeli newspaper about the recently appointed commander of the officer training school of the Israel Defence Forces (IDF), General Avi Gil (Yehoshua, 2014). The article reported that, as part of his changes to the curriculum, Gil had decided to teach IDF officer cadets about the work of the organisation 'Breaking the Silence' [*Shovrim Shtika*].[1] Breaking the Silence is a well-known Israeli NGO staffed by IDF veterans, and its work is very controversial in Israeli society. It gathers testimonies from soldiers who served in the Occupied Palestinian Territory and, using these testimonies, campaigns for the end of the occupation of the West Bank and Gaza on the grounds that it is immoral. Gil had asked the cadets to read some of these testimonies as part of their preparation for officer roles. He was immediately attacked by right-wing groups for his decision. For Breaking the Silence, however, this was a media coup. In an opinion piece responding to this development, its executive director, Yuli Novak, was quick to draw parallels between the values of an IDF officer and the values of the organisation:

This week the commander of Bahad 1[2] reminded me of ten years ago, of the days when I myself commanded cadets in an officers' course. As staff at the

---

[1] A note on transliteration: throughout this book I have adopted the style of the *International Journal of Middle East Studies* when transliterating Modern Hebrew, with the exception of some proper names in wide circulation.

[2] 'Bahad 1' is the Hebrew acronym for *bsis hadrakha 1*, the IDF officer training school.

officers' school, we saw our mission as to educate the cadets in profession-alism and values. First and foremost on the list of the values I taught stood truth. We talked about 'speaking the truth', 'reporting the truth', 'taking responsibility'. At the school there was a zero tolerance policy on harming this value. A cadet who lied – he wouldn't be an officer. A cadet who hid something – he wouldn't be an officer. Like then, so today I believe that it is preferable to strive for the truth than to attempt to deny it. (Novak, 2014a; my translation)

She further revealed her aspirations for the curriculum change:

The commander of Bahad 1 decided this week, knowingly or not, to open a small window to the cadets into the reality of the occupation. If he per-severes with this, and is not subdued by the calls for silence from the right, I wait to see the results with bated breath. Perhaps from this exposure an understanding will arise among the young commanders that there is no moral or enlightened way to rule over another nation. Perhaps after under-standing that, they will themselves demand – as soldiers and officers – to go back and carry out the mission for which they enlisted to the IDF: to defend the state, not to occupy and oppress.

   This small episode presents a condensed example of the web of interactions that I want to explore in this book. It poses two ques-tions: firstly, why did the commander of the IDF officer school think that it would be pedagogically useful to expose his cadets to testimo-nies designed to demonstrate the immorality of the occupation they were about to help enforce? Secondly, why did the executive director of Breaking the Silence believe that this development represented a promising political opening? What I will show in this book is that these two questions are in fact two sides of the same question: how is ethics implicated in the production of militarism in Israel?
   As the remarks cited above make plain, in Israel there exists a strange continuity between a military ethical pedagogy of speaking the truth, and an activist ethics of testimony. The contention of this book is that this connection tells us something important about the changing nature of Israeli militarism, both its hold on the soldiers who serve in the IDF and its resilience against strategies of public cri-tique. Ethics has acquired a peculiar importance in the workings of Israeli militarism, one which casts doubt on the efficacy of political challenges which seek to mobilise a purely moral critique of Israel's

military engagements. Rather than providing a means for the restraint of military violence, ethics has become part of an arrangement which makes violence easier for the military to commit. By taking a detailed look at the ethical activities associated with war and the military in Israel, this book will show the conditions which make this possible.

Moreover, though, this book also contends that the Israeli case has significant implications for how we should think about the relationship between ethics and war more generally. For the present moment is one in which the role of ethical activity in contemporary warfare is expanding and changing dramatically, and in which military ethics is staking increasingly profound claims on political legitimacy. In this environment, politicians describe their latest military adventures in moral language, and soldiering is presented to the public and to recruits as the acme of moral commitment. The study of military ethics, especially the body of doctrines known as 'Just War Theory', continues to entrench its role in the academy. Yet it has also been increasingly institutionalised in programmes of military training, and thereby worked carefully into the processes by which soldiers are socialised to fight. Correspondingly, resistance to contemporary wars has also increasingly drawn on ethical practices and discourses of morality. Anti-war movements and human rights organisations often appeal to moral standards as a means of generating public opposition, seeking to constrain militaries and the state through moral scrutiny. Ethics has therefore become an increasingly important terrain on which war and military activity is understood, legitimated, and contested.

Based on a study of the Israeli case, a central claim of this book is that this particular turn to ethics has become useful for practitioners of military violence and corrosive of the critical and political capacity to engage with and resist that violence. Furthermore, the book argues that this is made possible by the strength and sophistication of *militarism*, an ideological force which is capable of mobilising ethical effort in the pursuit of military violence. What this study reveals is that ethics can in fact offer powerful support to militarism at a number of levels. Indeed, under certain conditions, ethics can function as a weapon of war. In the specific context explored in this book, ethics has become a facet of the ongoing colonial dispossession of Palestine through Israeli military violence. It is of course important to be clear that this is not an intrinsic tendency of ethics. Rather, it is a consequence of the specific way in which ethics has been deployed in the service of Israeli militarism. The purpose of this book, then, is to capture this specificity with a view to revealing the limits and possibilities of ethics for constraining the violence of war.

The Moral Army Mythology

Why study Israel as means of addressing these issues? In the first instance, Israel has had no small role to play in military activity in the contemporary era. It has been a major and frequent participant in wars in the Middle East region since its creation. Furthermore, its role as a leading practitioner of counterinsurgency warfare, and as a node in the global circulation of arms, military technology, and security practice more generally, recommends it as an important and influential case (Gordon, 2010; Graham, 2010a: 226–62, 2010b; Khalili, 2010, 2013: esp. 44–64; Weizman, 2012; Halper, 2015). The centrality of the Zionist colonisation of Palestine in the broader context of our 'colonial present' should also underscore the significance of studying war and the military in Israel (Gregory, 2004: 76–143; Collins, 2012). Yet there is another much more precise reason to focus on Israel, and that is the particular prominence of ethics and morality in debates about war in Israel/Palestine and in Israel's self-perception as a military power.

The Israeli military often describes itself as 'the most moral army in the world'. Indeed, this was a phrase that I encountered many times during the research for this book. There are typically two instinctive and opposed kinds of reaction to this claim: the first affirms its truth; the second rejects it out of hand as a propaganda claim. Unsurprisingly, neither of these views quite capture the significance of this belief. Without question, it has been a useful and cynical, if unsubtle, claim to make in apologist Israeli public relations, or *hasbara*. Yet at the same time a great many Israelis genuinely believe in, or at least aspire to embody, this claim. We will meet many of them in the pages to come. This does not just include the general public. It includes military personnel, philosophers, educators, and even some anti-occupation activists. When placed alongside the colossal violence exercised by the IDF, this is a significant puzzle. It suggests an extremely strong ideological system which must surely have a powerful impact on Israeli militarism. Reflecting on this claim, what this book aims to explore is not whether in practice the IDF is a moral army, but rather why and how it became important to make this claim, and what the consequences of this have been.

The moral army mythology is far from new. It is arguably older than the IDF itself. Its origins are often traced to the pre-state doctrine of 'self-restraint' [*havlagah*] in defending Zionist settlements in Palestine. Yet the moral army mythology is also bound up with a wider belief in Zionism as the bearer of a moral mission and in Israel as a moral exemplar, a 'light unto the nations'. Following the Holocaust, and especially following the Eichmann trial, the memory of the near elimination of European Jews has been used to buttress Zionist claims to the moral high ground, and to frame those who threaten Zionism as potential perpetrators of genocide (Zertal, 2005; Perugini and Gordon, 2015: 30–7). This became an especially powerful idea during the Arab–Israeli wars of 1967 and 1973, where (despite its overwhelming military superiority, nuclear weapons, and superpower backing) Israel was portrayed as under existential threat. More recently, as the danger from conventional Arab armies has receded, this discourse has shifted its attention to the spectre of a nuclear-armed Iran and the rocket arsenals of its regional proxy, Hezbollah. Meanwhile, other enemies, including the Palestinian Liberation Organisation and more recently Hamas, have been identified as 'terrorists' and branded as irreconcilably evil and genocidal, sanctioning violence against them which is portrayed as purely defensive in nature. Israel continues to claim moral superiority against its rivals in this way.

Another long-standing feature of the claim to a moral army has been the construction of a specific mythology surrounding the morality of Israeli soldiers themselves. One of its founding narratives is the story of the *Lamed He*, the thirty-five soldiers killed in an ambush in the 1948 war because, according to the legend, they showed mercy on an elderly shepherd who then reported them to the local Arab militia (Ha'aretz, 2009). The IDF's much-vaunted value of 'purity of arms' is often traced back to episodes such as these. Testimonies from soldiers themselves have also had a crucial role to play in generating the mythology. One such classic text is *Siah Lohamim* ('Soldiers' Talk'), an anthology of recorded conversations, letters, and articles from soldiers who fought in the Six Day War of 1967 (Shapira, 1968; translated as, Near, 1970). The book acquired iconic status in Israeli society, giving the moral voice of the soldier a central place in the cultural reception of the war. The participants are recorded giving their thoughts about the war, with a special emphasis placed on their reservations and moral difficulties. They openly discuss their feelings towards Arabs, the morality of warfare (including 'purity of arms'), and their joy at the Israeli conquest of Jerusalem. Indeed, as scholars have noted, the final text was carefully edited by Amos Oz and Avraham Shapira to accentuate the impression of the moral conscience of the soldiers and to leave out more unsavoury stories from the original transcripts (Piterberg, 2007: 232–8). What emerged most clearly from *Siaḥ Loḥamim*, and other texts like it, was a seemingly authentic soldier's voice, speaking in conversational Hebrew and employing soldiers' slang, with apparently strong values and a moral sensibility.

This long historical genealogy of the moral army mythology notwithstanding, claims regarding the morality of the Israeli military have reached a new level in recent years. As later chapters will demonstrate in detail, the IDF now actively pursues the consolidation of the moral army mythology. This is evident most clearly in the drafting of its much-vaunted ethical code, 'The Spirit of the IDF', in the 1990s, and also in the growth since then of pedagogical initiatives designed to encourage soldiers to discuss ethical issues. Israeli politicians, spokespersons, and senior military officials have also often sought to publicly defend Israeli military actions on the basis of the moral army mythology.[3] Meanwhile, these claims have also become newly contested internationally, provoking major and repeated controversies. A key turning point in this respect was the 1982 Lebanon War, a self-proclaimed 'war of choice' launched by Prime Minister Menachem Begin and his Defence Minister Ariel Sharon. The massacre of Palestinian refugees in the Sabra and Shatila camps in Beirut, perpetrated with the full complicity of Israeli forces, became a focal point for this new wave of criticism. It marked a shift in Palestinian practices of memory-making in favour of discourses of martyrdom emphasising violence at the hands of Israel, which chimed with a growing emphasis on suffering

---

[3] For example, in a speech to the UN General Assembly after Israel's assault on Gaza in summer 2014, Prime Minister Benjamin Netanyahu said: 'No other country and no other army in history have gone to greater lengths to avoid casualties among the civilian population of their enemies [. . .] Israel's citizen army – the brave soldiers of the IDF, our young boys and girls – they upheld the highest moral values of any army in the world. Israel's soldiers deserve not condemnation, but admiration. Admiration from decent people everywhere.' (Israeli Ministry of Foreign Affairs, 2014).

and trauma in international humanitarian discourses (Khalili, 2007: esp. 33–8). This was further amplified during the First Intifada, which again succeeded in attracting international sympathy for the Palestinian cause and condemnations of Israeli violence through media portrayals of confrontations between unarmed protestors and the Israeli military. More recently, moral condemnations of Israel have been repeatedly prompted by human rights reportage into Israeli actions in the Occupied Palestinian Territory, and especially Gaza, which has been pursued by the UN and international NGOs (Fassin, 2011: 200–22; Perugini and Gordon, 2015: 38–40). This has also increased pressure on the IDF and the Israeli State to respond to these accusations by doubling down on their moral army rhetoric.

Yet it would be a mistake to portray the new ethical initiatives of the IDF purely as cynical and reactive response to this growing vein of international criticism. There is a more complicated set of factors of work which also originate from social and political changes within Israel. The nature of domestic debates over the moral army mythology within Israel helps to underscore this. One of the most interesting and significant forms that these debates have taken is the expression of dissent through soldiers' testimony. Again the First Lebanon War was a key turning point, in that it propelled soldiers' testimony in new, more political directions. A group of soldiers returning on leave from their first deployment in the war established a protest group called 'Soldiers against Silence' [*Ḥaiyalim neged Shtiḳa*] and used their testimonies to contradict the claims of the political establishment about the war and the treatment of Lebanese and Palestinian civilians by Israeli forces (Levy, 2012: 52–4). This trend continued during the First Intifada, including a range of literature and poetry composed by soldiers (see Mendelsohn-Maoz, 2011) and a notable anthology of soldiers' testimonies gathered by Ilana Hammerman and Roli Rosen detailing the widespread abuses of the period (2002). Since the Second Intifada, this production of soldiers' testimony has reached new heights. A 'new wave' of Israeli cinema (Morag, 2013), including most prominently the Oscar-nominated *Waltz with Bashir*, has focused on the experience of soldiers in coming to terms with the moral implications of their military activities, with the participants ranging from the lowest ranks (such as *Lebanon*) to leaders of the General Security Services (*The Gatekeepers*). More significantly still, the organisation Breaking the Silence has achieved notoriety for its dissemination of soldiers' testimonies.

There has been a vitriolic response from the Right to these expressions of protest. Right-wing groups and senior politicians, including cabinet ministers, have attacked Breaking the Silence as 'traitors' and as contributors to the de-legitimisation of Israel. Indeed, in late 2015 government ministers announced their intention to ban the organisation from both the army and the education system. Yet, beneath the political fanfare, it is also important to ask how much of a threat such activities really pose to the military and to the state. For these expressions of dissent through soldiers' testimony also display a fundamental ambiguity. This is because the moral army mythology is often buttressed as much through soldiers' demonstrations of moral anguish as through assertions of moral clarity. Indeed, this has long been recognised: in 1948, Prime Minister David Ben-Gurion famously distributed Natan Alterman's poem *Al Zot* ('About that') to all IDF units precisely *because* it detailed the violence of a massacre in Lydda (Morris, 2004: 489). His aim was to give the impression that the military took such episodes seriously. Indeed, the phenomenon of soldierly displays of contrition has become sufficiently widespread in Israel to acquire a (usually pejorative) label, *yorim ṿebokhim* ('shooting and crying'). Expressions of moral ambiguity can therefore also work to enlist such ostensibly critical and oppositional voices in support of the moral army mythology. Soldiers' own (sometimes fierce) attacks on the military and political establishment are often presented merely as further evidence of the existence of an Israeli military conscience. Indeed, for this reason, the production of soldiers' testimony has not simply originated from critical groups in Israeli civil society. As I will show in this book, it has also arisen, and has indeed been encouraged, within the Israeli military itself, often in the framework of military ethical pedagogy. This has made soldiers' testimony an effective vehicle for disciplining as well as expressing political dissent in Israel – and for this reason the importance of such practices of soldiers' testimony is a major theme of this book.

All this should serve to underscore that the moral army mythology is not simply an exercise in whitewashing. Instead, these ethical activities are sophisticated ideological practices which depend as much on ambiguity and moral qualms as they do on justification and exculpation. What they suggest is that the deployment of moral critiques, including through soldiers' testimony, is far less threatening to the military than the right-wing reaction to this phenomenon would suggest.

Indeed, a closer examination will show that this sort of practice has in recent years become extremely useful for the IDF. Explaining this fully requires us to put these activities in the sociological context of Israeli militarism and, more precisely, to understand them as a *part* of Israeli militarism, rather than merely as a reaction against it.

The Ethics of Israeli Militarism: Key Arguments

Israel has long been studied as an example of a militarist society.[4] A wide array of features point in this direction: the conscription and reserves system;[5] the high cultural value attached to the military and military service; the large number of former military commanders with careers in politics; the common resort to force in foreign policy; the prominence of the arms and homeland security industries; and the involvement of the military in a large number of activities normally considered beyond its institutional purview, including education for high-school diplomas, Jewish conversion courses, agricultural settlement, immigration and absorption programmes, youth and charity work, theatre and music, cultural programmes for soldiers, and so on.

Yet, for the avoidance of confusion, it is important to be precise about the term 'militarism'. It is not reducible to the prevalence of war, or particular features of the military in society. Rather, militarism describes a particular interaction between military activity and social relations (Shaw, 1991, 2013). In the words of one prominent scholar of the Israeli case, '[m]ilitarism comes into being only when the use of military force acquires legitimation, is perceived as a positive value and high principle that is right and desirable, and is routinised and institutionalised in society' (Ben-Eliezer, 1998: 7; cf. Mann, 1987). However, it is also important to note that militarism, as Alfred Vagts originally observed, is not reducible to an enthusiastic 'love of war'

---

[4] This literature is large and diverse but important introductions and overviews can be found in: Kimmerling (1993, 2005), Ben-Eliezer (1998), Ben-Ari and Lomsky-Feder (1999), Peri (1996b), Maman et al. (2001), Levy (2007), Barak and Sheffer (2010), and David (2013).

[5] Under this system, the majority of Jewish Israeli citizens aged eighteen are drafted for a period of military service. Men serve for three years and women for two years. Exemptions are normally only granted on religious or medical grounds. Furthermore, combat troops are eligible to be called up for reserve duty until the age of forty.

(1959: 17). This means that militarism can often be a highly ambiguous and even involuntary process. It implies the state of being in thrall to war, of being influenced by, dependent upon, and caught up in military ways. More recent sociological approaches to militarism allow us to clarify this insight by showing how war can become bound up with a wider set of social practices and structures (Stavrianakis and Selby, 2013). This includes an array of phenomena not normally understood as artefacts of war-making, such as popular culture, gender relations, or the labour market, which tie people's everyday activities, understandings, and identities to the pursuit of war and military activity. In this way, we can think of militarism as an *ideological* force, in the sense of a set of material and discursive practices which are 'embedded in everyday life' (Ben-Eliezer, 1998: 8; cf. Althusser, 1971) and which serve to make war seem desirable and normal.

Although Israel has long been a militarist society in this way, and for a wide variety of reasons, in this book I will highlight several important social and political shifts which have created a crucial role for ethics in this arrangement. In other words, I will show that ethics has become a crucial part of the way in which war-fighting and war-preparation are made to seem normal and desirable in Israel. Ethics has thereby become integral to the way in which Israeli militarism has developed, transformed, and retrenched itself. There are five different but related dimensions to this claim which are explored throughout the book:

First, ethics has become an important part of a project to make the military more attractive to recruits and to produce more motivated soldiers. In this sense, ethics has become an important part of a new mode of what might be termed 'militarist governmentality'. Military participation is increasingly framed as an opportunity, indeed a privileged and unrivalled one, for soldiers' individual self-betterment and moral improvement. Likewise, the IDF is increasingly interested in more than simply the technical capacity of soldiers to perform well on the battlefield. It promotes a regime of governmentality aimed at the formation of soldiers as ethical subjects who monitor and strive to enhance their conduct and who believe strongly in the righteousness of the army for which they fight. Ethical capacity has been added to physical fitness and battle-readiness as a feature of all-round military preparedness.

This first aspect is intimately related to the ways in which the IDF has reorganised itself in response to changing social realities, not least the growth of neoliberalism and the changing models of organisational culture and individual motivation it brings (cf. Cowen, 2008: 198–229). Since the 1990s, a new model of encouraging military mobilisation has gradually been adopted. The IDF has begun to complement conscription and the reserves system with professionalisation and competition in the labour market as means of recruitment (Cohen, 1995, 2008: 54–106; Ben-Eliezer, 2004; Levy, 2007: 147–79). While this transition remains incomplete and has occasionally been reversed, its effects have still been significant. There is a growing tendency to incentivise, rather than oblige, military participation from the population (Levy et al., 2007). Ethics has played an important role in this process. It has been used to forge professional and corporate identity in the IDF and has been central in various attempts to encourage soldiers to couple individual projects of self-cultivation with military participation, such as pre-army preparatory programmes or educational courses for soldiers. This has fostered a kind of militarism in which conduct during military service becomes a barometer of good character; it speaks a truth about the soldier as a subject.

Second, ethics has become crucial to the ideological legitimation of military violence in Israel. This role is not as straightforward as propaganda or whitewashing, and neither is it aimed at the legitimation of specific military acts or categories of acts. Rather, it is to generate a pervasive ideology of ethical soldiering that inculcates a belief in the IDF as a moral army with strong values. Significantly, this frequently includes rather than precludes engagement with the moral difficulties and dilemmas that soldiers face during military service. However, it is important to be clear that this emphasis on military ethics is not aimed at a reduction in the level of violence used against Palestinians. Rather, it is tailored to produce IDF soldiers imbued with a sense of their moral mission. Indeed, military ethics is used to promote this ideological belief *alongside* the enormous violence wielded by the IDF precisely in order to maintain soldiers' motivation to participate in it.

This second function of ethics is closely related to recent attempts to prevent declining combat motivation in the Israeli military as a result of the changing nature of operations (Catignani, 2009: 17–27) and wider societal trends. Yagil Levy has argued that growing casualty and bereavement aversion in Israeli society has produced a 'death hierarchy', in which exposure to military risk is stratified by social class and ethnicity (2012: 71–108). At the bottom of this hierarchy stand

Palestinians, who are increasingly viewed as expendable in military operations for the sake of preserving the lives of those further up the hierarchy (2012: 147–80). In addition, the difficulties entailed in contentious military tasks such as occupying and policing Palestinian civilian centres have encouraged Israel to carefully manage the exposure of its soldiers to risk and to the tasks of maintaining occupation (cf. Mann, 1987; Shaw, 2002). The IDF has been particularly concerned to avoid high profile cases of conscientious objection as a result of such operations. Strategies for reducing Israeli soldiers' exposure have included the use of proxies such as Palestinian security forces (Gordon, 2008: 169–96); innovations in the architecture and management of checkpoints, barriers, and curfews (Hanieh, 2006; Weizman, 2007: 139–60; Ophir et al., 2009; Khalili, 2013: 183–96); and the use of increasingly remote and deadly forms of military violence, such as airstrikes and drones (Weizman, 2007: 237–59; see also Ron, 2003: 113–88). Alongside these efforts, there has been a need for an accompanying ethics which can provide moral legitimacy for the increased violence required by many of these arrangements, as well as uphold a sense of moral legitimacy in situations where military contact with civilian populations remains unavoidable.

Third, and related to this, ethics has proven particularly useful in Israel's pursuit of counterinsurgency warfare. The recent intensification of Israeli counterinsurgency (Catignani, 2009; Khalili, 2010, 2013) has made the ethical demeanour of individual soldiers an important site of intervention for the IDF. This mode of warfare, in which the aim is not to defeat the enemy in a pitched battle but to intervene violently in the surrounding society to isolate and deprive it of support, often necessitates prolonged periods of contact between the occupying force and the occupied civilian population. Anthropological understandings of 'culture', 'happiness', and 'human terrain' have become important discourses in mediating this encounter (Gonzáles, 2007; Gregory, 2008; Zehfuss, 2012b; Khalili, 2014). Counterinsurgency also relies on a relatively decentralised structure of decision-making in which individual officers and even soldiers are required to make choices with potentially significant tactical, strategic, and moral implications. All of these requirements make counterinsurgency a demanding and often frustrating task for troops, not least in the Israeli case (Ben-Ari, 1999; Grassiani, 2013).

Ethics has helped to calibrate the more flexible and variegated deployment of force required in such warfare. Importantly, this role should not be equated simply with the restraint of violence. Counterinsurgency can be just as violent as conventional warfare, often more so in a settler–colonial context such as Israel/Palestine. Rather, the role of ethics is to help manage violence at the individual level that counterinsurgency demands (Coker, 2008: 134–8). This might mean restraint in one moment, but could just as easily mean a sudden and massive deployment of force in the next. Likewise, it might mean the use of force by one infantry unit, and the simultaneous exercise of restraint by another. It is this necessity for flexible switching and discretion at a low level which ethics, through its focus on individual conduct, is able to facilitate, thereby helping to regulate the violent encounter between occupier and occupied in counterinsurgency.

Fourth, ethics has come to play an important role in the continuing consolidation of militarist identities. The production of ethical soldiers with a strong sense of moral purpose has come to complement and reinforce other processes of militarist identification. Most significantly, the ethical soldier is a highly gendered subject, acquiring a heightened sense of his masculinity through the ethical exercise of self-control (cf. Sasson-Levy, 2008). Ethical training modifies Israeli military masculinities. It involves the incorporation of dispositions and sensibilities, such as 'empathy' and 'sensitivity', which are (problematically) coded as 'feminine' and produced through interactions, real and imagined, with women. This gendered dimension to ethics is all the more acute in the pursuit of counterinsurgency, which prompts many of these shifts in military masculinities and modifies the role of women (cf. Enloe, 1993: 10–38, 2000: 235–87; Duncanson, 2009; Khalili, 2011). These transformations in military masculinities notwithstanding, the privileged form of subjectivity at the heart of the ethics of Israeli militarism remains a masculinised one, even if the participation of women is often central to its production.[6]

Ethical activity has also become crucial for the continued construction of notions of ethno-national belonging and citizenship through militarism (cf. Helman, 1997). In recent years, the social basis of IDF manpower has changed significantly. A greater number of troops from

---

[6] This bias was unfortunately also reflected in the research for this book, in which the vast majority of my respondents were men. As a result, although I have remained attentive to the gendered dynamics of this discourse, I have been unable to properly examine the implications of these findings for women's militarism. In conscious recognition of this, I have adopted masculine pronouns throughout when referring to the ethical subject of Israeli militarism.

the socio-economic 'periphery', such as Mizrahim, Ethiopian Jews, and Russians, have been recruited (Sasson-Levy, 2003a; Levy, 2007: 117–25, 229–36; Sasson-Levy and Levy, 2008), and large numbers of national-religious soldiers are also joining the ranks (Cohen, 1997, 2013; Levy, 2014; Rosman-Stollman, 2014). These developments, especially the entry of religious soldiers, have required significant changes in military structures and procedures, such as new educational institutions, new units, and an enhanced role for the military rabbinate. This growing diversity has also presented a number of challenges to the maintenance of unified ethno-national militarist identities. In response, various ethical activities and discourses have helped to reconstruct these by attempting to forge connections between private moral communities and a national military collective. In addition, ethical discourses have also consolidated the hierarchies which maintain the national moral standing of dominant groups, especially secular Ashkenazim, through the displacement of racialised stigma on to the moral transgressions of 'peripheral' groups, such as Mizrahim or Ethiopians.

Fifth, and finally, ethics has played an important role in disciplining political contestation against Israel's military engagements. Recent years have witnessed a growth in the moral criticism of the conduct of the IDF from various Israel civil society groups and international organisations (Levy, 2007: 128–45; Marteu, 2009). Although it is important not to overstate the extent of the sympathy for such criticisms within Israeli society – confined as they often are to the political margins or to a particular social milieu – their media prominence and international reach have amplified their significance. As suggested above, though, such discourses need not pose a threat to militarism if they can be mediated and de-politicised through an ethical response. Indeed, their effective anticipation in this way might even serve to selectively recruit them in service of the moral army mythology. As such, I interpret the function of much of the ethical and pedagogical activity associated with the IDF as an effective strategy for the pre-emption and appropriation of such discourses. Furthermore, I also challenge the idea that the mobilisation of moral criticism is always a politically productive means for countering militarism.

Together, these five threads make up the central argument of the book concerning the relationship between ethics and militarism in Israel. Although distinct from each other, it is also easy to see that in many ways they are mutually reinforcing. Both the shift to neo-liberal strategies of military organisation and the intensification of counterinsurgency emphasise the centrality of the individual ethical soldier. Counterinsurgency produces peculiar ethical challenges in maintaining ideological combat motivation, as well as new forms of ethical military masculinity. The ideological legitimation of violence through ethics is clearly linked to the disciplining of political dissent. However, these mutual reinforcements should not give a misleading picture of harmony in Israeli militarism. The growing social diversity of the IDF has undermined the basis for a unitary moral discourse about the nation and its wars. The entry of national-religious soldiers into the IDF has posed a number of challenges to secular militarist discourses, not least concerning the role of women in the military. Counterinsurgency and occupation-at-a-distance have generated new forms of violence which require new forms of legitimation. The mythology of a moral army has been publicly attacked and undermined, even as these discourses of critique are reappropriated. Other scholars have also observed these trends, suggesting that Israeli militarism faces a 'gap of legitimacy' from its narrowing societal base (Levy, 2009), growing tensions between secular and religious troops (Cohen, 2013; Levy, 2014), and 'confusion' between military professionalisation and the model of a 'nation-in-arms' (Cohen, 2008; Libel, 2013).

In this regard, one further point to make is that ethics has been a crucial means through which many of these tensions and contradictions in Israeli militarism have been negotiated and managed. The flexibility and ambiguity inherent in the ethics of Israeli militarism has allowed it to adapt to various needs and circumstances. Ethics has provided a framework in which resistance and challenges to militarism can emerge but then be contained. This is therefore an ideological system which possesses a much higher tolerance for moral and motivational ambiguity than appears at first glance. Indeed, we should not automatically interpret increased opposition to occupation or particular military operations, growing uncertainty about their morality, or clashes between religious and secular discourses, as necessarily indicating a weakness in militarism. In fact, ethics has been crucial in negotiating these ambiguities and converting them into a source of strength.

Chapter Outline

It remains to outline the contents of the six chapters which follow. In the first chapter I give background to the argument made in rest of the

book by explaining theoretically how it is possible for ethics to promote militarism. I start by discussing the ways in which the recent 'ethical turn' has been militarised and put to use by militaries in support of
violence. Drawing on the anthropology of ethics, feminist theories of
International Relations, Foucauldian theories of governmentality, and
the psychoanalytic critique of ideology, I then give a detailed account
of how ethics can come to perform this militarist function. Although
it is designed to be as accessible as possible to the general reader, this
chapter will be of particular interest to scholars of international political sociology and international political theory. Other readers principally interested in the empirical argument as it applies to Israel may
prefer to skip or skim this section.

In the second chapter, I move on to examine the doctrinal and philosophical architecture underpinning Israeli military ethics. The analysis
centres on the production of the IDF ethical code ('The Spirit of the
IDF') in the 1990s and early 2000s. The chapter shows that the ethical
code was never intended to act as a meaningful restraint on Israeli
military violence. Rather, I argue that IDF ethical doctrine is primarily
designed to supplement militarism with a neoliberal emphasis on the
cultivation of the soldier as a free individual and ethical subject. I chart
a shift from a discourse of 'professionalisation' in the first version of
the document to an approach in the subsequent version which made
a greater attempt to shape soldiers' moral character and Jewish-Israeli
identity. I then show that this context is crucial for understanding the
implications of philosophical debates in Israel about the recent successive assaults on the Gaza Strip.

The third chapter moves on to discuss ethical pedagogy in the IDF.
It analyses the ways in which Israeli officers and soldiers are encouraged to relate to the values expressed in the ethical code. I examine
the pedagogical approach in ethics classes and courses arranged for
senior IDF officers, as well as the use of more innovative techniques
such as theatre-based education with regular soldiers. Throughout
the chapter I stress that ethical education in the IDF is primarily concerned with shaping soldiers as ethical subjects, particularly through
ascetic practices of self-examination and above all through testimony
solicited from soldiers themselves about their military experiences.
I also show the crucial role of military ethics in the ideological legitimation of violence, and particularly counterinsurgency warfare, through
the emphasis it places on preserving soldiers' human image. It is this,

rather than meaningful accountability or reductions in violence, which ethical pedagogy in the IDF primarily achieves.

The fourth chapter is also concerned with ethical pedagogy but focuses on a different site of educational intervention. It examines the work of Israeli pre-military academies in shaping soldiers as ethical subjects. I make the argument that, contrary to existing literature which portrays these academies as primarily a religious phenomenon, a far more productive approach to understanding their work is to view them as institutions which are concerned with the moral and ethical development of their students. As such, pre-military academies represent a particularly intense example of the nexus between ethics and militarism explored throughout this book. I highlight continuities between formal ethical education in the IDF and informal education at these academies, including a notable reliance in both on soldiers' testimony as a pedagogical technique, and explore further dynamics of the ideological legitimation of violence through ethics.

The fifth and sixth chapters then take the book in a different direction. They are concerned with the work of Breaking the Silence, which I argue should be considered just as much a facet of the ethics of Israeli militarism as those elements considered in previous chapters. This is because, despite the latent political objectives of the organisation, its testimonies and campaign offer a critique of the occupation which is primarily articulated in a moral register. In the fifth chapter I devote attention to the process of gathering testimonies and reflect on the consequences of this for those who testify to Breaking the Silence. I assess the diverse motivations of those giving testimony and examine the effect the process has on their political trajectories. I also examine internal debates within the organisation about the purpose of the testimonies project, particularly the question of whether the aim of testimony should be to bring about a political transformation in the testifier. I show that, despite the often vigorous attempt to reduce the personal dimension of the testimony process, this element often comes to supersede the public information objectives of the project. Using psychoanalytic theory, I argue that the ethical practice of testifying to Breaking the Silence remains caught in an oscillation between affects of guilt and anxiety which has been bequeathed to the soldiers by the ethics of Israeli militarism. I acknowledge that this has occasionally produced important political and personal openings for the testifiers concerned. However, my conclusion is that overall these ethical responses limit the political consequences of the testimony process.

In the sixth and final chapter I look at the educational and public campaigning activity of Breaking the Silence. I argue that the moral discourse employed by the organisation often ends up suppressing the more fundamental political questions it seeks to raise. In particular, I look at how its educational work in pre-military academies (where it has been very active) is often transformed from a political discussion into an opportunity for students at these academies to prepare themselves ethically for military service. As such, the chapter demonstrates not only how the ethics of Israeli militarism limits the effectiveness of political activism, but also how ethics is then able to make that activism useful for militarism. These two chapters therefore work together to demonstrate that the ethics of Israeli militarism constrains and appropriates forms of political contestation against military rule, even when ethical approaches are mobilised by ostensibly radical groups for political purposes.

1 | *Militarising the Ethical Turn*

We are now in the disturbing position of having nothing left with which to decide political questions but the most fragile and uncertain tools. It is time, perhaps, to write treatises on ethics.

(Bernard Henri-Lévy, *Barbarism with a Human Face*, 1977)

I think [the Libya] war was probably launched by two statesmen. . . Hillary Clinton and Sarkozy. More modestly, [by] me.

(Bernard Henri-Lévy, Interview, *New York Magazine*, 2011)

The Philosopher Who Started a War

In March 2011, the French philosopher, Bernard Henri-Lévy, was in Benghazi negotiating with the Libyan Interim Transitional National Council. Days earlier he had telephoned the French President Nicolas Sarkozy, an old acquaintance of his, to ask him if he was interested in recognising the Libyan opposition to Muammar Gadhafi. When Sarkozy indicated that he was, Lévy rented a private plane with a friend, flew to the Egyptian–Libyan border, and hitchhiked his way into Tobruk in a car delivering vegetables. From there, he made contact with the Libyan rebels and informed them of Sarkozy's desire to co-operate. When the rebels asked for assurances, Lévy called Sarkozy and urged him to send a positive signal. He warned Sarkozy: 'there will be a massacre in Benghazi, a bloodbath, and the blood of the people of Benghazi will stain the flag of France' (quoted in Erlanger, 2011). Sarkozy then issued a statement greeting the formation of the transitional council; the rebels, headed by the former Justice Minister Mustafa Mohammed Abdul Jalil, decided to pursue the initiative. Lévy returned to Paris, where he greeted the Libyan opposition delegation when it arrived there the following week. He accompanied Jalil to meetings with President Sarkozy, which led to official French recognition of the transitional council as the legitimate government, and also later with US Secretary of State Hillary Clinton, who subsequently lobbied the Obama administration to take military action. By mid-March, the UN Security Council had backed a resolution authorising the use of force to protect civilians in Libya. By the end of October 2011, after a wide-ranging NATO bombing campaign and the success of the popular uprising, Gadhafi was dead and his regime had fallen. Lévy's dreams had all come true. He was so pleased with his efforts that he subsequently wrote, directed, and indeed starred in a film about his Libyan adventure, *The Oath of Tobruk*, which also received a special screening at Cannes.

We should of course be cautious about Lévy's glamorous version of events. It is more than likely that this story has been deliberately exaggerated to enhance his role. But it is also striking that this narrative has not been officially contradicted by either the French or American governments. In all probability, this is not because the story is completely true; instead, it is because it is *useful*. It suits the political protagonists that this war is seen as having taken place at the urging of a famous philosopher with humanitarian credentials. This bolsters the official narrative that the war was fought with a moral purpose: to support the overthrow of an evil dictator who was trying to massacre the civilians of Benghazi.

This is not the only war against supposed evil-doers in which Lévy has sought to play a role in recent years. His recent documentary film, *Peshmerga* (another Cannes special screening), followed first-hand the struggle of the Kurdish militias, against ISIS. And, pertinently for this book, Lévy also embedded himself as an observer in an Israeli military unit during the war in Gaza in 2014. As he said in a subsequent interview:

I was in Gaza during the last war . . . and I saw how careful the Israeli army was with the civilian population, how gentle they were with Palestinians, how cautious they were before entering a house [. . .] I went through Gaza City and saw the importance of the devastation and what I can say is that it was a terrible war but a war with targets. The goal of the war for Israel was to suppress the rocket launchers. What is the goal of the war of Hamas when the rockets are out, what is it? You know what it is, it's what they say in their charter – to obtain by killing the liquidation, annihilation of Israel. (quoted in Hyzagi, 2015)

Once again, in these remarks the idea of a moral struggle of a good, 'gentle' army against evil barbarity – discourse which is also recognisable from the tropes of Israeli military public relations – appears to guide Lévy's interpretation of events. The IDF clearly had very good reasons for embedding this philosopher with its troops. He provided a useful authority for its version of events.

Lévy's example is of interest to us not simply because of his remarkable promiscuity in attaching himself to fighters in modern conflicts, including the Israeli military. His intellectual and political trajectory is also directly relevant to the history of the turn to ethics in warfare with which this book is concerned. It is a parable of what can happen when ethical reasoning puts itself at the service of military power. Lévy had been in his earlier years a pioneering member of the 'new philosophers' in France, a group of renegade intellectuals who relentlessly courted media attention in the political foment of the post-1968 period, and who helped to shape a new and influential concept of ethics. Led by Lévy, they attacked the established Left for its supposed affinities with Stalinist totalitarianism, and called instead for what has been described as an 'anti-political ethics' (Bourg, 2007: 297), characterised by a mistrust for political organisation and the direct pursuit of power. In this context, ethics meant the studied avoidance of absolute 'evil' through a meliorist gradualism. The priority became the protection of basic freedoms and human rights against a supposedly proliferating totalitarian barbarism, whose amorphous character has since constantly shifted from Nazism, to Stalinism and Maoism, and more recently to representations of 'fundamentalist Islam'. According to this vision, the revolutionary transformation of society could no longer be hoped for. Instead, the only reliable guide for action would be an ethics of avoiding the worst – an ambition for 'the least of all possible evils', as Eyal Weizman has put it (2012: esp. 37–9).

The new philosophers were not an isolated group. They emerged at a time in which ethics had become a newly invigorated field of intellectual activity in France, a development which is often called 'the ethical turn' (Rancière, 2006; Bourg, 2007; Vásquez-Arroyo, 2016: 25–62). This was a diverse movement, giving rise to a range of sophisticated philosophical work which was not reducible to the crudity and publicity-seeking of the new philosophers. As it has spread and transformed across the Western world, its variety has only increased. Yet this general turn to ethics, for all its diversity, has also left significant, identifiable legacies with which it is important to grapple. As the anthropologist of ethics, Didier Fassin, has put it:

A significant evolution of contemporary society has been the banalization of moral discourse and moral sentiments in the public sphere, the insistence on suffering and trauma in the interpretation of a multiplicity of social issues, the focus on human rights and humanitarianism in international politics, as well as the invocation of ethics in a wide range of human activities, from finance or development to medicine and research, from the rediscovery of bodily practices of the self in religious and secular worlds to the social expectation of the subject's autonomy. . . (2014: 433)

To summarise further, one could say that the effects of the ethical turn have been simultaneously universalising and individualising. On the one hand the turn to ethics has tended to abstract away from concrete political antagonisms, often directing our attention towards the decontextualised plane of 'humanity' and the absolute evils which confront it (Rancière, 2006: 7–9). On the other hand, it has also valorised a return to the individual self, away from collective struggle or institutions, as a means of cultivating the values on which this moralising discourse depends (Bourg, 2007: 9–10). These assumptions have become steadily more widespread, provoking ongoing debates about their political merits (e.g. Badiou, 2001; Vásquez-Arroyo, 2016). A key claim of this book is that the military sphere has experienced its own ethical turn, one which draws on but also shapes these wider developments. Although the book does not undertake a wider evaluation of the merits of the ethical turn in society, it does nevertheless argue that this militarisation of the ethical turn should, at the very least, raise troubling political questions.

A whole range of ethical activities have been pulled closer and closer into the military orbit in recent years. Military interventions are now frequently conducted in the defence of 'humanity' against enemies whose evil and barbarity are established further and further beyond question. This invocation of humanitarian principles has often had the paradoxical effect of further legitimating and encouraging military violence (Coker, 2001; Douzinas, 2003; Fassin, 2011; Weizman, 2012; Zehfuss, 2012a; Perugini and Gordon, 2015). Furthermore, militaries have also sought to craft an image for themselves as bearers of good intentions and moral restraint. To do this, they have intensified their search for doctrines and pedagogies which can buttress their claim to practise ethics. This has produced an enormous growth in scholarly work on the ethics of war in the field of moral philosophy (Rodin, 2006) and has also led to the emergence of a body of practitioner-orientated scholarship discussing the teaching of military ethics to soldiers (Cook, 2004; Challans, 2007; Sherman, 2007; Robinson et al., 2008; Wertheimer, 2008). These developments have also been institutionalised through the establishment of dedicated academic journals, such as the *Journal of Military Ethics*, and the creation of scholarly institutions which aim to address policymakers and practitioners on the ethics of war, such as Oxford University's Institute for Ethics, Law, and Armed Conflict. Many moral philosophers, not least in Israel as later chapters show, now supplement their academic work with teaching at military colleges, defence ministries, and officer schools, a phenomenon which should be understood as yet another dimension of the contemporary militarisation of the university (Stavrianakis, 2006).

To be sure, this renewed pursuit of military ethics draws on long-standing intellectual traditions, especially Just War Theory (Walzer, 1977), and on the substance of well-established principles in International Humanitarian Law. Yet it has also aligned with, and been shaped by, recent changes in the character of war and militaries. The shift to 'irregular' modes of warfare such as humanitarian missions and counterinsurgency has prompted assertions of the renewed importance of ethics to contemporary soldiering (Coker, 2008: 134–8; Carrick et al., 2009; Van Baarda and Verweij, 2009). In addition, the increasing use of robotics and remote technology has encouraged militaries to claim that they are fighting 'virtuous wars' without casualties (Der Derian, 2009; Zehfuss, 2011). This growing interest in ethics has also dovetailed with changes in the motivational and organisational cultures of militaries, which increasingly supplement traditional hierarchical and disciplinary modes of organisation with an emphasis on cultivating the personal, psychological, and mental capacities of soldiers (Cowen, 2008: 198–229; Howell, 2015). Surveying these developments, one begins to suspect that militaries are not simply paying heed to ethics: they are positively suffused with it, in ways that shape their practice profoundly.

Yet this development has also had consequences for the content and role of ethics itself, which can no longer claim to be innocent of these military trends. As it acquires its new function, 'military ethics' is often presented as a subset of the wider field of professional ethics and reduced to a component of soldiers' professional development. This has meant that the literature on military ethics has by and large remained rigorously pragmatic and practitioner-orientated, giving it a highly circumscribed role. In the words of the editors of the *Journal of Military Ethics*, 'military ethics is at its core practical and professional. It is meant to be the handmaid of the profession of arms. It exists to assist thoughtful professionals to think through their real-world problems and issues' (Cook and Syse, 2010: 121). The revealing gendered metaphor of a 'handmaid' makes clear the proximate and subservient role to military violence these scholars envisage for ethics. In this framing, ethics becomes preoccupied with producing a doctrine which 'works' for the military, often by seeking to produce a 'right' answer to moral questions (cf. Hutchings, 2010: 161). But this emphasis also extends beyond those scholars who view themselves as working directly with or for the military. For example, even Christopher Coker's more critical restatement of the necessity of ethics in modern warfare is founded on Rortyian pragmatism, in which ethics is first and foremost desirable because it is *useful* for policymakers and practitioners (2008: 7–15).

In this book, I seek to show that these trends carry serious political risks for the ethical capacity to undertake independent and critical thinking about war. If we are to fully appreciate these dangers, it is necessary to start from a conception of ethics which views it as a domain of human activity like any other, rather than as the necessarily enlightened pursuit that it is often taken to be. In this chapter, by way of preparation for the empirical studies to come, I seek to develop a theoretical account of how it is possible for ethics, militarism, and war to become mutually reinforcing. In the following sections, I draw on the anthropology of ethics, feminist International Relations, Foucauldian theories of governmentality, and the psychoanalytic critique of ideology to explain this development. At the end of the chapter, I then offer a brief methodological account of how I generated the findings which are later used to substantiate these theoretical insights.

Towards an Anthropology of Military Ethics

How can ethics be a militarist practice? How can we think of ethics as a weapon of war? These propositions seem to challenge conventional usage of these terms, in a way which calls for closer analysis. Ethics and war are often intuitively imagined as a kind of antagonistic pair, in which greater emphasis on one necessarily comes at the expense of the other. Ethics is therefore typically but misleadingly conceived of as a reliably effective limit on war that can constrain its occurrence and excesses. However, this relationship is far from automatic. Rather, it is an assumption based on a certain simplistic understanding of ethics as an active set of moral norms modifying behaviour, norms which are often imagined as pacifist or non-violent. Thinking critically about the relationship between ethics and militarism requires a more careful distinction between ethics and morality. In particular, it requires a theory of ethics which is more sensitive to the role of subject formation.

The relationship between ethics and morality is certainly a matter of scholarly controversy. Acknowledging these disagreements, many scholars either opt to leave this question open or decide that their interchangeable usage prevents any consistent distinction between them (Hutchings, 2010: 7–8; Fassin, 2012: 5–6). In this book, however, I adopt the position that ethics and morality are at least *analytically* separable, even if they are often indistinct in practice. In this, I am following the theoretical innovations made in the anthropology of ethics, where this distinction is central (Fassin, 2012: 6–7; Faubion, 2012; Laidlaw, 2013: esp. 110–19). From this perspective, morality is the domain concerned with determining and achieving the good. Ethics, by contrast, is a set of practices carried out by the self on the self which are aimed at enabling the subject to behave effectively in a certain way. Put more succinctly, ethics is a practice of subject formation. The anthropology of ethics develops this perspective from the later work of Michel Foucault, whose analysis of ethics emphasises practices of subjectivation over the moral content of a normative system or the actual moral behaviour of individuals (Foucault, 1998b: 1–32, 2000a).

The crucial aspect of the anthropological enquiry is therefore to analyse the quotidian practices through which subjects seek to fashion themselves ethically. For example, Foucault undertook several studies of classical and early Christian ethics which focused on dietary, erotic, and pedagogical practices (Foucault, 1998b, 2005). Other anthropological studies into contemporary religious and moral practices have also adopted this approach (Fassin, 2012; Faubion, 2012). Similarly, anthropological enquiries into the formation of Muslim ethical subjectivities have examined pedagogical and sartorial practices

(Mahmood, 2005) and the culture of listening to sermons on cassette tapes (Hirschkind, 2006). In all these anthropological studies, the focus is much less on the content of moral codes and much more on the everyday bodily and intellectual practices through which subjects seek to shape their own behaviour and identity.

In practice, of course, there may be considerable overlap between ethics and morality. Deciding on a moral good and implementing it in practice will necessitate ethical work. Likewise, ethics commonly includes reference to some version of morality. However, ethics can also be directed to non-moral goals, such as professional excellence, self-enhancement, or political objectives (Hutchings, 2010: 5–6). Indeed – and here is the fundamental point – there is no reason why the goal of ethical practice cannot be preparation for participation in war. It is perfectly possible to imagine a set of ethical practices which would be aimed at producing a more effective soldier. It is at this point that ethics might converge with a militarist project. What this study therefore attempts to do is to situate Israeli military ethics in the context of such everyday subjective practices, highlighting the ways of thinking, speaking, and acting encouraged by Israeli military ethics which work to shape and enhance soldiers' subjectivity.

The subjective effects of military ethical practices run far deeper than is currently recognised. In the practitioner-oriented literature, military ethics is generally conceived of as a feature of military training and the professional development of soldiers which helps to improve discipline and compliance (Robinson et al., 2008; Wertheimer, 2008; Carrick et al., 2009). For many such scholars, the contribution of military ethics is limited to these functions. In addition, some scholars have argued that military ethics education can make an extra 'moral' contribution beyond this. Distinguishing between 'functional' and 'aspirational' approaches, Wolfendale argues that the latter model also prioritises the development of soldiers' autonomous 'moral character' as 'virtuous people' (Wolfendale, 2008: 161; see also Challans, 2007; Carrick, 2008: 188). However, this distinction assumes that the only 'functional' contribution ethics makes is in ensuring 'correct behaviour' (Wolfendale, 2008: 165). In fact, military ethics can also make significant ideological and motivational contributions beyond this, which can contribute to making war and military participation seem desirable and normal. The 'functional' contribution of military ethics is not simply to enhance military governance narrowly defined as compliance-building.

It also contributes to the production of a sense of soldierly 'moral character', which is crucial to the formation of ideologically motivated soldier-subjects and thus to the consolidation of militarism.

To grasp this, we must understand morality as embedded in a wider process of subject formation through ethical self-fashioning. This is the crucial insight to be drawn from the anthropology of ethics. For this reason, it is analytically important to insist on the possible distinction of ethics from morality. This is not because in the case of Israeli militarism one finds them separately. Rather, it is because it is only as part of a set of wider ethical practices designed to produce soldier-subjects that the importance of the invocation of morality can be properly appreciated. Given that military ethics can play a role in the formation of soldier-subjects for whom war is made to seem a normal and desirable activity, it can be thought of as an aspect of *militarism* as well. This wider process of ethical subjectivation holds the key to a critical understanding of the militaristic effects of the moral army mythology.

Ethics and Militarist Governmentality

This emphasis on the role of subject formation in militarism in studying military ethics also builds on the insights of feminist International Relations scholarship. This work has drawn attention to the significance of the differentiation and consolidation of gendered identities in war. Feminist IR has shown that subjects are produced and coded as masculine or feminine depending on their differential participation in war, meaning that gendered subject formation – both within the ranks of the army and throughout wider society – is essential to the perpetuation of militarism (Enloe, 2000, 2007; Hutchings, 2008; Segal, 2008; Sjoberg and Via, 2010; Conway, 2012). Indeed, gender has also been shown to be essential to understanding the way in which military ethics works. As Jean Bethke Elshtain argued, the principal paradigm for considering the role of ethics in war, Just War Theory, rests on an inherently masculinist discourse which is concerned with producing the male soldier as a 'just warrior' and domesticating the female civilian as a 'beautiful soul' (Elshtain, 1995; see also Sjoberg, 2006; Owens, 2010; Kinsella, 2011).

Yet this feminist sensitivity to processes of gendered subject formation in militarism can also be extended to incorporate wider practices of subjectivation, not least ethical self-fashioning, in the functioning of militarism. This is where a Foucauldian analysis of militarism as a form of *governmentality* is particularly helpful. As a form of governmentality, militarism not only acts on subjects, it also *produces* them (Butler, 1996: esp. 1–31, 63–131; Foucault, 2002b). Foucault describes governmentality as an exercise in 'the conduct of conduct', whereby the production of subjects through a close management of individual behaviour becomes the decisive intervention in the exercise of power (2002b, 2008a: 87–114). Ethics, in which subjects take it upon themselves to direct their own conduct and fashion themselves through self-cultivation, therefore has great potential significance in the functioning of these relations of power, as Foucault himself observed (2000d, 2005: 251–2). This should indicate that ethics is potentially a very powerful contributor to militarism.

However, this connection between ethics and governmentality has generally been overlooked in Foucauldian studies of contemporary militarism. Scholars have instead tended to interpret militarism as a form of biopolitics, in which the imperative to 'make life live' is guaranteed by the use of violence to eliminate threats to the population (Foucault, 1998a, 2004; Reid, 2006; Dillon and Neal, 2008; Morton and Bygrave, 2008; Reid and Dillon, 2009; Evans, 2010; Basham, 2013: 4–8). This has been combined with an emphasis on the role of disciplinary techniques and embodied practice in the shaping of soldiers as agents of this biopolitical project (Higate, 2012; Basham, 2013; McSorley, 2013). Militaries are accordingly understood as disciplinary structures *par excellence* whose function is to produce 'docile bodies' capable of exercising violence on behalf of the state. Through careful training and socialisation, processes of surveillance, instruction, repetition, and drills, these soldier-bodies become the object of an intense 'anatamo-politics' in which movements, sensibilities, and emotions are carefully controlled. Such processes also acquire powerful gendered, racial, and class dimensions which layer identities with military significance (Basham, 2013).

Yet, as I will show in this book, it is necessary to combine these perspectives on militarism with a focus on the role of ethical conduct. Increasingly, and especially in neoliberal forms of government, individuals are being made 'subjects of their lives' (Burchell, 1995: 29–30) through the promotion of value systems and a culture of freedom in which they are made responsible for conducting themselves (Burchell, 1995; Rose, 1995, 1999; Foucault, 2008b; Dean, 2010: 19–21, 26–7).

This greater margin for freedom in the conduct of individuals has increased the prominence of ethics as a component of liberal modes of government. I argue that militaries have not been exempt from these trends, least of all the IDF. Understanding Israeli militarism as a form of (neoliberal) governmentality requires attention to these micro-practices of ethics as well as to interventions at the level of popula-tions or bodies. What is needed is an examination of the relationship between ethics as a 'technology of the self' (Foucault, 2000c) and mili-tarism as a 'political technology of individuals' (Foucault, 2002a).

Closer examination of Foucault's work gives an indication of the kinds of ethical practices which such an analysis would explore, as well as some of the modifications necessary to apply his thinking to studying the role of ethics in contemporary militarism. Foucault traces the genesis of modern forms of governmentality to the Christian pas-torate, which he identifies as 'a prelude to governmentality through the constitution of a specific subject, of a subject whose merits are analyti-cally identified, who is subjected in continuous networks of obedience, and who is subjectified through the compulsory extraction of truth' (2008a: 185). He therefore describes the modern Western subject as the product of an 'incitement to discourse' about his or her conduct (1998a: 17–36), the result of the exhaustive expression of inner truths through practices of 'avowal' (2014). Crucially, then, testimony has a foundational role in Foucault's analysis of subject formation and governmentality.

At one point Foucault specifically identifies the modern military as a descendant of the pastorate. He describes the emergence a specific form of military governmentality in which

[. . .] waging war became not just a profession or even a general law, but an ethic and the behaviour of every good citizen of a country; [. . .] being a soldier was a form of political and moral conduct, a sacrifice, and devotion to the common cause and common salvation directed by a public conscience and public authority within the framework of a tight discipline; [. . .] being a soldier was no longer just a destiny or a profession but a form of conduct. (2008a: 198)

One possible interpretation of the growing significance of military ethics to militaries might therefore be to view it as an accentuation of the pastoral nature of military governmentality. This transformation of militarism into an ethic of good conduct would not only help to underpin military discipline but also increase the identification between soldiers' individual ethical selfhood and their military participation. This interpretation might also help to elucidate the important role of soldiers' testimony in military ethics. The pastoral 'incitement to discourse' would invite soldiers to speak about their experiences and ask them to locate and judge the truth of themselves in their military-ethical performance. However, it is important not to overstate the significance of ethics as a form of pastoral power. As I argued above, military ethics is not simply about ensuring compliance with procedures or about the ruthless subordination of individual behaviour to military goals. Indeed, as I show later in the book, the IDF is not particularly interested in its soldiers' actual compliance with its ethical code. Likewise, soliciting soldiers' testimony should not primarily be interpreted as a form of discipline. It can also be an opportunity for individual self-fashioning, a means of protest, and a tool of ideological legitimation. All this suggests that we also need to look beyond the model of the pastorate for understanding the potential role of ethics in militarism.

Foucault himself gradually recognised that ethics was not reducible to a tool of pastoral power. His study of classical Greek and Roman, and especially Stoic, ethics led him to argue that not all ethical systems were premised on the analysis, condemnation, and discipline of the inner truth of the subject's conduct. In fact, a key theme of his later work is the contribution that ethics, including practices of truth-telling, could make to self-cultivation – what he called 'the care of the self' (2005: 31–78). Foucault reconstructed in great detail the techniques of self-care prescribed by Stoic ethicists. He discusses their methods of listening, reading, writing, and speaking, and their methods for testing and examining themselves, all of which he considered under the rubric of 'asceticism' (2005: esp. 315–487). Foucault contrasts this form of asceticism with the self-abnegation and self-renunciation characteristic of the Christian pastorate. Instead, he suggests that Stoic asceticism was characterised by the pursuit of self-enhancement. There are also intriguing moments when he compares these preparations, albeit figuratively, to armour and military fortifications (2005: 325). Indeed, writing in the discipline of military ethics, Nancy Sherman (2007) has also argued that Stoic techniques can provide powerful tools for soldiers struggling to maintain motivation in military adversity.

For Foucault, this ascetic ethics of self-care also corresponds to a particular form of truth-telling, one which is not so concerned with the examination of wrongdoing through confession. The important truths to be told are not primarily *about* the subject, they are *directed to* the subject in order to help bring about a transformation (2005: 327). Significantly, this does not preclude recounting one's past actions and experiences, which remains an important aspect of ascetic ethics. However, this self-examination is undertaken not in order to discern an inner truth but in order to assess one's progress towards desired goals or to consider how one might have acted differently. Occasionally, this process of self-examination will require a degree of frankness, candour, and even courage. At this point, Foucault notes the importance the Stoics attached to *parrhesia*, the practice of frankly or courageously speaking the truth to others.

Parrhesia is often interpreted as a practice of 'speaking truth to power' – and indeed there are several points at which Foucault explicitly analyses it as such, especially in his final lectures (2010, 2012). However, it is important to note that Foucault identifies *parrhesia* as a pedagogical as well as a political technique, making it a highly ambiguous and reversible ethical practice. As some scholars have already argued, *parrhesia* provides an attractive framework through which to analyse the production of soldiers' testimony in Israel (Morag, 2013: esp. 180–210; Shavit and Katriel, 2013). Tamar Katriel and Nimrod Shavit have further observed the similarities between *parrhesia* and the Israeli proclivity for 'straight-talking' (known as speaking *dugri*), along with its militarist significance:[1]

In the Greek polis, fearless speech was reserved for men-citizens of proper class who could profess personal, moral and social qualities that grounded their assertive stance and legitimated their public critique. In Israeli culture, somewhat similarly, speaking *dugri* has been associated with the idealised and highly gendered image of the Israeli-born Jew, the Sabra, which became the hallmark of the new Jewish-Zionist (masculinist) identity during the Israeli nation-building era, and later with Israel's militarist ethos and the soldierly role. (2013: 93; see also Katriel, 1986)

---

[1] It is also significant that *parrhesia* has been adopted as Hebrew word, meaning 'in public'.

As I will demonstrate in later chapters, this conceptual framework of self-care, asceticism, and *parrhesia* is particularly important for understanding the significance of ethical practice, and especially soldiers' testimony, for the functioning of Israeli militarism as a mode of governmentality. This may appear a surprising claim, particularly since Foucault appears at several points to suggest that asceticism would be effective in frustrating structures of obedience such as the modern military.[2] Such difficulties can however be minimised by concentrating on the ascetic emphasis on self-fashioning and constant self-improvement, which has much more obvious military applications. Indeed, the role of ascetic self-cultivation in militarism makes considerable sense when wider trends are considered, including the shift to neoliberal modes of military governance (premised on incentivising the individual soldier), the intensification of counterinsurgency (premised on the individual modulation and application of violence), and the consolidation of militarist identities (premised on individual self-image).

While understanding militarism as governmentality certainly elucidates the role of ethics in the formation of the Israeli soldier-subject, from a Foucauldian perspective the co-existence of ethics and contemporary militarism cannot help but appear uneasy and paradoxical. The practices of soldiers' 'self-care' that I will describe in subsequent chapters seem far removed from the positive portrayal given to them in Foucault's final lectures, and is an outcome which a governmentality approach to militarism has difficulty in fully accounting for. This may have something to do with Foucault's own interiority to the ethical turn, in which his later work marked a key milestone (Bourg, 2007: 321–33). Yet this is also because a governmentality approach misses the ideological dimension of militarism, in which ethics can have a potentially powerful role in legitimating violence. Foucault was famously resistant to the term ideology, which he tended to associate with a vulgar Marxist account of base/superstructure relations in which ideology is effectively a kind of misperception (Vighi and Feldner, 2007: 142–5). However, as I will now explain, an emphasis on ideology need not be this crude. Insights from the psychoanalytic

---

[2] 'There is, I think, a profound difference between the structures of obedience and asceticism [. . .] Asceticism is a sort of exasperated and reversed obedience that has become egoistic self-mastery. Let's say that in asceticism there is a specific excess that denies access to an external power' (Foucault, 2008a: 207–8, see also 2000d, 2005).

critique of ideology can reveal further dimensions of the ethical subject formation at work in Israeli militarism. Most significantly they
can also help explain how an ethical culture of 'self-care' might arise
within deeply embedded structures of military discipline and violence.

Militarism as Ideology

Understanding militarism as an ideological formation does not mean
simply focusing on the role of ideas without consideration of its relationship to social practice or materiality. At least since Althusser, the-
orists have had a concept of ideology which is of necessity implicated
in 'ideological apparatuses', that is, sets of institutions and practices
which produce and sustain ideology (Althusser, 1971). As such, ideology *is* a material practice, one which forms 'the imaginary relationship
of individuals to their real conditions of existence' (1971: 152–9). It
is therefore impossible to conceive of social practice without ideology,
which plays a central role in maintaining social structures. Moreover,
it is crucial to add that, for Althusser, ideology interpellates individuals
as subjects, making subject formation – rather than sets of ideas – the
crucial factor to be appreciated (1971: 160–5).

We do not need to adopt a crude distinction between 'science' and
'ideology', between 'real conditions' and their misperception, to maintain this position. In his psychoanalytic reconstruction of the concept
of ideology, Slavoj Žižek explains that the crucial question is not the
truth or falsity of the beliefs which make it up, but rather the way
in which certain beliefs – true or false – entice the desiring subject
into continued participation in social practices (2012: 8). These beliefs
may or may not be true, but it is not their truth which determines the
subject's belief in them: it is the way in which they capture the subject's desire. Yet psychoanalysis also starts from the premise that these
desires cannot be explained purely with reference to the conscious
thought of the actors involved. Instead, it emphasises the importance
of *unconscious* desires and drives in accounting for ideology, a claim
which requires further elaboration.[3]

---

[3] Although I will attempt a minimal reconstruction of the tenets of the psychoanalytic critique of ideology here, it goes without saying that this will remain
partial and incomplete. The best introductions to the theoretical framework
deployed here are offered by Chiesa (2007), Edkins (1999: 87–124), Fink
(1996), and Žižek (2008b).

In its Lacanian variant, psychoanalysis holds that 'the unconscious is structured like a language', meaning that even individual desires are always articulated in a socially given language (referred to as 'the Symbolic'). Since this language is social and does not only belong to the subject, he or she is necessarily alienated when articulating desires in its terms (Lacan, 2004: 203–15). Moreover, it stands to reason that if everybody is alienated in the Symbolic, then there is no consistent, reliable articulation to which it can be reduced. This means there is no totalising language which can fully describe reality or articulate the subject's desire ('there is no Big Other', in Lacanian terms). Alienation therefore implies a gap between the Symbolic order and the world it purports to describe, a gap which cannot be fully covered (Fink, 1996: 29–31). It is this un-Symbolised excess which Lacan terms 'the Real'. Not only, therefore, do subjects make radical compromises on their desires by entering into the Symbolic realm: they will also never be able to satisfy those desires, even in these compromised terms, since the Symbolic order is characterised by incompleteness.

It is this situation – this subjective predicament – that can tell us something new about ideology. Žižek's contribution is to have shown how ideological formations take advantage of such a predicament and how subjects can become trapped by their desires in an ideological snare (2008a, 2008b). For Žižek, the Symbolic can take the form of social norms that keep the political *status quo* in place. From this perspective, we can understand nationalism, religion, and indeed militarism as Symbolic frameworks through which subjects attempt to articulate desires (2008b: 111–22). In this, Žižek is not far from other forms of discourse analysis in which such languages become widely shared and powerful forms of social mediation that shape acceptable modes of thinking. However, as a Lacanian, Žižek also insists that the Symbolic realm always fails to cover an excess produced by the desiring subject. Ideological formations cannot purely survive on the basis of their Symbolic instantiation. They must necessarily engage the Real of our desires and attempt to grapple with this un-Symbolised excess (2008b: 122–44).

It is in its engagement with the Real that Žižek has shown that ideology can function most powerfully. Once it begins to manage and discipline our engagement with the Real, ideology can not only disguise the gap in the Symbolic but also harness 'the hidden kernel of enjoyment' for its purposes (2008b: 144). Fantasy plays a crucial role here. It intervenes to smooth over the anxiety prompted by the encounter with the inconsistencies and incompleteness of the Symbolic order. Understanding this mechanism of fantasy means making a crucial Lacanian distinction between the object of desire and the object *cause* of desire, the characteristic *in* an object which makes it seem desirable (also known as the *objet a*). Lacan explains that, in a situation of fantasy, the *objet a* functions as a lure by provoking feelings of desire in the subject without fully presenting an object for it (Fink, 1996: 59–61; Lacan, 2004: 263–76). It therefore simulates the experience of desire in a pattern of continuing frustration and insatiability; Lacan calls this 'surplus enjoyment' or *jouissance*.

The claim of this book is that Israeli militarism takes the form of an ideology: it conditions subjects to desire war and military participation and it produces unconscious fantasies which obscure its failures and inconsistencies and which produce *jouissance*. Ethics, moreover, has a crucial role to play in sustaining this ideology. Although these ideological contributions are manifold, they could be summarised under three broad headings. Firstly, Israeli military ethics produces a Symbolic order in which certain key values and discourses associated with war-fighting and military activity are presented as the expression of the soldier's desire. The moral army mythology is precisely one such example. The task of ethical pedagogy, as I will show in later chapters, is partly to make soldiers identify with the proclaimed values of Israeli militarism, to make soldiers *want* to embody them, and thus to embed them in their unconscious.

Secondly, ethics helps to sustain a set of unconscious fantasies which cover over the inconsistencies of this Symbolic order when it is confronted with the Real of the colonial violence of occupation. Like many things in war, the plausibility of the desire to be a moral army does not easily survive first contact with the enemy. This poses a problem for a military which presents itself as moral to its soldiers and which encourages them to identify as such. Accordingly, military ethics provides an array of techniques and activities for the soldier-subject to carry out which generate 'surplus enjoyment' and which distract from the fundamental, structural, and constitutive impossibility of ideas such as a 'moral army' or 'enlightened occupation'. In other words, military ethics functions as an unconscious fantasy.

Thirdly, ethics also helps to sustain militarist ideology through the prioritisation of affects of guilt over anxiety. Ethics promotes ways of thinking and acting which focus scrutiny on the conduct and shortcomings of the individual soldier, rather than on structural or political factors. Soldiers are encouraged to find explanations for any apparent moral failing within themselves. This encourages feelings of guilt, rather than a more dangerous questioning of the Symbolic order which might result in anxiety. For these soldiers this anxiety would be all the more acute considering how strongly they are encouraged to view themselves and construct identities as members of a moral army. This final ideological contribution is more than mere de-politicisation, therefore. It entails the production of militarist subjectivities which are less capable of effective political critique and activism and which tend instead to reach for individual ethical solutions to moral problems. Indeed, this prioritisation of guilt over anxiety also disciplines activism by regularly translating political acts into ethico-pedagogical interventions. In this way, as in the example which opened the book, the testimonies and educational activities of Breaking the Silence are often framed in Israeli military ethics as an impetus to moral improvement rather than political critique. This often makes such activities more effective in buttressing militarism than in mobilising against the occupation. As later chapters in particular show, these ideological effects of the ethics of Israeli militarism do not go unchallenged. However, as I shall also argue, what makes the ethics of Israeli militarism so strong, and its effects so enduring, is that it is *unconscious* and therefore extremely difficult to dislodge.

Notes on Method

The research for this book began as an enquiry into the role of soldiers' testimony in political discourse surrounding war in Israel, and an investigation into whether such practices could play a role in the disruption of prevalent patterns of militarism. That it ended up as a broader analysis of the role of ethics in Israeli militarism is a product of findings and connections made during the research, rather than a hypothesis generated in this abstract. Breaking the Silence were naturally a central case study for the initial research plan, and my original research strategy was to place the organisation in a wider historical and social context. My preliminary analysis of the organisation had noted its striking continuities with earlier forms of soldiers' testimony in Israel (including literature, anthologies, cinema, and political movements) and also the prevalence of militaristic tropes in its political discourse (the centrality of the soldiers' voice, the focus on primarily masculine experiences, a longing for an earlier heroic era, and so on). I wanted to find out why Israeli militarism seemed to generate this kind of protest, and what kind of transformations in militarism this might portend or foreclose. My suppositions were driven mostly by existing critiques of the 'shooting and crying' genre, which often criticised this kind of soldiers' testimony for being a conscience-clearing exercise for soldiers rather than a genuine political challenge. I was interested in deploying a Foucauldian approach to analyse soldiers' testimony as a product of a confessional 'incitement to discourse' which may have been linked to a regime of military pastoral power.

I set out to conduct fieldwork in Israel for a period of about six months. The first stage involved conducting interviews with activists involved in producing soldiers' testimony and observing these practices as closely as possible. The aim would be to glean information from them regarding the institutions, movements, and social practices which were driving or encouraging their activities. I then envisaged a second phase to follow up on these insights in order to analyse the wider field of social practices in which they emerged. From an early stage, the fieldwork challenged several of my key assumptions. The activists I encountered did not correspond to the idea I had of what testifiers would be like. Most of them considered themselves to have very strong political motivations for what they were doing, and many were hostile to the suggestion that their decision to give testimony arose from a need to express guilt. Furthermore, interviews with testifiers did not yield clear suggestions as to what kind of pastoral institutions I should look to analyse.

However, the fieldwork also yielded a few unexpected early insights which were to prove fundamental to the development of my analysis. The key element was my discovery of the relationship between Breaking the Silence and pre-military academies [*mekhinot kdam-tzva'iyot*]. These academies offer a year of voluntary informal education to high-school graduates before enlistment to the IDF. At the time Breaking the Silence offered lectures and tours to a large number of these academies, which meant that quite a common feature of their curricula was exposure to soldiers' testimony. After watching one such lecture at an academy, I became very interested in these institutions. Further fieldwork led me to discern a strong role for soldiers' testimony in their ethical pedagogy. The observation of this link became a crucial guiding discovery for the rest of my fieldwork. I soon became intensely interested in how wider practices of ethics in the IDF both encouraged and also made use of the practice of soldiers' testimony. In hindsight, this realisation dawned agonisingly slowly. Indeed, I probably did not grapple with its implications fully until one evening when, after I had introduced my work to a group of pre-military academy students, their teacher commented that I was clearly also interested in *education*, even though I had not mentioned it in my summary of the research. Over time, I gradually became aware that ethics education at pre-military academies was contiguous with a wider set of pedagogical strategies and approaches being deployed in the IDF itself, which prompted my interest in the IDF ethical code and the ways in which it is taught to soldiers. I therefore expanded my pool of potential interviewees to philosophers, educators, and military personnel who had been involved with IDF military ethical pedagogy.

The more of these interviews I conducted, the more I realised that it is impossible to understand the doctrines and teaching of Israeli military ethics without reference to soldiers' testimony, and likewise impossible to understand soldiers' testimony in Israel without reference to the doctrines and teaching of military ethics. Moreover, in these interviews I also began to encounter modes of giving testimony which did not match my earlier critique of 'shooting and crying' at all: the educators I spoke with eschewed this understanding of what testimony was for, and several of them even criticised Breaking the Silence for indulging in this practice. At the same time, as my interviews with activists continued, I was beginning to rewrite my account of the work of Breaking the Silence. I increasingly viewed it as a more complicated phenomenon than the straightforward label of 'shooting and crying' would suggest. However, I also began to notice other ways in which the work of the organisation had become implicated in the ethics of Israeli militarism.

By the end of the fieldwork, therefore, I had made the crucial analytic connection between testimony and wider social practices; but I had not made it in quite the way I had envisaged. I had found it through observation and encounter, rather than interviews with testifiers, and I had observed it unfolding as an ongoing tension between pedagogy and activism rather than in any sequential relationship between the two. Moreover, I had been forced in the process to re-evaluate several assumptions about the nature of the mode of ethics I was studying. In fact, and somewhat disquietingly for someone who had begun the project from a Foucauldian premise, the mode of ethics conformed much more closely to an ethics of the care of the self than to a regime of pastoral power. This discovery revealed to me the inadequacy of interpreting militarism purely as a form of governmentality and led me to embrace the additional theoretical explanations drawn from psychoanalysis and the critique of ideology I have outlined above. The result was not only a more sophisticated understanding of how militarism works, both in Israel and in general, but also an appreciation of the shortcomings of certain ethical approaches as a means of resisting militarism. The arguments presented in the rest of this book are the result of these discoveries.

2 | 'The Spirit of the IDF'

On 14 October 1994, delivering his speech in acceptance of the Nobel Peace Prize, Prime Minister Yitzhak Rabin made the first public use of the IDF (Israel Defence Forces) ethical code. Its principal author, Professor Asa Kasher, had provided Rabin's advisers with an extract of the document at their request several months before the text was finally approved.[1] Rabin spoke as follows:

The history of the State of Israel, the annals of the Israel Defence Forces are filled with thousands of stories of soldiers who sacrificed themselves – who died while trying to save wounded comrades; who gave their lives to avoid causing harm to innocent people on the enemy's side.

In the coming days, a special Commission of the Israel Defence Forces will finish drafting a Code of Conduct for our soldiers. The formulation regarding human life will read as follows, and I quote:

In recognition of its supreme importance, the soldier will preserve human life in every way possible and endanger himself, or others, only to the extent deemed necessary to fulfil this mission.

The Sanctity of Life, in the view of the soldiers of the Israel Defence Forces, will find expression in all their actions; in considered and precise planning; in intelligent and safety-minded training and in judicious implementation, in accordance with their mission; in taking the professionally proper degree of risk and degree of caution; and in the constant effort to limit casualties to the scope required to achieve the objective.

For many years ahead – even if wars come to an end, after peace comes to our land – these words will remain a pillar of fire which goes before our camp, a guiding light for our people. And we take pride in that. (Rabin, 1994)

This speech tells us something about the importance of the IDF ethical code for Israel's self-presentation and self-perception. This is not simply evident in the choice of this particular value, 'human life'.

---

[1] Author interview with Asa Kasher.

40

It is present in Rabin's portrayal of the IDF as the avatar of the nation and, moreover, as the ethical subject which must absorb, practise, and be judged by such values. If Israel is to prove its dedication to the value of human life, this speech suggests, it is the IDF which must be shown to express them. Indeed, it is striking that, elsewhere in his speech, Rabin consistently makes use of *military* examples to support his claims and, paradoxically, to demonstrate his commitment to peace:

As a military man, as a commander, I issued orders for dozens, probably hundreds of military operations. And together with the joy of victory and grief of bereavement, I shall always remember the moment just after making the decision to mount an action: the hush as senior officers or cabinet ministers slowly rise from their seats; the sight of their receding backs; the sound of the closing door; and then the silence in which I remain alone.

That is the moment you grasp that as a result of the decision just made, people will be going to their deaths. People from my nation, people from other nations. And they still don't know it . . .

As a former military man, I will also forever remember the silence of the moment before: the hush when the hands of the clock seem to be spinning forward, when time is running out and in another hour, another minute, the inferno will erupt.

In that moment of great tension just before the finger pulls the trigger, just before the fuse begins to burn; in the terrible quiet of that moment, there's still time to wonder, alone: Is it really imperative to act? Is there no other choice? No other way?

And then the order is given, and the inferno begins.

It should be made explicit, if it is not already obvious, that in these words *Rabin is testifying*. This is the same Yitzhak Rabin who, only a few years previously as Minister of Defence, had ordered that Israeli soldiers should *break the bones* of Palestinian demonstrators during the First Intifada (Peri, 1996a: 341, 354); the same Rabin who, as a commander during the 1948 war, had signed the order to expel the thousands of Palestinian inhabitants of the towns of Ramleh and Lydda (Morris, 2004: 429). Through his testimony, however, the impression we receive of his military career is rather different. This was the first of many moments I shall explore throughout this book when the IDF ethical code has occasioned soldiers' testimony and reinscribed the past in this way. Through such moments of testimony recalling moral judgements, an interior space is carved out inside the soldier, the space of reflection, restraint, and decision. This is the space in which Rabin, 'the military man', is left with his moral qualms, and in which he must confront 'the silence in which I remain alone'. Indeed, says Rabin, 'of all the memories I have stored up in my seventy-two years, what I shall remember most, to my last day, are the silences. The heavy silence of the moment after, and the terrifying silence of the moment before'. It is this silent space which has formed Rabin as a subject and it is here, furthermore, that the ethical code he is announcing will aim to do its work.

* * *

Military ethical codes are often presented as mechanisms for restraining the violence of war. In the Israeli context, this has undoubtedly been a common argument. The IDF ethical code (also known as 'The Spirit of the IDF', *Ruah Tsahal*) is a constant reference point in apologist accounts of Israeli state violence, both in the pronouncements of the IDF Spokesperson and in the wider media. The code is presented as evidence of moral military conduct and a commitment to reduce the level of casualties, especially civilian casualties. More critical observers have noticed the incongruence between the proclaimed values of the ethical code and, for example, the high number of civilian casualties in Israel's recent military assaults on Gaza. For some, this incongruence is demonstration that the ethical code of the IDF is ineffective or too commonly ignored, the implication being that greater enforcement and accountability are necessary (Sagi, 2011; see also Harel, 2009a).

Another set of critical observers see the code and its practical interpretations differently. They do not view enforcement as the main issue. Instead, they view the entire edifice as an exercise in the justification and legitimation of violence (Al-Khalidi, 2010; Chamayou, 2015: 127–34). No matter how well enforced, they argue, the ethical code is designed to allow for the deployment of force in a way which suits Israeli military and political objectives. These arguments are closely aligned with the critique of the practice of state 'lawfare', whereby states develop legal arguments designed to vindicate their pursuit of war (Hajjar, 2006; Weizman, 2009, 2010, 2012: 99–138; Halper, 2010, 2014; Jones, 2015; Perugini and Gordon, 2015: esp. 70–100). These critics view the Israeli experience as an attempt to reconfigure the boundaries of International Humanitarian Law (IHL) to suit state and military interests. Accordingly, they also observe a convergence between ethics and law, or a 'judicialisation' of ethics (Chouchane, 2009).

These critiques touch much more closely on the true function of the IDF ethical code than apologist accounts. Yet they miss an important dimension of Israeli military ethics, which is its role in the formation of soldier-subjects. Analysing the IDF ethical code requires an answer to the question: for whom was it written? Existing critiques make it clear that the code was certainly *not* written to save Palestinian lives – quite the contrary. What is less clear, however, is the intended *audience* for these elaborate doctrines. In the view of those drawing comparisons with 'lawfare', it appears to be some combination of the international community, foreign and domestic public opinion, and to a much lesser extent the military itself. My view, however, is that the IDF ethical code was primarily written for soldiers themselves, with the explicit aim of improving their willingness to fight. The IDF ethical code is therefore not the product of a benevolent moral attitude to Israel's enemies but is instead a part of an ensemble of governing technologies designed to address a range of motivational, organisational, and ideological problems faced by the IDF. The solution to all of these problems has been to cultivate the Israeli soldier as an ethical subject.

As discussed in the previous chapter, militarism has often been understood as a form of biopower which is fundamentally concerned with the management of human life through the selective application of violence. Its principal aim is therefore seen as governing soldiers and citizens as bodies and populations. Writing about military ethics, scholars have also argued that more deliberative and personal modes of ethics do not suit this mode of biopolitical governmentality. Instead, biopolitics is seen as encouraging the reduction of military ethics to the probabilistic management of risks to populations through violence. Schwarz notes the tendency for biopolitics to produce a codification of ethics:

When the socio-political mandate that informs the norm is centred on a calculable humanity and focused on the abstract idea of the survival of mankind, it is perhaps not surprising that contemporary theories about ethics, specifically in the context of war and just war theory, are turned into something calculable and predictable, framed as formulas or algorithms with which to determine ethical behaviour. (Schwarz, 2013: 145; see also Hutchings, 2010: 161)

This tendency is often associated with a growing role for machines in war-fighting, and in particular the rise to prominence of drone warfare

(Schwarz, 2015). In the case of the IDF ethical code, Anat Matar has further argued that its biopolitical tendencies are evident in the way that it assumes a perfect circularity between its values and the behaviour of soldiers, thereby aiming to 'conquer the individual' (2006: 9).

These observations are telling but they are also insufficient. For biopolitics does not always depend on a flattening of individual ethical behaviour. Regimes of military ethical governance also seek to engage the soldier as a subject, which requires them to cultivate and not diminish soldiers' individual ethical faculties. In this sense, it is important to understand the principles behind the ethical code not only as biopolitical but also as *liberal*, in that they seek to promote and direct soldiers' individual freedom (Rose, 1995; Foucault, 2008b: esp. 51–74, 129–58; Dean, 2010: 43–4). As Graham Burchell observes:

Liberalism, particularly in its modern versions, constructs a relationship between government and the governed that increasingly depends upon ways in which individuals are required to assume the status of *being the subjects of their lives*, upon the ways in which they fashion themselves as certain kinds of subjects, upon the ways in which they practice their freedom. [And] to the extent that practices of the self are what give concrete shape to the exercise of freedom, that is to say, are what give a concrete form to *ethics*, there opens up a new, uncertain, often critical and unstable domain of relationships between politics and ethics, between the government of others and practices of self. (1995: 29–30, emphasis added)

The important role of unstable freedom in liberal government undermines the idea that contemporary biopolitical military ethics merely pursues the impersonal reduction of risk. Indeed, as this chapter will show, it is precisely the encouragement of practices of individual freedom which has been at the heart of the reasoning behind the IDF ethical code.

While this emphasis on freedom has certainly created challenges, it has generally been a source of dynamism rather than weakness. The problem of how to produce ethical soldiers has been continually posed and answered anew in different and often contradictory ways. But this has also been the means by which ethical disagreement, ethical failure, and even ethical transgression are made part of this ensemble of governing technologies and a marked feature of Israeli militarism. Indeed, it is here that the role of ideology becomes crucial. For one crucial aim of this new ethical freedom has been to generate the impression of a voluntary and participatory 'Spirit of the IDF', in which the views and deliberations of all soldiers matter. This ethical spirit is designed to be deeply immersive in that it can register and reflect every individual experience, even when they deviate from widely held norms. As this chapter will begin to show, this also opens up a crucial space for testimony in ethical discussion and military ethical pedagogy.

The Origins of the IDF Ethical Code

The first recommendation to produce an ethical code for the IDF was made in 1991 by Major General Ilan Biran after he returned to Israel from a year studying with the US Marine Corps.[2] In a letter he sent to the then Chief of Staff, Ehud Barak, Biran recommended, among many other things, that the IDF should develop a code of ethics similar to the code of the Marines. Barak was enthusiastic about the idea and he established a committee responsible for the drafting of the document led by the head of the IDF Human Resources Directorate, General Yoram Yair. The rest of the committee comprised the Chief Education Officer, the Judge Advocate General, and the philosopher Asa Kasher from Tel Aviv University. Kasher undertook the greater part of the work to prepare the text of the code and he is widely credited as its principal author.[3]

The preparatory committee worked from 1992 to 1994 before submitting a final draft to the General Staff, which was finally approved in December 1994. It was titled 'The Spirit of the IDF: Basic Values and Principles'.[4] The code was structured in three parts, with a preface describing the sources and purpose of the code, followed by a list of basic values and their definitions, and finally a more detailed series of norms to guide behaviour in specific circumstances. Eleven basic values constituted the core of the document: pursuit of

---

[2] The account of the drafting of the first version of the ethical code in the following two paragraphs is derived from the author's interview with Asa Kasher.

[3] Kasher had been working with the army as a teacher of military ethics for a number of years already. His involvement in the process of drafting the code of ethics would mark a major step in the evolution of his career towards his present status as a public intellectual. Kasher's influence on military ethics in Israel has been both marked and controversial, and consequently his thinking will warrant significant attention throughout this chapter.

[4] See Appendix A.

the mission, responsibility, integrity, personal example, human life, purity of arms, professionalism, discipline, loyalty, representation, and camaraderie.

The immediate context for the introduction of the code of ethics was the wider process of professionalisation in the IDF led by Ehud Barak. By the early 1990s, the IDF faced growing problems of manpower and resources. Owing to the wider socio-economic trends associated with neoliberalism, the secular Ashkenazi elite which had traditionally provided the IDF with its main combat troops had turned away from military participation and towards the market as a source of social advancement (Levy, 2007: 147–79). Likewise, the defence budget had been steadily cut from 25% to 13% of GDP in the decade to 1995 (Cohen, 1995: 241). Responding to these trends, Barak wanted to move the IDF towards a professional model, a 'small and smart army' rather than a 'people's army' (Cohen, 1995, 2008: 83–106; Ben-Eliezer, 2004). Recruitment became more selective, the reserves were cut, and administrative staff were laid off. A new managerial culture was instigated, which Ben-Eliezer has described as 'influenced by neo-liberal managerial-business-marketing ideology', incorporating such approaches as Total Quality Management (2004: 55–6). Barak also attempted to rein in the large of number of non-military social programmes undertaken by the IDF, famously claiming that 'those who do not shoot will be cut' (Ben-Eliezer, 2004: 55–6).

Meanwhile, the IDF's attitude towards those who did shoot changed. The IDF began to regard itself as a competitor with other sources of employment and therefore introduced market principles to encourage greater enlistment to combat units, including increased pay and a client-based approach towards soldiers (Ben-Eliezer, 2004: 57–8; Levy, 2007: 147–9). The individual soldier was viewed less as a member of a collective national project, and increasingly as *homo economicus*, as an individual who would freely choose to become a soldier because it would give him an opportunity to enhance himself through military participation (cf. Foucault, 2008b: 225–33, 267–80). To increase the attractiveness of soldiering as a choice, the IDF also pursued a strengthening of corporate identity and the development of professional standards. In particular, attempts were made to enhance the officer corps through new and revamped training programmes (Libel, 2010, 2013: 283–4, 2014: esp. 91–3).

The introduction of an ethical code, aimed not just at officers but at all soldiers, was perhaps the clearest manifestation of the neoliberal drive towards professionalisation. Kasher's basic conception of how an ethical code should operate derives from his claim that the IDF should be understood as a professional military operating in a liberal-democratic society (1996).[5] The role of the military in such a society is, according to Kasher, to make it possible for individual citizens to enjoy the rights they hold, the right to life being paramount among them. This emphasis on the right to life is a symptomatic liberal concern, showing the importance of the citizen not only as a rights-bearing subject but also as the object of biopolitical power (Foucault, 1998a: 133–60, 2004: 239–64). These obligations require the liberal state to preserve the life of its population, if necessary through the use of military force. As Kasher stresses, building an army and fighting wars is in fact a 'moral duty' of the state (1996: 39–41). However, this creates a paradox, since in Kasher's conception the soldiers who are sent to defend the population are also considered 'citizens in uniform', whose lives also need protecting. This biopolitical justification for the use of force therefore finds expression in two different values of the ethical code: 'pursuit of the mission' (defined as protecting the population) and 'human life' (which requires the IDF to safeguard human life as far as possible in its missions).[6] What is most curious about the inclusion of these biopolitical dimensions in the ethical code, however, is that soldiers thereby become both the subject and object of this liberal duty of care. Consider the following passage from Kasher's textbook, *Military Ethics*:

By means of its norms the army says to the soldier: you are also important to us. It is not just upon you to protect the lives of others meticulously because their lives are important to us, but also to protect your own life because your life is also important to us. (1996: 52; my translation)

The state's biopolitical obligations are redoubled inside the soldier-subject here: soldiers must defend citizens, but they are also citizens themselves; the lives of soldiers must be protected by the state, but soldiers are also responsible for carrying this out. By instantiating

[5] This claim is of course widely disputed. For alternative views on the question of democracy in Israel/Palestine, see Yiftachel (2006) and Azoulay and Ophir (2012).
[6] See Appendix A.

these duties in an ethical code for soldiers, the state therefore attempts to fulfil them by cultivating soldiers who are, in Burchell's words, 'subjects of their lives' – simultaneously living beings, armed professionals, and ethical actors (1995: 30). The zone of ethical reflection inside the soldier becomes the space where the biopolitical rationale for the use of military violence is folded back upon itself, thereby producing a subject.

Anat Matar has observed a biopolitical tendency in the very grammar of the ethical code (2006: 4–11). It makes incessant use of Modern Hebrew's 'future-imperative' tense, thereby conflating what will be with what is expected (Matar, 2006: 9). The clearest example comes in the preface:

The Spirit of the IDF is the code of ethics according to which all the IDF's soldiers, officers, units and forces *will* comport themselves, and it *will* serve in molding their patterns of action. They *will* educate and critique themselves and their fellows in accordance with the Spirit of the IDF.[7]

For Matar the ethical code therefore takes on the quality not of the law, but of a much stronger 'superlaw' that aims to 'conquer the individual'. It is a language which does not prescribe as such but which instead purports innocently to render explicit what is already true by definition (2006: 7). Indeed, Kasher described it to me in exactly these terms:

a code of ethics is an upgrade of the relationships with value systems and with identity and with norms within the organisation. Even if you don't have a code of ethics they are there. But they are implicit and they could vary from one person to another and some persons could even have wrong conceptions. When you have a code of ethics it's shared to a significant extent and you can show why certain marginal conceptions are wrong and should be gotten rid of. And it's shared by everyone, so it's an upgrade.[8]

However, one should not be tempted into concluding that this circularity removes the role for ethical subjectivity. The individual who is 'conquered' in such statements does not thereby disappear; in many ways, he acquires an enhanced importance. In fact, even the

---

[7] See Appendix A [emphasis added].
[8] Author interview.

stark prefatory statement quoted above acknowledges the necessity of education and critique.

This is where Kasher's precise understanding of ethics as a feature of professionalism acquires its significance. An important aspect of this view is that the role of an ethical code is not to impose a certain vision of what the professional standards should be:

The subject matter of professional ethics is commonly held to consist of principles and rules of the form 'thou shalt' or 'thou shalt not', meant to regulate activity in a certain professional arena. To my mind, this is a wrong portrayal of professional ethics. (Kasher, 2005: 73–4)

Kasher instead claims that the values of the code are 'products of [professional] understanding, not its constitutive ingredients' and, in a sense, are therefore reflections of the prior free choices of the individuals they seek to guide (Kasher, 2005: 74). In order to make this impression convincing, however, it is necessary to generate a sense of involvement in and ownership of the ethical process on the part of the soldier. The code must invite soldiers' free participation as ethical subjects, encouraging them to implement the code as a reflection of their own decision (cf. Rose, 1995: 57–60; Dean, 2010: 43–4).

The most obvious way in which this effect is achieved is that the ethical code has no legal authority or enforcement mechanism. It only has meaning insofar as soldiers are prepared to use it themselves. The content of the code is also important for achieving this. For Kasher, this means that the values of the ethical code must seem achievable and therefore relatable to the soldier. He describes these values as embodying a 'practical ideal':

a 'practical ideal' is a set of values or principles that lends grounds to reasoned decisions, that are *practical*, not just in the sense that these are actions and patterns of behaviour but also in the sense that these are decisions that are not beyond the capacity of any normal individual, in a standard situation, within the professional context of his activity. In order to implement any decision pertaining to right behaviour – as inferred from the practical ideal – such a person must *know* what the decision is and *want* to implement it. The term 'ideal' does not purport to place the right behaviour on the horizon and thereabouts, where it cannot be reached, but one can always approach it. The term 'practical ideal' emphasizes the following: 'I know' and 'I want to' means 'I can'. (2002a: 102–3, emphasis in original)

Significantly, this position does not imply that soldiers must simply internalise and act upon given commands. The subjective element is much stronger than this: the soldier *must want* to implement the practical ideal. By acknowledging the importance of this 'I want to', Kasher has indeed touched upon, as all ethical systems must, the question of the subject's desire. He is outlining a theory of ethics, contrasted explicitly with one based on law (either Israeli or international), which emphasises the willingness, rather than simply the obligation, of the soldier-subject to identify with certain values. This conception should also be recognised as ideological. Žižek observes the 'post-modern' tendency for the superego to demand not obedience but enjoyment: the subject must no longer simply obey the law regardless of his preference but rather pursue what authority demands as if it were the product of his free choice (2008c: 313–99, esp. 344–5). With the adoption of Kasher's ethical code, the IDF manifested precisely this tendency. The public values of Israeli militarism were to be made unconscious and enjoyable. At the same time, however, the behavioural changes these values might seem to imply were left entirely optional. Indeed, its effectiveness as an ideological document depended precisely on the extent to which it remained unenforceable. This innovation is the subjective index of a shift from the model of a conscript 'people's army' to a more professional, and perhaps ultimately 'all volunteer', IDF.

It is nevertheless something of a risk to rely on the free decision of individuals to underpin the appeal of an ethical code. The challenge becomes one of encouraging adherence to and identification with its values while still allowing for soldiers' free choice. This was especially difficult in a setting where, as in the 1990s, the demographic composition of the IDF was becoming more diverse. Kasher's proposed solution to this problem of ethical diversity was the creation of a list of 34 detailed norms to supplement the 11 basic values.[9] These norms have three basic functions: showing how the values should be expressed in practice; showing the extent to which they should be expressed; and helping to resolve dilemmas between competing values (Kasher, 1996: 185–229). By circumscribing the ethical process in this way, Kasher aimed to guide the free decisions of soldiers. Indeed, these norms would assist with the cultivation of a specific ethical faculty which would inform these

---

[9] See Appendix A.

decisions, a faculty which Kasher refers to as *shiḵul da'at* [judgement, or discretion].

The Hebrew term *shiḵul da'at* translates poorly into English. Although 'judgement' is an accurate rendering of its sense, the two words that combine to make the Hebrew term do not translate well separately for this purpose. *Shiḵul* can be understood to mean 'consideration', but it also has the connotation of 'weighing' different possibilities, opinions, and decisions. *Da'at* translates as knowledge or wisdom and conveys the sense that this judgement is informed and taken from a position of understanding. The ethical faculty of *shiḵul da'at* is of crucial importance for understanding military ethics in Israel, even though its precise meaning and scope are subject to some disagreement. Kasher's vision of its role is a relatively restrictive one. Although he acknowledges that it is impossible to fix one way of doing something in advance and that the soldier's free judgement therefore assumes crucial importance, he stipulates that judgement should be constantly informed by the 'practical rules' [*klalim ma'aśiyim*] provided by the 34 norms of the ethical code:

It is important to understand that practical rules do not take the place of judgement [*shiḵul da'at*]. On the contrary, they are designed to enhance it. In order for there to be judgement [*shiḵul da'at*], it is necessary for there to be consideration [*shiḵul*], and it is necessary for there to be knowledge [*da'at*]. The practical rule is a part of that knowledge [*da'at*]. Judgement [*shiḵul da'at*] is carried out with the help of the practical rule. Just as it is impossible for there to be a practical rule not followed by judgement [*shiḵul da'at*], so it is impossible for there to be judgement [*shiḵul da'at*] without a practical rule before it. (1996: 188; my translation)

However, Kasher acknowledges that the difficulty of relying on this faculty of judgement is precisely that this personal involvement of the soldier in the ethical decision risks escaping the bounds imposed by the norms. When the norms are no longer taken into consideration, the decision ceases to be the result of judgement [*shiḵul da'at*] and becomes the product of unreliable 'personal deliberation' [*hitlabtut 'ishit*]:

Personal deliberation [*hitlabtut 'ishit*] is not invalid, it could even have strong personal value, but it is important to understand that it does not have any professional or moral value in itself [. . .] If the personal deliberation [*hitlabtut 'ishit*] leads to a correct outcome, it is likely that it will have a psychological value from the point of view of the natural inclination of the soldier to act according to it. Despite this, if the personal deliberation [*hitlabtut 'ishit*] leads the soldier to an incorrect outcome, which, for example, risks loss of life in circumstances where endangering life is forbidden, then this positive psychological value is dwarfed [. . .] by the negative content of the mistaken decision and by its bad consequences. (Kasher, 1996: 216; my translation)

This dangerous personal excess of subjective involvement in the ethical process, which he acknowledges is unavoidable, is precisely what Kasher is attempting to constrain through his conception of professional ethics. *Hitlabtut* (which can also be translated as 'wavering' or 'having doubts', as well as 'deliberation') must be disciplined and channelled into more objective judgement, no matter how painful it makes the decision: 'there is no escape from judgement [*shiḳul da'at*], however professional, moral, principled, difficult, profound, and shocking it must be' (1996: 228).

By seeking to marshal the free decisions and judgements of the individual soldier in the new IDF ethical code, Kasher therefore made a typically liberal contribution to the project of professionalising the IDF and rejuvenating Israeli militarism. He attempted to incorporate a new kind of governmental and ideological strategy, one which sought not only to involve soldiers in Israeli militarism as obedient bodies or a national collective but also to invest them as subjects in its proclaimed values. Yet he also introduced a necessary instability in making use of this subjective element of freedom, one he acknowledged could not be fully controlled. Kasher's highly ambitious project was therefore highly likely to come up against alternative conceptions and to struggle in capturing the variety of possible militarist subjectivities. Indeed, no sooner had Kasher's code been accepted by the General Staff and announced with great fanfare in Rabin's speech than the effort to alter it began in earnest.

Redrafting the IDF Ethical Code

Kasher presented his code widely before it was first adopted, seeking feedback and possible improvements. One such presentation was attended by Colonel (later General) Elazar Stern, then head of Bahad 1, the principal training institution for IDF officers. Stern was a member of Israel's national-religious community and was a prominent figure in new generation of religious soldiers entering the ranks of the IDF. During the question and answer session, Stern raised his hand and commented that what struck him about the proposed code was that there was nothing specifically 'Jewish' about it. He asked Kasher why 'love of the land' [*ahavat ha'arets*] was not among its basic values, since this seemed to him a key aspect of soldiers' motivation to serve in the IDF (Stern, 2012: 191). Over time, a wave of criticism in this vein developed with Stern at the forefront.[10] It did not come simply from a religious perspective, however. In an article published in the right-wing *Tekhelet (Azure)* magazine in 1997, Tzvi Hauser (then an instructor in the IDF's Leadership Development Institute, and later cabinet secretary to Benjamin Netanyahu) set out a strong statement against Kasher's code from a secular right-wing point of view (Hauser, 1997: 47–72). He also upbraided Kasher for failing to include 'love of the land' as a value (1997: 54–9). Yet Hauser went further, accusing the code of representing the spread of 'post-Zionism' in the IDF and the weakening of Jewish Israeli identity:

> . . . the main failing of Spirit of the IDF is the fact that it is purposefully devoid of any Zionist or Jewish content. The code is designed in such a way that the army of every democratic country in the world could adopt it without changing a word. The new IDF code does not reflect or demand any sense of commitment to any of the central tenets of the Zionist idea: It mentions nothing about the loyalty of the army to the Jewish state and Jewish national sovereignty, nor does it provide any expression at all of the country's bond with world Jewry. . . As far as actual ideological content, the code obligates the IDF to uphold and defend the 'democratic character' of the State of Israel – and nothing more. It embodies no values such as 'patriotism' or 'love of the land', and therefore signals an abandonment of the basic points of consensus that were the ideological heritage of the IDF up until the publication of the code. (1997: 53)

Kasher responded fiercely to these accusations. Firstly, he argued that it was not practical for a code of ethics to mandate the object of a soldier's love. Secondly, he argued that the inclusion of the values

---

[10] Author interview with Ya'akov Castel.

of 'human life' and 'purity of arms' showed that Jewish values had a certain influence over the document. Thirdly, he rejected altogether the necessity for the code to be 'Jewish' or 'Zionist' in character. He argued that professional ethics, in his conception, does not require such a character but instead demands fidelity to the principles of 'democracy', since that has the strongest influence on the nature of the society in which the profession must operate.[11]

Initially, the General Staff accepted Kasher's arguments. Once the code was announced, however, the backlash grew in intensity. Stern immediately drew up his own separate code of ethics for the officers at his academy ('The Values of an Officer'), arguing that while he accepted Kasher's code he would also demand additional standards from officers, including 'love of the land'. He also wrote a letter to the new Chief of Staff, Amnon Lipkin-Shahak, criticising what he called 'The Neutral, Universal, and International Code' (Stern, 2012: 192–3). Within a year the controversy had grown and had even entered electoral politics. In the context of the Oslo Process, the decision to exclude 'love of the land' was widely interpreted as abandoning a commitment to annexing the occupied territories of the West Bank. The National Religious Party added a promise to introduce 'love of the land' into the code to its manifesto for the elections of 1996, and even made this demand during negotiations to enter Netanyahu's first coalition government. Faced with this pressure, Lipkin-Shahak convened a meeting over the issue where it was agreed that, although the code should remain unchanged for five years until 2000, it would then be possible to review it if problems had arisen.[12]

In the interceding years, Stern was gradually promoted through the ranks of the IDF and in 1999 was appointed Chief Officer of the Education and Youth Corps, giving him responsibility for the ethical code (Stern, 2012: 152–3). Immediately after the elapse of five years in 2000, he decided to open the code for review, seizing the opportunity 'like a blessing from heaven' (Stern, 2012: 193). Stern informed Kasher of his intention to form a wider team to review the code and attempted to include him; but Kasher was opposed to any major revisions, and after some initial meetings the two men clashed badly. According to Stern, when the decision was made to embark on significant changes

[11] Author interview with Asa Kasher; see also Kasher (2002b).
[12] Author interview with Asa Kasher.

Kasher simply got up and left the room, 'slamming the door behind him' (2012: 194).

Stern delegated organisational responsibility of the committee to Colonel Ya'akov Castel, the head of the IDF education department within the Education and Youth Corps.[13] He also appointed several academics and military figures to the committee, many of whom were chosen through personal connection.[14] The group included Professor Avi Sagi (who was Stern's youth movement leader), Professor Daniel Statman, Professor Shaul Smilansky, Professor Moshe Halbertal, and Major General Yishai Beer. Most of the academics involved were specialists in either moral or Jewish philosophy. Moreover, as far as I am aware, the committee was all male. This core team, with the assistance of other contributors at various points, set about a lengthy consultation and discussion process.

Taking Kasher's code as a starting point, they worked to reformulate the text, discussing minute details for hours in lengthy meetings that occasionally 'started in the early evening and adjourned at sunrise' (Stern, 2012: 195). Stern and Castel were also greatly concerned that the document be seen as representative of both the IDF and wider society. Accordingly, drafts were circulated to focus groups across the army, ranging across the different branches and among different ranks, and to several representatives in civil society from a range of social groups. This included literary figures associated with the Israeli left (such as Amos Oz and A.B. Yehoshua) and figures associated with *Gush Emunim* and the settler movement (such as Yosef Ben-Shlomo).[15]

After one and a half years of discussions, the new code was finally adopted in 2001. The document made three major kinds of changes to the original.[16] The first was in the wording of the values, changes which were mostly stylistic in nature but which occasionally also affected content.[17] The second was the inclusion of three 'fundamental values', set above and apart from the basic values. And the third was the removal of the detailed 34 norms which Kasher had written. Together, these revisions reflect a significant change in the thinking

---

[13] Author interview with Ya'akov Castel.
[14] Author interview with Avi Sagi.
[15] Author interview with Ya'akov Castel.
[16] See Appendix B.
[17] Most notably the value of 'purity of arms'; see below.

underpinning the document, especially in its attitude towards the soldier as an ethical subject. Indeed, this change in the pedagogical approach represented a much more significant departure than the changes in normative content or concessions to any specific political or religious agenda.

Despite Stern's commitment to including 'love of the land' and connecting the code with 'Jewish values', as well as the influence of the national-religious movement in pushing for its alteration, most of the changes made did not especially reflect national-religious demands. It is true that the sought-after 'Jewish' elements were introduced. However, their place in the document is carefully circumscribed and the result is hardly a transformation in its character. Israel is now identified as a 'Jewish and democratic state' in the preamble, whereas it was not before. In addition, one of the fundamental values is 'patriotism and loyalty to the state' [*'ahavat moledet vene'amanut lamedina*]. Yet this is not the 'love of the land' [*'ahavat ha'arets*] formula that was originally demanded. The committee instead opted to use a formulation suggested by A.B. Yehoshua, 'patriotism' [*'ahavat moledet*, or 'love of homeland', more literally translated].[18] In the precise wording of this value, Israel is defined as 'a democratic state which constitutes a national home for the Jewish people', which is in fact a slight departure from the language of Israel's Basic Laws. Although this is only a semantic difference given the document's lack of legal force, the alteration was made because of the perceived need to motivate Druze and Bedouin troops.[19] It underscores the point that the code was not simply adjusted to reflect national-religious demands. The aim, at least in theory, was to increase the range of possible subject positions from which the code might be embraced in reaction to the growing social diversity in the army.

The difficulty, however, was finding a means to constrain this diversity even as greater room was made for its inclusion. The convenor of the steering group made precisely such a point in interview:

if in the past there was one hegemonic ethos, that permeated everyone [*ethos ehad hegemoni, shekulam hulhlu 'alpiv*] . . . in the '90s, there was the beginning of disagreements over what the correct values were in Israeli society.

---

[18] Author interview with Ya'akov Castel.
[19] Author interview with Avi Sagi.

So when you enlist lots of people from different ideological communities, with different systems of values, and they naturally bring these values inside the army, and you give them means of violence, you give them a weapon, then you have to create a kind of mental and ethical regulation [*leyatser 'eyzeh 'asdara mentalit 'erkhit*] according to which everyone will act. Otherwise everyone will act according to the values which they bring from home, which is something very problematic in a military system.[20]

Whereas Kasher had attempted to respond to this difficulty through the creation of a set of norms, the approach of the new committee was different. Instead they decided to abandon these norms and to focus on simplifying the code and making its language less formal. In addition, rather than elaborating specific rules to help decide on cases where there appeared to be a conflict between basic values, three much broader 'fundamental values' (defence of the state, patriotism, and human dignity) were included to help soldiers navigate such dilemmas. The apparent puzzle which needs to be solved, however, is how this relaxation of the format and style would still be able to achieve the goal of 'creating a kind of moral and ethical regulation'.

A perception which many of the members of the committee shared was that the previous code was not accessible enough for the soldier and did not sufficiently engage him as an ethical subject.[21] Committee member Avi Sagi, who as a reservist in the Education Corps had attempted to teach Kasher's code, commented that:

. . . it was so unfriendly to the officer. Many of them told me it is better to learn how to deal with computers than with this code. Soldiers and officers have to receive decisions in the conditions of battle, in conditions of warfare, and they have to use judgement [*shikul da'at*]. They have to make use of their own considerations regarding the specific situation they confront. And this is a problem that the old code didn't allow for. The earlier code turned the officers (mostly – less the soldiers) from being a subject to being an object. They gave the data to the computer and received the right answer. That was the problem that we, that I encountered as a reservist who had to explain this.[22]

---

[20] Author interview with Ya'akov Castel [my translation].
[21] Author interviews with Moshe Halbertal, Avi Sagi, and Ya'akov Castel.
[22] Author interview [my translation].

Ya'akov Castel, the convenor of the committee, concurred on this
point when he described the purpose of the change in tone:

the practical meaning of this is to give much more weight to the discretion
[shiḵul hada'at] of the commanders. If I am a commander in the army and
I need to act, according to the perspective of Asa Kasher, if I learn my profession in a serious way, I will come to the one appropriate answer and
all the commanders will come to the same decision. There is just one
appropriate, legitimate answer. In the second perspective, two different
commanders − or more than two different commanders − will arrive at
different solutions, and they will both be appropriate. So it's not chaos.
The spectrum is limited. It has limits. But still the weight of the judgement
[shiḵul hada'at] of each commander in dealing with it is much greater in
the second perspective. The first perspective turns them into automatons
[aṭomaṭim] to a certain extent.[23]

From these statements we can see that the drafters of the new ethical
code wished to grant a greater role for the soldier's faculty of 'judgement' [shiḵul da'at]. Although Kasher also sees a role for individual
judgement, and he further denied in interview that he believed that
there can be only one correct answer in dealing with dilemmas, it is
clear that the abandonment of the norms and the changes in the code's
language were seen as a move away from his more restrictive understanding of shiḵul da'at.

However, the intended result of this decision was not that the standards would be lowered and soldiers would be expected to identify
with the code less. This is where a simple language of greater or lesser
freedom fails to account for an ideological dimension. As Judith Butler
has made clear, individuals can be made more compliant not only,
or even primarily, through the wider dissemination of stricter norms.
Instead, it is their subjective constitution and their resultant willingness to exercise power *over themselves* which constitute the crucial
factor (1996: 106–32, 167–200). The motivation behind making
the tone of the document less formal was precisely so that it could
be more readily applied by soldiers themselves in assessing their own

[23] Author interview [my translation].

behaviour, and therefore that its injunctions would be more keenly felt. Indeed, part of the reason why so many extensive consultations with soldiers took place was to ensure that this effect would be achieved. Avi Sagi described the purpose of these meetings with soldiers as follows:

The question was how to translate the values in such a way that the soldier will be able to use them, to interpret their own situation in the framework of the values. That was the question. The dialogue was very important. It was not important in the way that one soldier or officer will say to us: I don't accept, I don't agree with the value of human dignity. That wasn't the question. [It] was always a question of translation and interpretation. And the writing of this code in a familiar way, in a friendly way. That was the point.[24]

What is clear from this statement is that, despite the greater role for the soldier, the values of the code remained non-negotiable. The changes in tone were not designed to grant soldiers greater leniency but rather to ensure soldiers would in fact be more inclined to identify with its values.

Elazar Stern himself touches upon the way in which a less formal language can actually be more exacting for the soldier. Emphasising firstly 'the need to simplify some of the texts and make the code easier for regular soldiers to comprehend', he then illustrates his point with reference to a particular value:

I suggested we replace the term 'integrity' that appeared in the code with 'honesty'. Integrity, as far as I understood the term, is something that depends on others who observe you. Honesty on the other hand is something more personal; it is about you opposite the mirror. It's sharper and deeper. (2012: 195)

Stern's trick here is to pretend that he is not referring to 'something that depends on others who observe you', as he claims Kasher's code does. Instead, he argues that this impetus to behave honestly can come from within. However, a more psychoanalytic perspective reveals this

---

[24] Author interview.

claim to be fundamentally ideological. No individual can exist without a socially derived language in which his or her desire can be expressed. Even the personal mirror image of which Stern speaks depends on a prior identification with these values.[25] The ideal which the soldier must live up to is therefore no different in content or origin from Kasher's image of professional excellence. The only difference is that Stern's version is more internally entrenched within the subject and more aligned with the soldier's tendency to judge himself in the mirror. Stern makes the claim that the subject is pursuing self-realisation in pursuing standards which are unique and internal to him, exercising his own 'judgement' at every stage, while simultaneously offering a list of immutable values whose content is entirely socially given.

This greater emphasis on the soldier's identification with the values of the code has significant consequences. Whereas Kasher's code offered a 'practical ideal', a target which the soldier could always reach if he wished, the second code actively inscribes a gap between the soldier and ideal behaviour in its ethical architecture. One minor but revealing change made (at the suggestion of Moshe Halbertal and Yishai Beer) to the opening words of the preface makes this clear. Kasher's original version had read:

The Spirit of the IDF is the moral and normative identity card of the IDF as an organisation, which stands [zo ha'omedet] as the foundation for all actions carried out by all men and women soldiers in the framework of the IDF . . .[26]

After revision, however, the current version now states:

The Spirit of the IDF is the moral and normative identity card of the IDF which it is appropriate that should stand ['esher ra'ui shete'amod] as the foundation of the activities of all men and women soldiers in the framework of the IDF . . .[27]

---

[25] 'It is only after the emergence of the ego-ideal *qua* symbolic identification that the subject is properly individuated at the level of the Imaginary, and his ego is consolidated' (Chiesa, 2007: 81).

[26] See Appendix A.

[27] See Appendix B.

Ya'akov Castel considered this alteration to be of immense importance:

> It's a big difference . . . As soon as you say 'it is appropriate that it should act like this' you are saying that it is an educational document . . . You are constantly educating the soldiers to reach this standard, with the clear knowledge [that] there is a gap [*pa'ar*], there will always be a gap between . . . common human behaviour [*hahitnahagut ha'enoshit harovahat*] and the appropriate standard [*haraf hara'ui*]. We will try to reduce this gap as much as possible – that is our role, as an institution and as commanders.[28]

This recognition of the residual, irreducible gap in the subject has several important effects. Firstly, it extends rather than limits the authority of the ethical code. In psychoanalytic terms, it enhances the role of the superego, the punitive internal demand to obey, since the demands of the code are by definition impossible to meet. In fact, in the classic logic of the superego, the more one attempts to obey it, the guiltier one feels. Secondly, the ethical process no longer depends on successful compliance to be effective and engaging. Whereas Kasher's code posited a circularity between existing practice and the values of the code, the new code can function perfectly well, perhaps even better, if its standards are regularly not met. Thirdly, as will be shown in more depth later, this gap creates a crucial opening for testimony in the ethical process. Speech becomes the medium in which this gap can be registered, as past failings are recalled, analysed, and learnt from, thus sealing off the failure and reaffirming a renewed commitment to succeed.

This is the true significance of the new 'Jewish' elements in the code. By drawing on national and religious symbols, the new version not only addresses the challenge of pluralism in the IDF by providing focal points for common loyalty. It also strengthens individual identification with the values of the code by providing a cultural anchor (one could say 'master-signifier', or 'quilting point') for its values (cf. Chiesa, 2007: 88–96; Žižek, 2008b: 95–110). The new fundamental value of 'love of homeland' should be interpreted in just this way: not only is the 'homeland' intended to provide a shared reference point for all soldiers, it is also deemed capable of commanding such loyalty that it can be the object of their 'love' and thus an intense focus of identifcation.

---

[28] Author interview [my translation].

For Kasher, by contrast, it is hopeless to demand love from soldiers, since it does not constitute a 'practical ideal'.

A value such as 'love of homeland' makes it possible to see how, in spite of its familiar language and its greater role for the discretion of the soldier, the new code ends up demanding a much greater loyalty from him. Indeed, on this basis it is clear that the liberal logic present in Kasher's code is much more pronounced in the second version. The strategy is paradoxically to depend *even more* on the subjective involvement of the soldier and his free personal decisions, all the while making the practical ramifications of the values of the code even less specific. By aiming to implant its standards even deeper inside the soldier himself and by mobilising the inevitable gap that appears between its impossible standards and actual behaviour, the new code took this tendency to its extreme and produced a much stronger ideological edifice as a result. It is only with these important differences in mind that we will be able to approach the most contentious value of the code and to understand what underlies the philosophical debate surrounding it.

'Purity of Arms' and the Assaults on Gaza

The most vaunted and emblematic of the values of the IDF ethical code is undoubtedly 'purity of arms' [*tohar haneshek*]. In Kasher's original, the value appears as follows:

The soldier will use his weapon and his power to vanquish the enemy only to the degree required, and will exercise self-restraint in order to prevent unnecessary harm to human life, body, honour and property.[29]

Its meaning is further elaborated beneath:

Purity of arms among IDF troops means the restrained use they make of their weapons and their power in the implementation of missions, only to the extent necessary for their attainment, without unnecessary harm to human life, body, honour and property, whether to troops or civilians (especially the defenceless), during war and security operations as well as during times of peace and tranquillity.

[29] See Appendix A.

In the new code, however, the value acquired a different definition:

The soldier will use his weapon and his power only for the fulfillment of the mission, and only to the extent required, and he will maintain his human image even in combat. The soldier will not use his weapon or force to harm non-combatants or captives, and will do all he can to prevent harm to their lives, bodies, dignity, and property.[30]

The committee members paid particular attention to the reformulation of this value in new version of the code because, in their view, Kasher's original language was at best 'misleading'[31] and at worst 'simply dangerous'.[32] These concerns related to its relationship to the key principles of *necessity* (restricting targets to those necessary for achieving legitimate military objectives), *distinction* (distinguishing between civilians and combatants), and *proportionality* (using force proportionate to the military value of the target) in evaluating the use of military force. These three principles are crucial features of the International Humanitarian Law of armed conflict (International Committee of the Red Cross, 1977: 21–31; Hajjar, 2006: 23), but they also reflected wider moral concerns. Moshe Halbertal's own understanding of the requirements of morality in warfare incorporates these principles, for example, Halbertal (2013). Kasher's version of 'purity of arms' does emphasise 'necessity' but blurs the 'distinction' between civilians and soldiers ('whether to troops or civilians') and does not make an explicit demand to reduce disproportionate force, even where the target is deemed legitimate.[33]

In response, Kasher claims that his code does in fact incorporate these requirements. He argues that, since these are principles of International Humanitarian Law, he paid regard to them in the requirement made by the twenty-first and twenty-second norms of his code (which were later abolished) to obey the laws of war.[34] He further argues that his code is stronger than the laws of war because it requires that force be used only when necessary even against other soldiers, and not

---

[30] See Appendix B.
[31] Author interview with Moshe Halbertal.
[32] Author interview with Avi Sagi [my translation].
[33] Author interview with Daniel Statman.
[34] Author interview with Asa Kasher.

just civilians.[35] He justifies this on the grounds that soldiers are in fact 'citizens in uniform' and therefore deserve the same protection. However, this position also has the possible implication that one might prefer the lives of soldiers over civilian life in certain cases. By contrast, the new version of the code draws this distinction more sharply, and puts a requirement on the soldier to reduce the harm to civilians as far as possible. This requirement exists even if it exposes the soldier to extra risk (Halbertal, 2013). Indeed, it is the starkest example of the way in which the new version, although more relaxed in tone and more trusting of the 'judgement' of the soldier, makes more exacting demands than the original. Notice, however, that while this value is certainly more exacting in theory, in practice it lacks all specificity.

Disagreements over the meaning of this value have acquired much greater significance as a result of the debates surrounding Israel's recent assaults on the Gaza Strip, in which the high number of civilian casualties has generated international controversy. The three principal engagements (Operation Cast Lead, December 2008–January 2009; Operation Pillar of Defence, November 2012; Operation Protective Edge, July–August 2014) have successively intensified, but also entrenched, a pattern of philosophical debates about what purity of arms should mean both in theory and in practice. In particular, these debates have received their impetus from a piece co-authored by Asa Kasher and Major General Amos Yadlin (former head of IDF military intelligence), in which they seek to adjust traditional doctrines of military ethics to the requirements of 'fighting terror' (Kasher and Yadlin, 2005). This article further blurred the distinction between soldiers and civilians by arguing that Israel has a greater duty of care towards its soldiers, citizens, and other civilians under its 'effective control' than to civilian bystanders in hostile areas (cf. Al-Khalidi, 2010; Khalili, 2013: 62–3, 206–7). This argument, originally devised as a doctrine justifying targeted assassinations, has had significant influence on IDF thinking about military ethics and the question of 'purity of arms'. Indeed, although the document was never formally accepted by the IDF, widespread claims have been made that it has

---

[35] Whether he is correct depends on one's interpretation of article 35 of the First Additional Protocol to the Geneva Conventions (International Committee of the Red Cross, 1977: 21).

underpinned ethical doctrine during recent Israeli attacks on Gaza (Harel, 2009d).

However, it is important to be clear about the precise contribution that IDF ethical doctrine makes in this context. In practice, it is far from clear that an ethical code with no enforcement mechanism would make a serious difference in the heat of battle. At an intuitive level, it is possible to imagine that it might help to encourage restraint. Yet determining the extent of such a nebulous contribution presents an almost insurmountable epistemological and methodological challenge. The IDF for its part has never conducted serious studies of this sort.[36] Indeed, the available evidence suggests that any professed concern to avoid harm to civilians has had a very limited impact on restraining IDF conduct in recent operations. Successive investigations have made it clear that IDF conduct in Gaza in recent years is inconsistent with International Humanitarian Law and the standards of the IDF ethical code, even in its more relaxed interpretations (for a sample see: B'Tselem, 2009, 2013, 2015; Human Rights Watch, 2009a, 2009b, 2010; UNHRC, 2009, 2015; Amnesty International, 2014; Physicians for Human Rights, 2015). This is even the case concerning the IDF's attitude to the lives of its own troops. Evidence is mounting that the IDF has on several occasions deliberately imperilled the lives of captured Israeli soldiers in pursuit of the so-called 'Hannibal Directive', according to which massive force should be used to prevent troops falling into enemy captivity (Amnesty International, 2015). Even Asa Kasher himself has been publicly critical of the way the Hannibal Directive has been interpreted in practice (Ha'aretz, 2015).

Moreover, there are also strong grounds for a very different conclusion: that ethical considerations made in the light of the code might in fact increase the level of violence overall. Eyal Weizman (2009) has argued that the complex modelling which militaries conduct of the likely civilian casualties resulting from a given action frequently bears little resemblance to practical outcomes. What such laboured calculations are more likely to achieve, he suggests, is simply the impression that such operations are morally or legally justified (2012: 99–138). Perversely, the outcome might be that such 'targeted' strikes will be

---

[36] Author interview with Asa Kasher.

more readily resorted to and that the number of 'accidental' civilian casualties will accordingly increase (cf. Owens, 2003). Indeed, as Craig Jones has demonstrated, the growing influence of Israeli military lawyers in providing targeting advice has actually had the effect of streamlining the legal justification of violence (Jones, 2015).

However, while these arguments suggest that the ethical code is not effective in restraining violence, they still do not help to specify the real function of military ethical doctrine in the facilitation of war, which is distinct from that played by 'lawfare'. To understand this contribution properly, it is necessary to recall the original purpose of the IDF ethical code, which had nothing to do with a desire to lower the level of civilian casualties. Aside from any examination of actual military conduct, the vague and optional character of the ethical code should make this very plain. Instead, as has been shown above, the immediate context for the emergence of the code was an agenda to turn the IDF into a more professional body and to motivate soldiers to serve more effectively by cultivating them as ethical subjects. Accordingly, I would suggest that the debate surrounding the value of 'purity of arms' has been far more consequential for the formation of the Israeli soldier as an ethical subject than for the actual conduct of warfare and its human cost. The questions which need to be answered when considering the value of 'purity of arms', therefore, are: what kind of ethical subject does this value, in all its various guises, presuppose and valorise; and how, in the context of the recent Israeli assaults on Gaza, has this idea of ethical subjectivity become militarily useful?

As demonstrated above, the ethical subject of the IDF ethical code is in the first instance the free individual of neoliberal governmentality, whose 'judgement' is the crucial ethical faculty. In the writings of Israeli military ethicists, however, this ethical subject appears useful not only in the context of the changing nature of the IDF as it becomes more 'professional' or socially diverse. Ethics also helps with the fighting of counterinsurgency warfare. In their interpretation, insurgents such as those Israel faces in Gaza have adopted a strategy which explicitly aims to undermine Israel's ethical capacity to justify its use of military force. Hence, insurgents choose to attack civilians rather than just soldiers, and moreover they choose to disguise themselves among the surrounding civilian population, making it harder to uphold the principle of distinction. According to Halbertal, the aim is to undermine the moral resolve of their opponent by 'goading Israel into an overreaction' (2009). This would lead to 'the shattering of Israel's moral legitimacy in its own struggle' (2009).

What is interesting about this view is that it presents soldiers' ethical motivation as a strategic resource. It is concerned with more than simply international legitimacy or legal deniability, though these may well be separate goals. It directly posits the importance of ethics for the winning of asymmetric warfare. As Halbertal tellingly puts it, 'in a democratic society with a citizen's army, any erosion of the ethical foundation of its soldiers and its citizens is of immense political and strategic consequence' (Halbertal, 2009). Accordingly, he redescribes the classic counterinsurgency strategy of separating the insurgent force from the local population (usually achieved through practices of confinement (Khalili, 2013)) as an ethical process:

Rather than being drawn into a war of all against all and everywhere, Israel has sought to isolate the militants from their environment: to mark them and 'clothe' them with a uniform, and to force them to a definite front. The moral restraints in this case are of great strategic value. (Halbertal, 2009)

Viewed from this perspective, the principle of distinction, so crucial to 'purity of arms' and the law of armed conflict, is therefore nothing more than the application of counterinsurgency strategy to moral principles.

This close affinity with the approach of counterinsurgency extends to the level of tactics as well. For what this process requires in practice is not simply doctrinal clarity but the careful and intricate deployment of soldiers as ethical subjects. Because of the nature of this new battlefield, the clear distinction between the insurgent and the civilian population must be actively inscribed by the diffuse efforts of individuals:

In a traditional war, the difficult moral choices are made by the political elites and the high command, such as whether to bomb Dresden or to destroy Hiroshima. But in this new kind of micro-war, every soldier is a kind of commanding officer, a full moral and strategic agent. Every soldier must decide whether the individual standing before him in jeans and sneakers is a combatant or not . . . (Halbertal, 2009)

Military ethicists writing in other contexts have also noted the significance of the rise of the 'strategic corporal' (Carrick, 2008: 192). Likewise, Halbertal observes that in 'micro-war' the ethical activity of each individual soldier becomes a vital constituent of the military apparatus. Just as the challenges of urban warfare spurred the IDF to develop 'swarm' tactics that reasserted control over the space of a hostile city through small teams tunnelling through the walls of houses (Weizman, 2007: 185–220), so asymmetric warfare in general requires ethical swarming, the multiplication and intensification of ethical effort to maintain moral legitimacy. Moreover, one can see how the neoliberal model of ethics one finds expressed in the ethical code has a vital role to play here. By implanting a new region of 'freedom' and 'judgement' inside each soldier-subject, and by dispersing responsibility to them, troops will become much better equipped to fulfil this function.

Yet it is not the case that soldiers must be depended upon as individual ethical agents purely because of this tactical dimension. Neither is it because this is a more reliable way of separating combatants from non-combatants. Rather, it is because the soldiers themselves are the *telos* of this process. It is their 'ethical foundation' which is the strategic resource and which motivates them to fight. A closer look at the philosophical debates about 'purity of arms' in asymmetric warfare demonstrates this clearly, for it shows that Israeli military ethicists privilege the interior world of the soldier ahead of tangible outcomes or political or legal criteria. Indeed, while there is a substantive difference between Kasher and his critics on the question of how far soldiers must go to protect civilian bystanders in war, this difference is much more consistently related to their different conceptions of the role of the soldier as an intentionally acting ethical subject than to the degree of their concern for Palestinian civilians. These different conceptions can be derived directly from the differing approaches embodied in the two versions of the ethical code, one which focuses on the articulation of clear, practical guidelines for the ethical soldier and another which focuses instead on the constant improvement of his moral character.

In order to understand this, it is first necessary to examine the body of moral philosophy on which these philosophers draw and from which this tendency originates, namely Just War Theory. The nucleus of Just War Theory developed in early Christian theology in the works of St Augustine and St Thomas Aquinas. More recently it has undergone a renaissance after the enormous success of Michael Walzer's restatement of the theory in his *Just and Unjust Wars* (1977; for alternative perspectives, see Owens, 2010). Just War Theory distinguishes between *jus ad bellum* (rightness in going to war) and *jus in bello* (rightness in fighting war), with 'purity of arms' clearly falling into the latter category. The consequences of such a distinction are enormously de-politicising, providing a framework for discussing military ethics which focuses on purity of intent in isolated, decontextualised incidents. Such an analytic move may seem defensible in a liberal context; but it is completely at odds with, for example, the theory of anti-colonial insurgency warfare, in which the political nature of each soldier's commitment and each military occurrence is stressed.[37] In making this distinction, therefore, Just War Theory already has a highly circumscribed understanding of warfare and the role of the soldier as an ethical subject.

The moral co-ordinates of Just War Theory are even more constrained when it comes to evaluating these intentions. Here the central principal is known as the Doctrine of Double Effect (DDE). Considering that this notion is an unreconstructed borrowing from Catholic theology, its intellectual weight in these debates is quite remarkable (for a critique, see Scanlon, 2008). Simply put, it holds that an action is not evil if the genuine intention behind it is good, even if the same action has obvious and predictable evil effects, so long as the act is proportionate to the achievement of the good intention. As Helen Kinsella has demonstrated, DDE (as originally expounded by Augustine and Aquinas) was developed well before the principle of distinction between combatants and civilians emerged (2011: 34–7). As she argues, the doctrine's greater concern with 'the innocence of the soldier than with the innocence of the one who may be killed' (2011: 35) leaves a 'startlingly ambiguous and flimsy legacy' (2011: 36) for the principle of distinction. Furthermore, contemporary scholars' attempts to rectify this legacy have merely compounded the problem. Walzer adds a

---

[37] The classic statements of such a view were made by Frantz Fanon (2001) and Mao Zedung (2000). Although Walzer does grant the validity of guerrilla struggle, he does so purely on the condition of its compliance with *jus in bello*. 'Terrorism', by contrast, is not so favourably regarded (Walzer, 1977: 176–206).

further caveat to DDE, also widely accepted in Just War Theory, that any double effect should be accompanied by a 'double intention' – that is, an intention to perform a justified act of war, *and* an intention to increase proportionality by reducing the harm to non-combatants. However, this focus on intention, present in the original formula of the doctrine and redoubled in Walzer's restatement, is highly solipsistic, depending entirely on the internal mental considerations of the soldier, rather than the external effects of his actions.

Israeli military ethicists, whether more or less permissive in their interpretation of 'purity of arms', all rely on DDE to make their case, as is evident in the content of the written debates between them. Responding to critics of their doctrine in the *New York Review of Books*, Kasher and Yadlin are at pains to reiterate the compatibility of their view with the terms of DDE:

. . . when a military force faces a mixed population of combatants and non-combatants in a territory not under its effective control, we follow Walzer's *Just and Unjust Wars*: 'Double effect is defensible' when 'the actor . . . seeks to minimise [evil involved], accepting costs to himself'. IDF Operation 'Cast Lead' included a variety of effective efforts to minimise collateral damage, including widely distributed warning leaflets, more than 150,000 warning phone calls to terrorists' neighbours, and non-lethal warning fire – unprecedented efforts in every respect. In our understanding of double effect 'cost' does not require jeopardy. (Kasher and Yadlin, 2009)

However, when critics of Kasher attack his position, they tend not to rely on the claim that civilians' lives should be privileged over those of soldiers and instead focus attention back on to purity of intent, which remains the decisive question. Hence Halbertal argues that collateral damage can only be justified when it takes on the character of preferring one's own life to that of another (as would be the case, for example, in not sharing food when both you and a friend are starving), rather than the character of intentional killing (which is 'such a terrible act that a person has to sacrifice his life and not do it') (Halbertal, 2013). Therefore, he argues, opting to proceed with an operation that will kill civilians when alternative, riskier means are available is immoral because such a decision involves preferring intentional killing over risking the lives of friendly soldiers and civilians. In the case of collateral damage, only after risk is assumed can it be said the death is not intentional and is therefore akin to preferring one's own life:

The attempt to bring collateral damage closer to the permitted status of preferring life becomes possible only if efforts are made to reduce this damage as much as possible. However, in contrast to preferring life, in collateral damage the attacker assumes part of the responsibility for the death of the attacked because his actions caused the death. Therefore, while we do not demand that a person endanger himself to save the life of his friend, it is absolutely possible that we will demand that he endanger himself to avoid hurting his friend through collateral damage. (Halbertal, 2013; my translation)

In this argument, then, the reasoning is not that risk should be taken because soldiers' lives should be risked ahead of the lives of civilians: the risk is taken because it is the only means available to demonstrate the required purity of intent. Indeed, while Halbertal is clear that good intentions alone are insufficient, and that they must be accompanied by actions reflecting them, these actions are nevertheless significant primarily insofar as they reflect and demonstrate a pure intention to 'let die', rather than a bad intention to kill.

Kasher and Yadlin's response to this criticism is also revealing. They argue that allowing risk to fall upon friendly soldiers or citizens is also an intentional act of killing:

[this] objection rests on the distinction between killing and letting die. In one course of action, the state lets some of its citizens die, while in the other course of action, the state kills some of the bystanders. If killing is always morally worse than letting die, then the state ought to follow the first course of action rather than the second [. . .] Our rejoinder is that under the present circumstances the distinction is of no crucial moral significance. Imagine yourself having to make a choice between pushing a blue button and pushing a green one. If you push the former, a missile is going to fire killing the terrorist and some bystanders. If you push the latter, no missile is going to be fired and the terrorist will explode in the mall. *The moral focus of the situation is on the level of your decision.* A decision to let citizens die is as morally significant as a decision to kill the terrorist and the bystanders. From the point of view of a democratic state, a decision to let citizens die when they can and should be effectively protected is *tantamount to a decision to kill them*. It is as morally wrong for the state to let its citizens die under such circumstances as it is morally wrong to kill them. (2005: 20, emphasis added)

This strange thought experiment demonstrates clearly that it is the intentional decision of the soldier which remains the privileged focus of their attention.

Yet it is not just at this level of imagined abstraction that the question of the soldier's intention remains crucial to the debate. The actual conduct of past operations has been subject to scrutiny by philosophers on these grounds. Kasher offered a lengthy defence of Operation Cast Lead in which he referred in detail both to his co-authored article with Amos Yadlin and to the ethical code of the IDF (Kasher, 2009).[38] In a letter replying to this article, Daniel Statman attempted to probe more deeply into the conduct of soldiers during the operation (2010: 3–8). Citing media reports and the collection of testimonies gathered by Breaking the Silence about the campaign, Statman suggested that soldiers were often reckless with regard to protecting civilians' lives. He quotes several soldiers and officers, including one who was told: 'this is a war and as in war there is no consideration for civilians, anyone who sees something – shoot' (2010: 4).

Statman reiterates his belief that soldiers must be prepared to risk their lives to protect civilian bystanders, and he directly addresses Kasher's claim that the state has a special duty towards its soldiers ahead of these civilians. Kasher makes the point that a state cannot be expected to risk its soldiers' lives to help the civilians of another state during a natural disaster, and therefore cannot be expected to make a similar effort in reducing collateral damage to civilians (Kasher, 2009: 65). Statman replies that the comparison with a natural disaster overlooks the intentional role of Israel in causing the death of civilians during Operation Cast Lead:

Although a state is permitted to refuse to provide help to people who are not its citizens if this imposes a burden or heavy risk, one cannot derive from this that it is permitted *to harm* those same civilians in order to advance its interests or defend its soldiers or civilians. (2010: 5; my translation, emphasis in original)

Once again Statman is invoking the importance of the prohibition on intentional killing, rather than disputing the principle that states

---

[38] Kasher wrote a similar piece after Operation Protective Edge in 2014, in which he rehearses exactly the same arguments (2014).

are allowed to prefer the lives of their soldiers. Kasher makes this clear in his response to Statman in which he explicitly invokes the importance of the distinction between killing *intentionally* [*bakavana*] and killing *knowingly* [*bayod'in*] (2010: 8–9). According to Kasher, if prior warnings are given and sufficient care is taken, then the responsibility falls upon the civilians who failed to leave and the target who stays in their vicinity. The intention to kill/be killed is now *Palestinian*, whereas the Israeli soldier proceeds *merely with the knowledge* that they will die (cf. Joronen, 2015). Kasher accepts that this latter scenario may have regularly occurred during the operation, but he challenges Statman to provide evidence of an active Israeli intention to kill civilians:

Does Statman *know* (from a trustworthy source, not from the foggy tales of 'Breaking the Silence') that there was an incident in which soldiers killed the neighbours of a terrorist with prior intention, as distinct from the intention to kill the terrorist? (2010: 9; my translation)

This challenge sits uneasily with Kasher's other published remarks (cited above) about the difference between killing and letting die. Previously he had argued that acting in such a way that might possibly allow a 'terrorist' to attack Israeli civilians in future is tantamount to killing those Israelis intentionally. Faced with the imminent prospect of certain Palestinian civilian deaths as a result of Israeli military action, however, Kasher insists that no such Israeli intention exists.

It is tempting to argue, following Agamben, that the entire exercise of distinguishing between intentional killing and letting die is simply the product of Kasher's biopolitical division between Israelis as citizens and Palestinians as 'bare life' (Agamben, 1998: 45–101). Some subjects (Israelis) can only be intentionally killed; others (Palestinians) can only be allowed to die. It is this sharp civilisational hierarchy, one might argue, which separates Kasher from his critics. What should not be overlooked, however, is that this biopolitical determination finds its expression in ethical terms. It is not simply that, for Kasher, the Palestinian bystander can only be allowed to die: the necessary, and more important, corollary of this is that the Israeli soldier can never intentionally kill him. A biopolitics perspective on this question can only take us so far, therefore. What it misses is that this production of 'bare life' is in fact merely the projection of an ethical vision in which the preservation of the soldier's purity of intent is paramount. The Palestinian bystander is never truly 'bare life'; he is only variously projected as such for the purposes of the differing imaginaries of Israeli military ethics. Crucially, it is the way in which these philosophers position the soldier as an ethical subject which is the principal factor in modulating this projection.

This can be most clearly seen in the fact that Kasher's response to Statman criticises his reliance on Breaking the Silence testimonies. I suggested above that the more demanding requirements of the new ethical code would create an augmented role for testimony in the ethical process as a way of mediating the inevitable failure to meet these standards. Statman's use of Breaking the Silence testimonies in his evaluation of Operation Cast Lead is direct evidence of this new possibility. Indeed, both Statman and Halbertal claim to read Breaking the Silence documents very carefully and find them to be reliable sources of information in evaluating the performance of the IDF.[39] Kasher, by contrast, has little tolerance for them. He takes a different approach when evaluating IDF operations. In his moral assessment of both Operation Cast Lead and Operation Protective Edge, for example, he repeatedly stresses that the use of non-official (i.e. non-IDF) sources to assess military actions is inherently unreliable (2009: 45, 2014).

Despite this assertion, in both articles Kasher nevertheless declares that *he* is in a position to clear the IDF of wrong-doing: 'the data collected so far permits us to conclude that a significant part of the criticism directed at Israel and the IDF during and after the operation was, to say the least, based on flimsy evidence' (2009: 46). This turnabout is revealing. It shows that Kasher is almost unable to contemplate an internal investigation of IDF conduct which would reveal major shortcomings. This is not the only time he has expressed such confidence. In an interview for the *Jerusalem Post*, he was even clearer:

. . . it doesn't matter where an accusation comes from, the IDF must take a look at it. The IDF must look into every story from B'Tselem, every story from Machsom Watch, every story from Amnesty International. Not because I rely on them. I don't. But you don't have to rely on them to do your work

---

[39] Author interviews.

properly. Look into every story. There's a tiny, microscopic proportion that has some basis, so look, check, find out. (Jerusalem Post, 2011)

Whereas Statman views Breaking the Silence testimonies as indicative of a wider culture of problematic behaviour, Kasher views such claims as fabrications to be exposed and, on a very small number of occasions, as evidence of isolated defects to be corrected. The consequence is that, when faced with the accusation that the IDF intentionally killed civilians, Kasher simply rejects this as formally impossible. In his view, professional, official investigations by the IDF do not find – could never find – widespread evidence of this. The whole point of Kasher's original ethical code was that it would embody a 'practical ideal', reflecting existing practice to a great degree. But if investigation or testimonies reveal that the code was widely ignored, then this ideal would no longer be practical; indeed, the IDF would no longer be professional or ethical. To ensure that this never happens, therefore, Kasher constrains his definition of intentional killing as much as possible and expands the number of occasions on which civilians are merely 'let die' as bare life.

This 'microscopic' role for testimony stands in stark contrast to the omnipresent, constitutive gap between ideal standards and actual behaviour in the redrafted ethical code. Thus, for Kasher's critics, it is entirely conceivable, even helpful, that testimonies should emerge which show that intentional killing occurred, and it is therefore not as necessary to circumscribe the conditions in which it could be said to have happened. Indeed, the fact that such episodes are examined through testimony is all the more evidence that the IDF is acting properly. For example, despite the concerns voiced in his letter, Statman still feels compelled to reaffirm that: 'I feel completely honestly that the IDF is one of the outstanding armies in the world in the area of morality in warfare, if not the best – and despite this there is still room for improvement' (Statman, 2010: 3). This approach to testimony as a means of improvement and as a mode of ethical activity is certainly more challenging than discrediting testimony altogether, as Kasher does. Yet it is precisely this willingness to engage with testimony as an ethical technology, even where it reveals flagrant violations of the code, that gives Israeli military ethics its power. It allows for a more flexible manipulation of the soldiers' ethical faculties and their deeper subjective involvement in military activity, which is after all the purpose of the ethical code. It also has the serendipitous effect of neutralising the political critique which motivates many Breaking the Silence testimonies. Testimony is reappropriated as a purely ethical activity, as a means to help the IDF improve and fight better, despite testifiers' often explicit aims to the contrary. It is this polyvalent deployment of the concept of 'purity of arms' which allows it to perform such a central role in Israeli militarism.

Conclusion: The 'New Spirit' of Militarism

In their path-breaking study of the changing legitimation strategies employed in advanced capitalist societies, Boltanski and Chiapello highlight a number of developments which provide clear parallels to the changing role of military ethics in the IDF. They argue that the capitalist mode of production requires a 'Spirit' to maintain itself, which they define as 'the ideology that justifies engagement in capitalism', the 'set of beliefs associated with the capitalist order that helps to justify this order and, through legitimating them, to sustain the forms of action and predispositions compatible with it' (2005: 8, 10). The 'Spirit of the IDF' performs precisely the same role with respect to Israeli militarism.

Boltanski and Chiapello note transformations in the Spirit of capitalism which are, roughly speaking, contemporaneous with the developments in Israeli military ethics I have surveyed in this chapter. They argue that the reaction against the bureaucratised, rationalised reorganisation of capitalism which took place in the 1960s produced a critique which stressed the importance of the development of the individual in a non-hierarchical setting. Instead of crumbling under this critique, however, capitalism reorganised itself to reflect such concerns through a new management culture in the 1990s. These management theories emphasised the importance of personal autonomy and freedom for motivating employees (Boltanski and Chiapello, 2005: 57–99).

Consequently, capitalist firms encountered the same dilemma we have seen Israeli military ethicists grappling with: how to motivate an organisation of liberated individuals, a dilemma which is all the more acute in a military setting. The IDF arrived at the same solution as new management culture:

the only solution is for people to *control themselves*, which involves transferring constraints from external organisational mechanisms to people's internal dispositions, and for the powers of control they exercise to be consistent with the firm's 'general project'. (Boltanski and Chiapello, 2005: 80, emphasis in original)

Indeed, although Kasher's code began this process, its efforts were subsequently deemed insufficient on precisely these terms. It was attacked for its impersonal style, its lack of ideological depth, and for its overbearing constraints on individual judgement. In response, the new code further entrenched this mode of governance and devolved even more responsibility to the individual level, relaxing externally imposed constraints. Yet in doing so it in fact worked to strengthen individuals' ideological commitment to militarism, just as the new management culture had bound its employees further to capitalism:

the new mechanisms, which demand greater commitment and rely on a more sophisticated ergonomics, [. . .] precisely because they are more human in a way, also penetrate more deeply into people's inner selves – people are expected to 'give' themselves to their work – and facilitate an instrumentalisation of human beings in their most specifically human dimension. (Boltanski and Chiapello, 2005: 98)

As we shall see in the next chapter, this idea of the soldier's 'human image' is in fact crucial to the pedagogical techniques developed to implement the ethical code. Indeed, it should be no surprise that Boltanski and Chiapello also refer to the primacy of corporate 'ethics' in achieving this new configuration of individual autonomy with institutional control.

Boltanski and Chiapello's argument about the dialectic of critique and reform in contemporary capitalism also has applications in understanding the debate about 'purity of arms'. In particular, the manner in which a formerly political critique expressed in soldiers' testimony has been used as a means for evaluating and enhancing ethical performance shows how militarism has been reinvigorated by this process. That testimony itself is a product of the reflections of the soldier on the conduct of battle, and not of those subject to their violence, underscores the privileged importance that the interior world of the soldier attains in the ethical vision of Israeli militarism. Furthermore, it is the peculiar fate of testimony that reveals how this 'New Spirit' of Israeli militarism is strengthened by the practice *within* the formal military sphere of ethical techniques that might otherwise be directed in opposition to it. As I shall show as the book progresses, this has the effect not only of implanting testimony in the IDF as a militarist ethical practice but also of reinscribing wider practices of soldiers' testimony in ways which serve to drain it of political significance.

3 | 'Keeping a Human Image': Teaching Military Ethics in the IDF

I think that the most important job of the education corps is to make sure that the spirit of the young people that come to the army will remain the same when they are out of the army. So the education corps is like a body guard of the spirit of the people who have served in the army. That was why I was so interested in it. In one way, the army has to deal with a socialisation process – that you have to become a soldier – and in [an]other way it has the role of making sure you don't become a war machine . . . The main important thing in . . . *Ruaḥ Tsahal* ['The Spirit of the IDF'] is to protect our soldiers to remain human beings, even [on the battlefield], even in war. All of what the Spirit of *Tsahal* [the IDF] does is to protect our soldiers not to do terrible things, even in war. This is a very important role.[1]

These are the words of Roni Sulimani, the former head of the education department of the Israel Defence Forces (IDF) Education and Youth Corps. His remarks are revealing, firstly, because they suggest that military ethics training in the IDF is designed primarily with the Israeli soldier, and not the Palestinian civilian, in mind. He frames military ethics as something which protects soldiers from the moral consequences of their military service. Yet, secondly, his comments also indicate that military ethics serves quite a complex ideological function. In his view, full identification with the 'war machine' is not the aim of Israeli military ethics. The goal is not to produce obedient automata who implement the orders they are given without question. The key to this ideological operation is helping soldiers to remain 'human beings'. This emphasis is in keeping with a Hebrew aphorism which appears in the 'Spirit of the IDF': *lishmor 'al tselem ha'enosh*, keep a human image.

I would take this claim one step further than Sulimani, however. The function of Israeli military ethics is not simply to preserve a pre-existing humanity which risks being eroded in war. Rather, military ethics is in

---

[1] Author interview with Roni Sulimani.

fact generative of a new kind of militarised humanity, a humanity which only acquires its full meaning when juxtaposed and contrasted with the violence of the war machine. It is precisely soldiers' *dis-identification* with the violent regime they serve which enables them to function effectively as militarist subjects. Military ethics in fact works to cultivate and mobilise this dis-identification, to make soldiers feel that they retain their humanity despite but alongside their complicity in violence. This depends not on the endless justification of any and all military activities but conversely on the often difficult but carefully managed confrontation with the reality of violence. The ideological success of military ethics resides in the tension this generates between the human being and the soldier, between the man and his uniform. This tension is in fact constitutive of the masculine, Jewish, and 'human' solider-subject. Military ethics thus produces an ideological fantasy of moral humanity which obscures without diminishing the deep structural violence of which it is a part. What is more, this process is so effective precisely because it does not depend on the level of success in reducing the number of ethical transgressions. By emphasising subject formation, Israeli military ethics can tolerate success and failure in equal measure, and perhaps even exhibits a bias in favour of the latter.

The Institutional Framework of Ethical Pedagogy in the IDF

Ethical pedagogy in the IDF is anything but systematic. To begin with, it is not at all integrated into disciplinary or accountability mechanisms which might translate greater awareness of ethical issues into changes in military conduct. As discussed in the last chapter, the ethical code itself is entirely optional and has no enforcement mechanism. Moreover, ethics is largely not discussed when past actions are formally reviewed for operational or legal failures. This is most clearly evident if we examine the most important such practice, operational debriefing [*tahkir mivtza'i*], in which commanders appraise the successes and failures of past military actions through interviews and discussions with soldiers. Commanders are in theory supposed to discuss the ethical issues which arose during a particular mission in the process of operational debriefing in what is known as ethical debriefing [*tahkir 'erkhi*].[2] In practice, however, this is rarely undertaken. In a research paper produced by Colonel Atar Dagan as part of his studies

---

[2] Author interview with Roni Sulimani.

at the Institute for National Security Studies, it was found that in only two out of fifty debriefings examined were ethical issues discussed.[3]

Particularly significant in this respect is that the findings of operational debriefings are used by the Military Advocate General (MAG) and Military Police Criminal Investigation Department to determine if further investigation of an incident is necessary.[4] It is notable that operational debriefings rarely ever lead to investigations or to accountability. Despite approximately 5,000 Palestinians, over 1,000 of them minors, having been killed by Israeli security forces in the occupied West Bank and Gaza Strip between 2000 and 2013, only seven Israel soldiers were convicted of offences related to the deaths of Palestinians in that period (Yesh Din, 2013: 1–3). Indeed, human rights organisations have raised concerns that operational debriefings are in fact often used to co-ordinate testimony between soldiers and evade legal sanctions (Yesh Din, 2011: 32–8).[5] Discussion of ethical issues is hardly conducive to such attempts to obscure wrongdoing, and helps to explain the absence of ethical discussion in such settings. This should reinforce the point that the purpose of ethical education is to protect the soldier, not to hold him to account.

Consequently, it is more common to find detailed discussion of ethical concerns with soldiers in educational forums which are insulated to a certain degree from the actual use of violence and from disciplinary structures. Even then, ethical pedagogy remains decentralised, undirected, and often haphazard. There is only a minimal level of consistency. All soldiers will be exposed to the 'Spirit of the IDF' document at some point in basic training, and its values are supposed to form the basis of any discussion of ethical issues. In addition, all soldiers must carry a copy of the code as part of their uniform. Beyond this, it becomes much harder to generalise about the practicalities. This is partly because of the amorphous nature of ethics as a topic of study. As well as being an independent area of interest in its own right, ethics can variously appear as an aspect of operational, legal, cultural, and

---

[3] Author interviews with Atar Dagan, Amos Harel, and Asa Kasher.
[4] For more information on the role of this procedure in the overall system of military and criminal investigations in Israel, see the second report of the Turkel Commission established to examine these procedures (2013: 335–46).
[5] Responding to such concerns, the Turkel Commission recommended in 2013 that separate investigations by the MAG should occur concurrently with operational debriefing but still suggested that debriefings should be made available to the MAG (2013: 378–83).

even religious education and training, all of which can change according to the precise unit and deployment in question.

However, this decentralisation is also a consequence of IDF organisational culture. There is no dedicated body in the IDF whose exclusive concern is ethics. The closest such body would be the Education and Youth Corps, although this is only one aspect of its broader remit. The Corps develops the materials, educational tools, and lesson outlines for classes discussing ethics, which are tailored to each specific rank and unit.[6] The Corps also trains personnel (normally draftees) to act as Education Officers. However, the role of the Education Corps is subject to a key educational principle in the IDF, which is that soldiers should receive all education and training from their commanding officer, or at least in their presence. The aim of this principle is to create an organic link between education and practice, drawing on the experience of officers rather than an externally derived and abstract approach to education which might not reflect military reality. However, this also means that the nature and emphasis of ethical pedagogy can change depending on the preferences of the commander, creating a great deal of unevenness and a lack of uniformity in standards. Indeed, despite the desire of figures such as Asa Kasher to professionalise ethical training and the widespread use of the language of 'professionalism' in relation to military ethics, this has not progressed far. As Kasher himself lamented to me, 'the very idea that an organised military force should have professionals, people who are professionals in education, professional in education of ethics, professional in terms of instruction of values, is alien to the IDF'.[7] This is true even at the level of officer training, despite repeated attempts to instigate the professionalisation of education (Cohen, 2008: 99–107; Libel, 2010). There remain a large number of different officer schools and military colleges, and each is strongly influenced by the preferences of their commanders.[8] According to Stuart Cohen, these colleges retain a

---

[6] Author interview with Roni Sulimani.

[7] Author interview.

[8] The most important among these institutions is 'Bahad 1' where all officers (both combatant and non-combatant) must complete a course, followed by specialised courses in their own corps. The most important military colleges are the Tactical Command College (Mekhlala lePikud Takti, or Maltak for short), which provides training to company commanders; the Staff and Command College (Beit Sefer lePikud uMate, or Pum for short), which provides courses

strongly 'anti-intellectual bias' and cling to 'the notion that there exists no substitute for practical hands-on experience' (2008: 102).

Another major source of both anti-intellectualism and decentralisation in IDF ethics teaching has been the reform of pedagogical doctrine which took place in 2004. This reform was initiated by the then Chief of Staff, Moshe Ya'alon (later Minister of Defence, 2013–16), and came to be expressed in the document *Yi'ud veYihud*, which roughly translates as 'Identity and Purpose'.[9] Ya'alon perceived a problem of declining combat motivation and sought to restore soldiers' sense of Jewish-Israeli identity as a remedy. In this he drew on his belief that the 'People's Army' ethos should be revived, returning the IDF to its militia-like roots but combining it with a new ethno-religious emphasis (Libel, 2013: 285–7). He also interpreted his efforts as part of a scaling back of the creeping professionalisation of the 1990s (Ya'alon, 2006). Ya'alon tasked General Elazar Stern, the IDF Chief Education Officer, with developing a strategy, and Stern quickly brought Professor Benjamin Ish-Shalom, the Director of the Jewish educational charity, *Beit Morasha*, into the process. Ish-Shalom had a formative impact on the *Yi'ud veYihud* document and its implementation, and sat on the final committee which approved it.

The Education Corps was given the formal responsibility of implementing the strategy, but crucially this was to be done in co-operation with external organisations, principally Ish-Shalom's *Beit Morasha*. In encouraging such collaborations, this new strategy has been a key element in the increasing privatisation of IDF education. At the launch of the new educational strategy, *Beit Morasha* became a major partner institution working with the Education Corps. Over the course of its activities in the IDF, *Beit Morasha* claims to have reached over 200,000 soldiers – as many as 25,000 per year (Beit Morasha, n.d.).[10] In recent years the pace of the work has slowed but many other organisations

---

for majors and lieutenant colonels; and the Institute for National Security Studies (*Mikhlelet haBitahon Le'umi*, or *Mabal* for short), where the most senior officers in the IDF are taught together with members of the Mossad and Security Services.

[9] The phrase *Yi'ud veYihud* is taken from the title of a well-known essay on the IDF by David Ben-Gurion.

[10] A promotional video (in English, aimed at American donors to the organisation) about the work of *Beit Morasha* in the IDF is also available on YouTube (Friends of the IDF, 2012).

have continued programmes originally developed under its aegis.[11] An increasing number of external organisations now contribute to IDF education. According to the Israeli State Comptroller's Report into education in the IDF in 2011, the number of educational activities involving external civilian organisations rose from approximately 700 in 2008 to around 2,050 in 2010. The range of external organisations involved also grew from a 'limited' number in 2009 to 'dozens' in 2011 (Israeli State Comptroller, 2011: 1599).

The *Yi'ud veYihud* strategy emphasises the importance of developing the Jewish-Israeli identity of soldiers, and their sense of the values that underpinned their motivation to serve in the IDF. It mandated the inclusion of the study of Jewish tradition and thought in officers' schools and in military college syllabi and was integrated into officer training at all levels. However, once again the emphasis was placed on the discretion and role of the officer rather than centrally maintained standards. In particular, *Yi'ud veYihud* emphasised that officers needed to acquire the tools to pass these values on to their soldiers and underscored the importance of the role of the commander as an 'educator in uniform'. A specific programme, called *Mahzabim* (a Hebrew abbreviation for 'education for IDF leadership in Jerusalem'), was established in 2007 to focus on improving the educational capacity of commanders and to encourage them to discuss values with their units (Libel, 2013: 287). Colonel Ya'akov Castel, the former head of the IDF education department who had also overseen the redrafting of the ethical code, led this programme.

Although the emphasis of the *Yi'ud veYihud* programme was broad, ethics formed a crucial component of its approach. In many ways, this document represented the pedagogical corollary of the changes made to the ethical code in 2000–01. Both processes were driven in large part by Elazar Stern and should in this sense at least be seen as a coherent whole. But ethics is also woven into the very fabric of the programme. To begin with, it was the moral difficulties entailed in maintaining the occupation of the West Bank and Gaza, especially during the Second Intifada, which contributed to the perceived need to develop the strategy. Discussing the logic behind the document in a newspaper interview, Benjamin Ish-Shalom remarked:

IDF soldiers are presented these days with missions of great gravity [*mesimot cevadot mishkal*] that require dealing with complicated conditions such

---

[11] Author interview with Shai Herskowitz.

as standing at checkpoints, arrest operations that expose them to immediate danger, guerrilla war, war in which civilians are injured and the distinction between the battle front and the home front is not clear. A war in which a soldier fights in Jenin in the morning and goes out with his friends to the shopping mall in the afternoon. This situation needs spiritual improvement. (Arutz Sheva, 2004; my translation)

Moreover, the emphasis the programme places on values naturally means that the reinforcement of Jewish-Israeli identity occurs through ethical work. The director of the Jewish and Israeli Identity programme at *Beit Morasha* emphasised to me the inseparability of values and identity.[12] Furthermore, the ethical code of the IDF is referred to in the *Yi'ud yeYihud* document as a major source of the values underpinning Jewish-Israeli identity.[13] Indeed, in a joint interview given with Benjamin Ish-Shalom, Moshe Ya'alon stressed that the aim of the programme was to give values such as 'purity of arms' and 'human life' a clear grounding in Jewish tradition (Makor Rishon Dyokan Magazine, 2006). In a similar way to the addition of 'Jewish' elements to the text of the ethical code, therefore, the *Yi'ud yeYihud* programme was designed to provide a cultural anchor for these values and thus to encourage identification with them. Describing its purpose and outcome, Ya'alon was furthermore clear that it was ethical discussions which the training ultimately aimed to generate:

The program exposes participants to important knowledge. It also legitimizes the discussion of values for those soldiers who already possess a firm grounding in values and equips them with tools that enable them to transmit those values to the soldiers under their command. Now, when a platoon commander has a discussion with a soldier, it is about ethical issues . . . The discussions of commanders, platoon leaders, and soldiers who attend this program are not academic. The program raises ethical issues that are translated into practical matters – such as rules of engagement, conduct in the field, and combat. It enables them to understand the concerns underlying these regulations. (Makor Rishon Dyokan Magazine, 2006)

The role of ethical pedagogy in this strategy is therefore both the strengthening of Jewish-Israeli identity and the alleviation of the moral

---

[12] Author interview with Shai Herskowitz.
[13] The contents of the document are summarised in the 67th Annual Report of the State Comptroller (2011: 1605).

difficulties of fighting counterinsurgency warfare. This was to be achieved through the promotion of values and moral character in soldiers through increased contact with private charities, religious communities, and educational foundations. The purpose of this pedagogical approach was manifestly not to promulgate and monitor clear ethical standards, and certainly not to instigate mechanisms of accountability and discipline. In this sense, the significance of ethical pedagogy in the IDF should be interpreted as firmly ideological.

Teaching Ethics to IDF Officers: Asceticism and Self-Examination

Despite Yaʿalon's reforms, the rhetoric of professionalism remains significant, especially at the level of officer training. From this perspective, Asa Kasher's emphasis on the importance of professionalism has been simultaneously highly influential but poorly realised in practice. On the one hand, one can without doubt detect the influence of this language in the approaches of the staff of military colleges. His textbook *Military Ethics* is still a fundamental guide for educators in the IDF and his personal teaching has cemented this influence. Summarising the teaching of ethics at the Staff and Command College, Lieutenant Colonel Amira Raviv emphasises that 'working in the field of ethics advances the professionalism of the officer' (Raviv, 2004: 53; my translation). Yet this emphasis on professionalism is also bound up with the production of other identities, not least ethno-religious sentiment. Thus, describing the work of the Tactical Command College, its commander hints at the subsumption of professional training into wider processes of ethical subject formation:

We develop the foundation of the profession of the officer in its normative aspect [*bahebaṭ haʿerchi-normativi*], in other words cultivating appropriate behaviour for a Jewish-Israeli officer in all situations; and thus in the professional aspect, in other words examining the facts in a professional way. In this way, the decisions of the officer in situations of difficulty will be ethical [*'erchiot*] and professional as one. (Davidi, 2004: 35; my translation)

The centrality of 'Jewish-Israeli' identity to this pedagogical approach, in keeping with the emphasis of the *Yiʿud veYiḥud* programme, is certainly evident here. Beyond its ambition to strengthen cultural and religious identification, however, I want to emphasise that this approach is fundamentally shaped by an *ascetic* ethical disposition. In particular, rather than focusing on compliance with professional standards, this pedagogical strategy encourages officers to work on themselves to improve their moral character and to develop ethical faculties.

Kasher characterises this rival ascetic approach as a non-professional and naïve application of moral theory to military activity – an attempt to 'shape character' rather than 'shaping [. . .] behaviour as people in military uniforms'.[14] Referring back to the importance of having detailed norms in the ethical code, Kasher stresses the importance of agreed and clear standards:

you can talk to them . . . for hours and days and weeks about human dignity . . . it's not enough. You have to do something else . . . in order for them to act properly. One thing you should do is to have norms in your code of ethics and not just . . . abstract values. Norms that would say 'okay, under such circumstances, this and that is what is required'. It's like a regulation, like rules of engagement, like a command; not a value, [. . .] something that hovers above your head, put in very abstract terms.[15]

This is very different from the more ascetic approach of other teachers of military ethics. For example, Moshe Halbertal's view on this question is precisely the reverse: 'the challenge is to make these rules part of the inner world of each soldier, and this takes more than just formulating the norms and the rules properly' (Halbertal, 2009). Halbertal's aim is to produce 'a certain understanding of the depth of the principles . . . of their sense and what they stand for and why . . .' This is to be achieved 'with a good narrative imagination, imagining life complexities, and building trust in judgement'.[16] He even invokes the Aristotelian concept of *phronesis*, or practical wisdom, to describe the faculty he wishes to cultivate. Halbertal is clear that this requires an extremely demanding ethical process:

In discussing the code of ethical conduct with Israeli officers, many times I encounter the following complaint: 'Do you want to say that, before

---

[14] Author interview with Asa Kasher.
[15] Author interview.
[16] Author interview with Moshe Halbertal.

I open fire, I have to go through all these moral dilemmas and calculations? It will be completely paralyzing. Nobody can fight a war in such a straitjacket!' My answer to them is that the whole point of training is about performing well under pressure without succumbing to paralysis. This is the case with battlefields that have nothing to do with moral concerns. Do I attack from the right or from the left? How do I respond to this new tactic, or to that? And so on. This is why moral considerations have to be an essential part of military training. If there is no time for moral reflection in battle, then moral reflection must be accomplished before battle, and drilled into the soldiers who will have to answer for their actions after battle. (Halbertal, 2009)

What Halbertal has in mind here is a recognisably ascetic form of ethics, one which is fully contiguous with more conventional military training and is aimed at preventing the 'paralysis' of the officer in combat. It involves a careful process of repetition, discussion, and elucidation. In fact, this approach appears very similar to the Stoic practice of *paraskeue* that Foucault identifies in ancient ascetic culture:

In the ascesis, the *paraskeue* involves preparing the individual for the future, for a future of unforeseen events whose general nature may be familiar to us, but which we cannot know whether and when they will occur. It involves, then, finding in ascesis a preparation, a *paraskeue*, which can be adapted to what may occur, and only to this, and at the very moment it occurs, if it does so. (Foucault, 2005: 320–1)

Indeed, given that *paraskeue* literally means 'preparation', it is striking that in IDF jargon ethics training is considered an aspect of 'mental preparation' [*hakhana mentalit*]. According to Foucault, a crucial element of this process is absorbing certain precepts and sayings (*logoi*) for use in moments of ethical deliberation. Quoting Seneca, he argues that through *paraskeue* the ethical subject will have these *logoi* 'driven into him, embedded in him'; they will be 'phrases that he has embedded in his mind by repeating them' (2005: 323). The aim of teaching the IDF ethical code is precisely the same. The basic values of the 'The Spirit of the IDF' function as *logoi*, with ethical pedagogy encouraging their absorption. Indeed, Daniel Statman, another Israeli philosopher teaching military ethics in the IDF, appeared to confirm this, emphasising to me that the ethical code must be 'drilled in the minds' of soldiers, and turned into a 'common language'.[17]

This ascetic outlook is echoed in the words of senior military personnel who regularly give lectures on military ethics to officers. Major General Yishai Beer, who served previously as Judge Advocate General and worked on the panel to redraft the ethical code, describes his view of the ethical process in direct contrast to a legalistic approach.[18] Criticising the trend for the increasing involvement of military lawyers in approving specific military actions (cf. Jones, 2015), he argues that a focus on law encourages only a minimum level of compliance and may give rise to a more permissive attitude once legal authorisation has been assured. Instead, he believes that moral training should be used to raise standards. Indeed, he is proud of the fact that, in its most recent draft, the Spirit of IDF makes no reference to Israeli or international law at all. Beer uses the metaphor of the driver of a car to justify his position: just as a driver should be in control of both the accelerator and the brake to ensure maximum effectiveness, so the officer should be in charge of both the application and the restraint of force. Beer's metaphor is notable for the way it interiorises the ethical process within the individual subject, creating an internal economy of force and restraint rather than an external legal or bureaucratic framework. It is the individual as a full moral and strategic agent who acts as the conduit for decisions, privileging the officer's personal judgement as a site of pedagogical intervention. By the same token, this leaves very few mechanisms for enforcement of standards or clear lines of accountability.

Another figure who has been frequently called upon to give lectures to officers is Colonel Ben Tzion Gruber, deputy commander of an armoured division and a personal friend of Moshe Halbertal.[19] Gruber also gives public speeches in the United States and in Israel, using a similar array of carefully selected videos (many of which come from UAV cameras over Gaza) to those he uses in lectures within the

---

[17] Author interview.
[18] The following two paragraphs are based on the author's interview with Yishai Beer.
[19] Author interview with Ben Tzion Gruber. Gruber claimed to give about fifty lectures per year in the IDF.

IDF.[20] Gruber fully adheres to Halbertal's view of 'collateral damage' questions, using the same language of necessity, distinction, and responsibility, and even claims to have influenced the philosopher himself.[21] Strikingly, one of Gruber's central metaphors for his pedagogical contribution is also vehicular. He describes his role as augmenting a soldier's moral 'brake-pads' [refidot]. This image also reprises Yishai Beer's notion of an internal economy of force and restraint within the soldier-subject, emphasising the importance of an inner ethical substance rather than structural or political factors. This is ascetic work precisely in the sense that it requires self-augmentation, an enhancement of one's internal capacity for self-control.

Yet the primary aim of this activity does not seem to be saving civilian lives. Instead, it is something more personal. Each time a soldier uses violence, Gruber contends, his ethical brake-pads erode slightly and, through a process of gradual attrition, they can eventually disappear altogether. This leaves behind a soldier who is no longer a human, but 'an animal'. The purpose of ethical training is to augment these human capacities through ethical work. Here we can also begin to understand the ideological importance of asceticism for 'keeping a human image', for allowing officers to dis-identify with the violence they exercise in order to continue functioning as military agents. Gruber told me that he drew directly on his own experience to develop this metaphor: 'you [. . .] lose something when you shoot, and when you kill your first enemy, you are not the same. I know this: you are not the same. You never killed someone. I killed a lot. I am not the same guy for sure'.[22] Furthermore, it is important to recognise that this ascetic effort to remain human is also a gendered, masculinising one. Sasson-Levy has shown that the construction of masculine identities among Israeli soldiers depends on a tension between 'thrill-seeking' and practices of 'self-control' (2008: 305–9). Gruber's language suggests that the gendered pursuit of masculinity through bodily discipline also extends to ethical self-regulation: he is concerned that he is not 'the same guy' he once was.

Once again, then, the principal aim of this ascetic self-cultivation is preserving the humanity of the soldier rather than protecting civilians. This

---

[20] I observed Gruber giving one such talk to journalists in Tel Aviv on 1 May 2013.
[21] By contrast, he described Asa Kasher as 'a disaster'.
[22] Author interview.

priority is often difficult to spot but it is undoubtedly present. Gruber explained to me how he would usually explain this in ethics classes:

. . . you have to stay a human being. Usually my phrase is as follows: if your sensitivity to [. . .] a baby after the war is not the same as before, we will never, ever win. That's what I teach my soldiers always. And when I say baby, a baby is a baby is a baby. Palestinian, Jewish, everyone. You have to be as sensitive to a baby after you fight as you used to be before. For me that's the litmus paper, you know?

This imagery stages an ideological fantasy, in which the constant struggle to maintain 'sensitivity' is both detached from yet dependent on the reality of military violence. It is detached in the sense that it is the soldier's *sensitivity* to the baby, rather than the welfare of the baby itself, which serves as the marker of humanity here. Yet it is also dependent on violence because fighting is just as much a part of the 'litmus paper' as sensitivity. The production of this particular sense of humanity relies on participation in fighting; sensitivity finds its demonstration in its survival of the encounter with violence. Moreover, this reference to the figure of the baby, grounded as it is in the domestic sphere of the family, is again gendered, producing an implicit comparison between fatherhood/motherhood and soldiering. The ascetic struggle to stay human while exercising violence becomes bound up with an effort to embody a gendered identity, thus further strengthening the fantasy.

This ascetic emphasis is also evident in the practical pedagogical techniques used to teach ethics to officers. Lt Colonel Amira Raviv describes the development of the approach adopted by the Staff and Command College as follows:

[W]e learnt that ethical education is not successful in activating internalisation processes [*tahalichei hapnama*] when the officer listens to lectures or to moral preaching; on these occasions he becomes just a passive element . . . It seemed that the way to create the most meaningful change was discussion based on incidents that the students brought from their own personal experience, or examples close to them, on dialogue, on the exchange of opinions, on persuasion and on experience using simulations and role play. (2004: 55; my translation)

In order to facilitate such activities, she also stressed the importance of 'creating an atmosphere of open-mindedness [*petihut mahshavtit*] and critical thinking' (2004: 55). She further mentions the importance of self-examination and of 'discussing positive episodes, as well as negative episodes – courageously and without bias. The whole way, we check ourselves in the light of [ethics] – whether we reached the goals we set ourselves, and whether there is room to improve' (Raviv, 2004: 55). The ascetic drive is obvious in these remarks, as is the atmosphere of frankness characteristic of *parrhesia*, the practice of candid truth-telling. It would seem from these comments that testimony by the officer is an important way of immersing him in the ethical process, of practising the relation of values to past behaviour, and of creating the impetus to improve. Indeed, this was confirmed in several of my interviews with those teaching ethics to IDF officers.

Moshe Halbertal appeared to take a very similar approach to soliciting testimony in teaching the value of 'purity of arms' to officers. He discussed his main pedagogical aims as follows:

I want them to come out with four very simple questions[23] they can ask themselves and teach to their soldiers. That's one thing. In the end it's not a philosophy seminar, so people have to internalise it and work with it. For a philosopher it's a big challenge to crystallise things. And also, while doing it, emphasising first of all that it's both professional and reasonable. And second that these principles are not going to disturb their capacity to reach their military goal but actually will be very constructive and helpful. And then . . . also listening very carefully. I learned a lot from them, listening very carefully . . . It's always an hour and a half, two hours' discussion. It's not a lecture.[24]

In this context, Halbertal stressed that the 'Spirit of the IDF' was in large part designed as 'a critical tool . . . a tool for self-examination'.[25] He also emphasised that discussing officers' past experiences was intended as an opportunity for self-improvement, not about exposing past trauma or guilt:

It's done in the spirit that they might have missed something, that they want to listen . . . it's not confessional . . . It's really not about: 'look I've done this terrible thing, how should I atone for that?' I don't think they're going to do that in this forum, if they are going to do that at all.[26]

---

[23] The four questions relate to his principles of necessity, distinction, responsibility, and proportionality – the last being added only in situations where sufficient information is available.

[24] Author interview.

[25] Author interview.

[26] Author interview.

This underscores my earlier argument that these ethical techniques are fundamentally ascetic, rather than pastoral, in their contribution to militarist governmentality. The principal aim is not exposing failures or generating confessions, but contributing to a sense of self-cultivation.

However, this does not preclude the possibility that difficult episodes might be discussed to this end. According to Yishai Beer, the discussions about officers' past experiences he has had while teaching ethics have been 'extensive and emotional'.[27] Generally, however, the most difficult accounts to discuss are those in which an officer claims that he or a comrade risked harm for the sake of saving civilian lives, and not episodes of violence against Palestinians:

. . . some of them have some guilt feelings and want to receive some kind of confirmation from me as if I'm some sort of Catholic priest giving clemency. I cannot. If you have a story, present it, let's talk about it but I . . . It never occurred to me that someone told me 'Hey, I murdered a civilian' or 'I killed a civilian'. They don't talk like that. But they tell the stories. Basically . . . most of them are about risk they've taken not to kill the innocent. So they want to receive some kind of confirmation from me that what they have done is fine because they know that I have also a military capacity, so I can give them my professional perspective regarding that.

Again, therefore, Beer's primary concern was not confession but eliciting what he called 'living examples' through discussion in order to relate the contents of the ethical code to practice. His classes specifically concern the importance of 'human dignity', one of the three fundamental values in the Spirit of the IDF. He begins by discussing the importance of respecting the human dignity of friendly soldiers before broadening the discussion to include enemy combatants and civilians. The continuing tension between this human element and the military instinct was directly present in Beer's view of the role of ethical education:

It's not, you know, intuitive for military commanders to think about your adversary's soldiers . . . I think it's very important. It's very problematic, but it's very important. It's problematic in the sense that soldiers are being trained to kill. They are hunters, you know. You teach a hunter how to hunt. It's quite complicated. But they are willing.

---

[27] The quotations in the following two paragraphs are drawn from the author's interview with Yishai Beer.

As I have already stressed, however, this 'problematic' tension between the 'hunter' and the 'human' should also be viewed as productive. The very difficulty involved in relating these values to the reality of war, combined with the often emotional nature of these discussions, engenders an ideological process through which soldiers can understand themselves not only as hyper-masculine 'hunters', but also as sensitive human beings.

A parrhesiastic ethics of testimony also facilitates this militaristic ideological process. Beer illustrated this point in another remark about a specific class he gave to officer cadets in training at Bahad 1, as part of the IDF's *Maḥzabim* programme. Underscoring to me how open and frank he perceived his discussions with officers to be, Beer mentioned that the *Ha'aretz* journalist Amira Hass (well-known for her left-wing views) was observing his class, and he claimed that she was 'amazed' and 'impressed by the openness of the discussion'. In a notable turn of phrase, Beer then observed: 'If Amira Hass can be in the audience of such a discussion, why on earth do you need *Shovrim Shtiḳa*? [Breaking the Silence]'. Not only is Beer drawing a direct parallel here between his own work inside the IDF and the work of Breaking the Silence, he is also showing the ease with which the political message of the group can be neutralised through reference to a shared aim of openness and moral improvement. His remarks illustrate the ease with which soldiers' testimony can be and has been absorbed by the IDF as a militarist practice.

A comparison with the approach of Asa Kasher in teaching ethics should further underscore the specific role of testimony in asceticism. Despite his emphasis on professionalism and the importance of having trained professional instructors in ethics, Kasher is certainly not averse to drawing on soldiers' experiences to demonstrate the application of the values to practice. He views it as an excellent resource to be combined with professional instruction. Yet it is also important to stress that Kasher remains more reluctant to dwell on negative stories. He gave the following example of a written assignment he used to give to officers he was teaching at military colleges:

I give them as a term paper the duty to write about someone's experience and analyse it. Most of the time they bring their own experience, and most of the time it's a bad experience, which means that they are afraid that they did not act properly, which means its self-criticism on grounds of the code, which I

. . . Okay, the fact that they bring their own experience is excellent. But that's no problem, that comes as no surprise. I mean, they are all very experienced and why should they bring some story from an old book? They have gone through numerous incidents that are of much interest. Secondly, the fact that they come up with self-criticism is fine. It shows that they are frank, serious, sincere, that they take it seriously. I like it. However, what I dislike is the concentration on the bad aspects. The whole idea of ethics is to improve your activity, not to remove you from bad experience but to make you become closer to good activity. Rarely do they bring . . . an example of a battle about which a person was decorated. So they are more in the business of removing themselves from the bad than turning themselves closer to the good.[28]

Many aspects of military asceticism are present here – the Stoic practice of 'self-writing' (cf. Foucault, 2000b), the focus on self-improvement, the endorsement of self-criticism, the importance of frankness and sincerity – but the crucial difference remains the level of willingness to incorporate discussion of negative incidents. Kasher would still prefer the emulation of heroic examples, rather than the exploration of past failings. Again, this is characteristic of his entire approach to ethics; it is the pedagogical corollary of his emphasis on the 'practical ideal'. The officers' lack of conformity to these expectations suggests that a more demanding and difficult ethical process, which takes failure more seriously, is more likely to engage their interest.

To integrate the preceding points about asceticism and testimony, I will offer one further example – this time drawing on a specific programme, rather than the more diffuse work of different instructors. This is a course for senior officers convened by Colonel Ya'akov Castel called the *Lev Aharon* programme, which was established in 2006. It is based at the Shalom Hartman Institute, a Jewish education centre in Jerusalem, which also counts among its academic members several of the philosophers involved in drafting the latest version of the IDF ethical code (Avi Sagi, Daniel Statman, and Noam Zohar). The programme caters for officers between the ranks of Major and Brigadier General, as well as staff who teach at military colleges and officers' schools. Between 1,000 and 1,500 officers now participate in the course annually, and approximately 6,000 had passed through it by 2013.[29] In accordance with the

---

[28] Author interview.
[29] Author interview with Ya'akov Castel.

Yi'ud ve Yiḥud educational doctrine, the programme aims to strengthen officers' Israeli and Jewish identity. However, to view the programme as a narrowly ethno-religious project is to miss its broader ethical and governmental framework. In keeping with a neoliberal rationality, this is achieved through the ascetic cultivation of individual values and moral character in an educational process which has been privatised to a religious educational foundation. The brochure of the programme makes this dimension especially plain and is therefore worth quoting at length:

Targeted at secular and religious Jews as well as non-Jewish officers, the seminars focus on values and morality, exploring the gaps between different sectors in Israeli society, the idea of Israel as a Jewish and democratic state, the history of the Jewish people, and Jewish heritage. The seminars enrich participants by introducing new viewpoints to their existing perspectives of Israeli society, providing them with new manners of understanding their culture, heritage, and personal relationship to Israel. The officers study two elemental IDF texts – the IDF Spirit, an outline of the moral responsibility of the IDF, and David Ben-Gurion's Yi'ud ve Yiḥud on the commitment of the Jewish people to serve in the IDF and the responsibility of the commander as an educator.

Lev Aharon seminars, which consist of an orientation, core seminar, and post-seminar follow-up session led by distinguished academics and experienced senior officers, provide participants with a break from their regular, stressful, regimented schedule to critically and emotionally explore various facets of Israeli society. The transformative seminars often provide officers with their first opportunity for intimate, unguarded, honest expression within the military framework. Many senior officers report that they are extremely proud to serve in a military that makes this type of open discussion an integral service component for its leaders. (Shalom Hartman Institute, 2012)

The ascetic emphasis on frank, open, and critical discussion and self-examination stands out from this description. Indeed, the course takes place over several months explicitly in order to allow time for reflection on recent practice – in other words, to encourage the possibility of testimony. Castel described this in detail:

It is divided into three parts. There is an orientation day. Afterwards they go back to their units, to their homes, to their families, to their units, and come back to the central process for an intensive series of lessons, which lasts between five days and ten days in a row. After that they go back to their families and their units and we invite them for another day between three months and half a year afterwards in order to hear two things: what they say in retrospect about what they did/went through [*ma she hem 'avru*]; and, no less important, whether they did anything with it, whether it influenced them in a concrete way, in their actions, in their behaviour in the army.[30]

This is particularly the case in discussing the 'Spirit of the IDF', to which one discussion session is devoted per course. In groups of ten to twelve, the officers go over recent examples from their military experience and discuss them in the light of the code. If no examples are forthcoming, then the convenor will make use of a case study from a prepared bank of examples. Generally, however, Castel reported that discussions were quite frank.

Often the examples discussed do not directly concern combat but interpersonal relationships in the army. Castel reported that several discussions had concerned cases of misuse of social media or accessing the personal data of other soldiers. One particularly interesting example he recounted revealed how ethics is also bound up with the management of racial hierarchies in the military:

A commander in whose unit there was a religious female officer – a young woman who came from a religious household – who developed a love affair with another Bedouin officer – a Muslim Bedouin. Now, the officer is in a dilemma about what do with this. That is, on the face of it, it's their private life. On the other hand . . . there are problems on both sides, not just on one side . . . Is it right to separate them and to send him or her to another unit? Because there are here lots of problems . . . there will be a lot of regrets in their communities [. . .] It's not simple: how far it is it permitted for a commander to be involved in things like this?[31]

In this case, ethics was explicitly used as a regulatory framework in which the tensions of the growing social diversity of the IDF can be managed. Other examples, however, were rooted more directly in

---

[30] Author interview [my translation].
[31] Author interview [my translation].

issues of battlefield morality. He referred to one example where an officer discussed his use of drones in Operation Cast Lead in Gaza:

In Cast Lead, we had a case of dilemma which a commander had in this unit about the limits of the use he made of [drones] and the argument that there was between two commanders about whether to do a particular mission or not, between two pretty senior commanders, who considered an argument about a moral dilemma there is here between the military benefit [*to'elet hatsva'it*] and the moral dilemma . . . It stirred me up ['*oti ze rigesh*] that they brought it into the class. Ultimately [. . .] the person who dropped the bombs did what he was told, but he wasn't sure that he acted in the correct moral way. He brought it into the classroom.[32]

This particular example illustrates very well how the ideological impact of such ethical discussions is contingent neither upon practical outcomes (since the order was still followed), nor indeed on an uncomplicated justification of the violence employed (since the officer remains unsure he did the right thing). Nevertheless, the very complexity and lack of consensus in this case contributes to the perception that this ethical reflection is powerful and meaningful, helping to achieve the desired consolidation of a value-based Jewish-Israeli identity.

This example is also noteworthy for its provenance in drone warfare, typically considered by critics to be a mode of violence which facilitates ethical disengagement (Coker, 2013: 109–45). It may be, however, that the call to recover a more reflective, 'human' approach to the use of drones has already been anticipated by militaries themselves. For it is precisely this human element which the *Lev Aharon* programme appears to wish to cultivate, effecting the mechanism of ideological dis-identification I have referred to in this chapter. Castel was very keen to emphasise the 'human' aspect of what the course achieves:

It's part of being a commander to be concerned with these questions. I really think that it makes them – and they testify to this – better human beings, more sensitive. They also say that it makes them better parents to their children, which is very, very touching to hear from them, that it makes them better partners to their spouses. It influences them in many ways as people. The army is interested in their functioning as officers, but as a by-product

---

[32] Author interview [my translation].

here we develop many benefits to the people as human beings ['*anashim cabnei 'adam*], which is a great benefit in the state of Israel – it's important to society. Not in the military field but there is here improvement in many ways.[33]

It is instructive to note the way that the development of the officer as a human being is also underpinned with references to family life, further demonstrating the connection being established ethical soldiering and the consolidation of domestic gendered identities. Contrary to Castel, however, I would submit that there is also a direct military benefit being garnered here, which paradoxically can only be achieved by this sense of distancing from purely military concerns. Such courses help officers to 'keep a human image' and this is in fact the core of their ideological contribution to militarism.

Teaching Ethics to Soldiers: Multimedia, Theatre, and 'Empathy'

As discussed above, part of the ambition behind providing ethical training to officers was also to enable them to hold discussions of ethical issues with their soldiers. Despite efforts to promote commanders as 'educators-in-uniform', the results of this strategy have been uneven. The Israeli State Comptroller investigated the success of the *Yi'ud ṿeYiḥud* strategy in 2011 and found that, despite a high willingness on the part of officers, many did not feel that they had the ability to hold discussions about values and identity with soldiers under their command (2011: 1607–11). In research conducted by the Education Corps, only around one quarter of officers surveyed reported having held such discussions with their soldiers (2011: 1608). Much more routine occasions for ethical pedagogy therefore occur during basic training and in subsequent sessions run by the Education Corps, often through privatised arrangements with external organisations.

In his recent account of the deployment of a unit from the Naḥal brigade to Hebron, the Israeli journalist Amos Harel observed the ethical training process which soldiers undergo. He notes that it first appears in basic training in the form of a week-long educational course which

---

[33] Author interview [my translation].

is supposed to cover cultural and societal issues (such as Zionism and state building) but which in practice focuses on 'mental and ethical preparation [*hakhana mentalit ve'erkhit*] for activities in the territories' (Harel, 2013: 339). Indeed, just as the officer training described above emphasises the importance of learning to apply theory to practice through repeated discussion of examples, so regular soldiers are encouraged to think about examples drawn from practice in order to promote what is referred to as the 'assimilation' [*hatma'a*] of values.

Unlike in the case of officers, however, there is a much stronger emphasis on visual material and active, even bodily, participation. In the class which Harel describes, the platoon commander first discusses with his soldiers the precise meaning of 'necessary force' in the value of 'purity of arms'. After this, the soldiers are shown several videos, each produced by the Education Corps and IDF Theatre, which depict scenarios in which the values of the Spirit of the IDF are deemed relevant and occasionally come into conflict. In one video soldiers come across a wallet containing one thousand dollars in a Palestinian home which is about to be demolished. The commander then leads a heated discussion about whether it would be permissible to take the money (answer: no). What is striking about this example is how the issue of looting is foregrounded and thereby completely obscures the question of the house demolition, which remains an unexamined, neutral part of the scenario. In another video, a soldier recounts how he and a friend beat and then strangled an arrested Palestinian who was sobbing too loudly. And a final scenario portrays soldiers abusing an elderly Palestinian at a checkpoint as revenge for a friend killed in a terrorist attack (Harel, 2013: 339–43). In all these cases, the discussion is designed to improve the smooth functioning of the military procedure at hand – whether it is demolition, arrests and detention, or maintaining checkpoints – and to shift the controversy to seemingly more individual, rather than structural, instances of violence.

The focus of such sessions becomes much more practical after basic training is complete and soldiers have been assigned to their units. Prior to deployment at checkpoints or other locations in the West Bank, all IDF soldiers undergo computer-based training developed by the IDF School of Law (Guiora, 2006; Adler, 2007). Contrary to the perceived role of military lawyers as effective only in justifying or legalising military operations from a distance, the IDF School of Law is also interested in the ethical formation of soldiers. Indeed, in its practical manifestation this legal training is in fact subsumed by wider ethical objectives. The software, developed in a project led by Major General Amos Guiora during his time as commander of the School of Law, works to accentuate the active involvement of the soldier as a subject in the ethical process. In his words,

The preferred solution was to avoid – unless field and operational circumstances dictated otherwise – 'standup' lectures to units whose soldiers were either in training or preparing for deployment, and instead to develop an interactive software, based on Hollywood movies and state-of-the-art graphics, to teach an eleven-point code of conduct. This code is based on international law and was formulated after careful analysis of other armies' practice.

Although other armies had indeed developed training material on this issue, means of effectively reaching the soldier were lacking. The client has to be 'hooked' to ensure – as much as possible – that a genuine learning process will take place. A training video with role-playing actors, as used in other armies, was found to be 'unnatural' and 'staged'. The goal was to devise an educational tool that the audience could relate to, not only in the context of present experience from before their military service. That tool had to be entertaining at least in its approach; it had to have a 'marketing edge' to it, or the soldier might disregard it. (Guiora, 2006)

The use of language inspired by neoliberal organisational culture is evident in this passage – the soldier is a 'client' to whom 'entertaining' training must be 'marketed' and who therefore chooses the moral pathway because he is incentivised. As Guiora adds, 'the use of the word "client" is intentional, since an educational mission that is not client oriented is a guaranteed failure' (2006).

What is also noticeable is the accentuation of the interactive element in this training. Although virtual, this software deploys a much more immersive approach to ethical training. The use of Hollywood films to illustrate certain dilemmas is designed to promote identification with the situation as well as to add an 'entertaining' edge. Indeed, as one lecturer from the IDF School of Law remarked, 'I have personally found that there is nothing as effective as a movie clip with a plethora of explosions and machine gun fire to ensure the undivided attention of a class' (Adler, 2007: 47). This tactic of immersion is apparently deemed crucial to the efficacy of the software, as an example shows:

The segment shown from the movie *Platoon*, which depicts a My Lai-like incident, is powerful in its images and sounds. Soldiers are seen burning huts and throwing grenades into dug holes that may well be hiding places. Children cling to their parents and beg that they not be taken from them. Against this harsh background, the camera focuses on the commander walking away deep in thought. (Guiora, 2006)

Following these clips, soldiers are shown animated scenes based on real events that have occurred under IDF Central Command, which controls the West Bank, and the software asks them questions about the best course of action. These animations can therefore also be considered a form of testimony. Indeed, as Giuora writes, 'confronting soldiers with real-life dilemmas that either his unit or similar units have experienced was seen as the most realistic and potentially effective approach' (2006).

The embodied dimension of ethical pedagogy is accentuated even further when an additional tool is used to teach ethical values: interactive theatre. Theatre workshops in which soldiers are invited to play roles alongside actors is commonly used by the IDF to prepare soldiers for situations they are likely to face on particular deployments. Harel reports, for example, that the IDF uses theatre groups to run 'simulations' in which soldiers pretend to be in a real-life encounter in the West Bank (2013: 336–9). Some of them take on the role of duty soldiers, while others might perform the role of settlers, left-wing activists, and even Palestinians. This can be used primarily as a technical tool without much consideration of ethical issues, as Harel reports in the session he observed. However, the IDF frequently uses interactive theatre as a means of ethical pedagogy as well. Indeed, in 2012, the Education Corps announced it would be expanding its use of such methods as a response to the growing number of controversial incidents involving Israeli and international activists (Walla! News, 2012).

In order to understand properly the role of theatre in ethical pedagogy in the IDF it is necessary to trace its origins, which once again lie with the *Yi'ud veYiḥud* programme and the organisation *Beit Morasha*. This developed in the early stages of the collaboration between the IDF and *Beit Morasha* and steadily expanded thereafter. In 2004, an Israeli television actress, who had also been a member of the IDF theatre troupe during her military service, began working as an educator in the IDF with *Beit Morasha*.[34] She experimented with drama-based methods with a group of officers as a means of exploring ethical issues and found them to be a successful way to involve the participants. The number of sessions was quickly increased and she began to work more and more with regular soldiers, often travelling to military bases in the West Bank to run workshops (in locations as diverse as Rama, Hawara, Itamar, and Yitzhar).

As her teaching methods developed, the workshops began to assume a regular format, which roughly proceeded as follows. A group of approximately thirty soldiers would take a day away from active duty and would join a session lasting three hours. After several warm-up exercises designed to encourage participation and allow her to get to know the soldiers, the soldiers would be divided up into six groups and each given a theme to work on. These themes included: humiliation at checkpoints, violence towards Palestinians, looting, handling the media, drugs and alcohol, and taking bribes. Occasionally, in response to a particular request from the commander, these topics might also reflect recent problems the unit had encountered. The soldiers were asked to develop short plays based on their experiences, which could either be something they were directly involved in or something they had seen. They assumed the roles not only of soldiers but also of Palestinians. After twenty minutes' preparation time, the soldiers would each perform their improvised sketch in turn, followed by a discussion about the moral implications involved in light of the values of the 'Spirit of the IDF'. The class would end with a summary from an officer who had been present throughout, who was usually a company commander or deputy company commander.

This exercise is perhaps the clearest example of the use of testimony as a form of ascetic 'mental preparation' in the IDF. The use of theatre in this way is another form of *paraskeue*: the values of the 'Spirit of the IDF' are being 'assimilated' through reflection on practice. Yet there are also additional features to this approach which reflect the

---

[34] Unless otherwise stated, the following account is based on two interviews by the author with the educator in question, Michal Feuras, which took place on 7 March 2013 [hereafter, 'first interview'] and 9 April 2013 [hereafter, 'second interview'], in Tel Aviv.

particular position of regular soldiers and which accentuate the role of emotions, embodied behaviour, and crucially gender. The well-being of the soldier was a key concern of these sessions, and the importance of protecting the human image of the soldier was a direct message which the convenor used to convey. She described this message, which is redolent with the language of maternal care, as follows:

Okay guys, you came to army as pure as you can get. Okay, you are pure. And my job, the army's job is after three years . . . because you will come out and you will be a citizen again . . . and my job is to make sure that at the end of the day when you look in the mirror you will be as pure as when you got here.[35]

This importance of the mirror image was in the convenor's view equivalent to invoking the idea of settling accounts with God, but in a more pluralist metaphor. Avoiding the need to confess sins was also a key element in her rhetoric:

. . . at the end of the day look in the mirror and say, even though the occupation is shit [. . .] even though I have to be here in this lousy checkpoint, I know that I did everything as I was supposed to do. I didn't do anything morally wrong . . . And I can look at myself and be a whole person. And not going . . . afterwards and saying 'al ḥeṭ sheḥaṭati lefaneikha' [forgive me for my sins] . . .[36]

It is clear that such an approach leaves the fundamental political reality ('the occupation is shit') untouched and unchangeable, displacing it through an emphasis on staying human. Indeed, her continued reference to the importance of remaining 'whole with yourself' [shalem 'im 'atzmekha] or 'with your actions' stages a fantasy of subjective completeness which is designed to suture the inherent contradictions of the idea of maintaining a moral occupation.

A crucial element of the way in which the convenor of these sessions would enhance their effectiveness was through the use of gendered language and through a manipulation of her gendered position.

---

[35] First interview.
[36] Second interview. The Hebrew phrase comes from the Yom Kippur confessional prayer.

Generally, a major constraint on the effectiveness of the Education Corps is seen to be that education officers are overwhelmingly women and that therefore they struggle to gain the respect of soldiers. The director of the Identity and Purpose programme at *Beit Morasha* also indicated to me that he thought male instructors were usually more suitable for the task. Yet the convenor of the theatre programme was adamant that her position as a woman in fact helped her to ensure effective participation in the sessions. Like most women working in the armed forces, she certainly had to make some adjustments to her usual manner of self-presentation (cf. Sasson-Levy, 2003b: 448–51). This was especially the case because she was recognised by the soldiers from her work on television and because she was quickly identified with a left-leaning, Tel Aviv background. To compensate she would make a particular effort to use military slang, for example, and would rely heavily on her religious knowledge and her background in *Beit Morasha* to overcome resistance from more religious soldiers.

Yet these adjustments in her language were not designed to efface her position as a woman but rather to allow her to make more effective use of it. As Cynthia Enloe has documented at length in her work on the role of women in supporting roles in militaries, it is most often through their perceived femininity that women in military roles make their crucial contributions (2000: esp. 35–49). When I asked her exactly how she felt being a woman helped her, the convenor of the theatre sessions responded:

I think it has to do with . . . I'm a very warm person and I didn't come there to judge them. I was not judgemental. And . . . I don't know if it's . . . it's kind of chauvinistic, or feminist, to say that I tried to get them in touch with their female point of view or whatever . . . I can't really prove it . . . But I got told a lot that it was good that it was from outside, it was good that it was a female, it was good that it was civilian, and it wasn't somebody that's inside. It's like you're so used to the crazy, crazy situation [and then] you're for three hours in a different place, with a different person, who speaks a different language, who makes you correlate things that you didn't think about . . .[37]

---

[37] Second interview.

There are many gendered elements to this statement which need to be analysed separately. Firstly, it is clear that she holds a perception that the soldiers needed to know that she supported them and that she was there to help and not to judge. On another occasion, she made clearer how her perceived femininity made this possible:

I always used to tell them, I'm on your side. That's very, very important to me: that first of all I think that what you are doing is very important and I really respect you, and I really appreciate the fact that you take care of me and my daughter, when I had a daughter, but before me as a civilian, and your parents and everybody.[38]

She therefore not only mobilised her position as a mother but also attempted to remind them of the (always gendered) context of their families in order to stress that she was there to support them. Rhetorical gestures such as this perhaps help to explain why soldiers were by all accounts more willing to discuss problematic behaviour in these drama workshops than in the context of operational debriefing.

Secondly, it also seems that being a woman helped to underscore the recreational and therapeutic side of the theatre sessions. As she also commented, this atmosphere encouraged participation and openness:

Usually there wasn't any hostility because – think about it – you're on duty for a long time and then comes this gorgeous actress from Tel Aviv (I'm joking!). Then I'm joking, and I'm playing with them. And I'm like: everything is going to be okay, you can tell me everything, we're going to speak about everything openly.[39]

Thirdly, it is also possible to see that not only was her perceived femininity crucial to this process, but also the soldiers themselves were being encouraged to adopt a supposedly more feminine disposition. It is the domestic, familial, and oedipal nature of the space created during these sessions that encourages testimony. More than this, however, it is supposedly feminine behaviour and supposedly feminine ways of, in her words, 'correlating things differently' which soldiers are being trained to take back to their military pursuits.

---

[38] First interview.
[39] First interview.

This last point needs greater examination, since it gets to the heart of the specificity of the sessions offered to regular soldiers as distinct from those given to officers. Whereas ethics training for officers tends to focus on developing repertoires of behaviour for particular scenarios and improving the ability to use discretion [*shiḳul da'at*] in applying values to practice, regular soldiers have relatively fewer opportunities to deploy such faculties. Thus, when the theatre sessions were used to train officers on a minority of occasions, the convenor altered the nature of the post-performance discussion to discuss alternate ways of doing things:

If it was with the commanders, if somebody in the audience would say 'Yeah, I would have dealt with it differently. I would have done this and that' I would call them to the stage and ask them to perform and show me how they deal with it. And then like train them or show them different aspects of being an officer, of commanding.[40]

Here the ascetic dimension of the training lies in the repetition and experimentation with different approaches. However, in the case of the sessions with regular soldiers, while the ascetic technique of self-examination is still being applied, the pedagogical process relied on a more overtly affective, gendered, and embodied processes. This reflects their position in the 'seam of encounter' – the face-to-face contact they would have with Palestinian civilians (Khalili, 2014: 7; see also Gregory, 2008). The crucial faculty being cultivated was no longer *shiḳul da'at*, therefore, but a purportedly feminine sense of 'empathy', as the convenor of these sessions repeatedly emphasised to me.

To fully grasp the importance of empathy for this activity it is worth quoting at length her fullest comment on this matter. It illustrates why theatre is particularly well-suited to this task, as well as the potentially disturbing rationale behind its use:

. . . it was something that my [acting] teacher, may he rest in peace . . . told us like one of the first lessons we had. And he told us: what is the most important thing that an actor should have? And everybody was like 'potential' and 'self-awareness' and 'self-confidence' and then nobody guessed it and he says 'empathy'. And I think that in order to be a better officer, a better

---

[40] Second interview.

soldier, a better person, a better everything . . . is *to understand the other person's point of view in order to make them or yourself do whatever it is necessary*. And now I'm going to say something that another teacher told me about empathy, [who was a] psychologist: the Nazis were very, very big in empathy. And why is that? Because empathy is not about being kind or . . . it's about being able to be in the shoes of the other. And why were the Nazis very empathetic? Because when the Jews got to Auschwitz they were told . . . there was music on, okay? And they were told to bathe and get food and that's [the] way, because they could be told as they got there 'you're going to be killed! Go to that side!' or whatever. The devious ways . . . that's because they understood what a person that is travelling for so long in a train . . . what they are thinking about, okay? And not make them . . . to calmly take them to the gas chambers, okay? Now, that's about empathy . . . it has nothing to do with the soldiers in the checkpoints, they have nothing to do with the Nazis . . . But I think that the empathetic point of view is very, very important to understand what it's like to be a Palestinian that has to cross checkpoints all day long, and to be in . . . in a traffic jam every day and to have his car checked every day and to have his kid watching or a Palestinian with his wife – to really understand what happens. And the soldiers were like . . . got to the empathetic point of view, or place, not the psychopathic way but the real empathic point of view.[41]

The disavowed but implicit comparison with the Holocaust, though striking, is not the central issue in this statement. It is in fact less surprising than it might appear. As beyond the pale and anti-Semitic as such comparisons are often held to be, historically speaking it has been common for Israeli soldiers to make these connections, as Ruth Linn (1991) has documented. The convenor of these workshops also noted the Holocaust came up 'very often' in the theatre sessions she used to run, even without prompting from her. The description of Nazi death camps she gives is also historically inaccurate in many ways, and mostly draws on the widespread but mythological anxiety in Israeli society about why Jews went to the gas chambers 'like lambs led to the slaughter' (Segev, 1993: 113).

Instead, the most relevant aspect of the above remark is the way in which empathy is posited as a means of control. It is described as a means of understanding the behaviour of Palestinians, and of accordingly learning to adapt one's own behaviour to reduce the friction

---

[41] Second interview, emphasis added.

between occupier and occupied. Empathy in this sense is supposed to act as a kind of checkpoint lubricant, aiming to make the task of maintaining military rule easier. Yet unlike mercenary anthropology, as deployed by the US in Iraq and Afghanistan, the principal focus of the cultivation of empathy in these theatre sessions is not in fact a form of 'cultural' education about the mores and sensitivities of Palestinian society (cf. Gonzáles, 2007; Gregory, 2008; Zehfuss, 2012b). Rather, and perhaps ironically, empathy is produced by processes of introspection. It is the soldiers themselves who generate the perception of what it is like to be a Palestinian at a checkpoint, either by imagining it or by putting themselves on the receiving end of simulations of their own violence and humiliation tactics in the scene. The 'Palestinian' in these performances is therefore only ever a projection of a specifically Israeli imaginary. This is why it is important to stress that, however practical in intent these simulations are, they primarily function as solipsistic and depoliticised moments of (gendered) subject formation. This becomes even clearer when the techniques employed for promoting 'empathy' in the post-performance discussion are examined:

I was very manipulative because I was always used to remind them of their own family . . . I used to use their families to make them understand: would you like somebody in the supermarket, while they're saying *neshek*[42] or 'open your bag' to say, 'now, okay take your hands, now raise your hands, now spread your legs, now fall to the ground', or to your little brother? Or to make them understand – now, there are kids who throw stones and are very, very . . . they make you mad, okay? I can understand the situation, okay? And they're eighteen. But I used to ask them, 'who here has a small brother or sister? Can you even imagine a cop – an Israeli cop coming to your brother or sister with their weapons on, speaking to them with their weapons after throwing whatever. Can you even imagine that happening?'[43]

Once again, situating the soldier in the always-already gendered context of family relations is crucial to activating the empathetic response. Meanwhile, the political reality – that Israelis and Palestinians in the occupied territories live under completely different legal regimes

---

[42] 'Weapon', the shorthand used by security guards in Israel to check customers for firearms.
[43] Second interview.

which make some actions against an Israeli unimaginable and the same actions against a Palestinian routine – is totally effaced in such moments. It is 'empathy' and not politics which appears to make the difference.

Perhaps the starkest example of this was that the convenor also analysed soldiers' lack of empathy in racial as well as gendered terms. She singled out the border patrol, where a disproportionate number of 'peripheral' troops serve, as a particularly problematic area:

It's a very anthropological, sociological situation. It's very interesting because most of the people in [the border patrol] are minorities, like you have Druze, you have very poor Mizrahim, Jewish people, and Ethiopians, and sometimes Russians, immigrants. It's interesting to see that they are the most abusive, most hateful. Like the hate or the political incorrectness is most in your face there.

By identifying the source of violence and racism in soldiers' ethnic origins, the structural violence and racism of the occupation is further obscured by the emphasis on individual or minority dispositions. Yet this also serves to reinforce a moral hierarchy which implicitly elevates Ashkenazi Jews not only to a position of superiority but also to a duty of hegemonic moral guardianship over the other components of the national collective.

Another key feature of these drama workshops was the emphasis on openness and candour in opposition to silence. At the beginning of each session, the convenor invited soldiers to write about a moral issue they had faced during their recent service on a piece of paper, which she would read as they prepared their improvisations. Although these papers were anonymous, one of the purposes of this procedure was to check that the plays performed corresponded to the most pressing issue facing the unit. Moreover, the papers were used to check for the presence of what is known in Hebrew as a *kesher shtika* ('conspiracy of silence'), which refers to a situation in which authority and personal dynamics within a group prevent problems and complaints from being discussed. In post-session debriefings with the commanding officer, the convenor of these sessions would always point out the existence of an apparent *kesher shtika* with the aim of helping the unit to work to resolve it. Silence was therefore perceived as an obstacle to military effectiveness, whereas sharing, reporting difficulties, and honesty (testimony, in other words) were considered advantageous to it. What is striking about this emphasis is its unintentional rhetorical resonance with the work of Breaking the Silence [*Shovrim Shtika*]. It is perhaps noteworthy that both this use of theatre workshops to explore moral issues and the first exhibition organised by Breaking the Silence began in the same year, 2004. When asked about this apparent similarity, Roni Sulimani, the director of IDF education who approved the programme, took this as no surprise:

. . . because [Breaking the Silence] act out the way their culture is . . . from my point of view it's good that soldiers are coming out and saying this is what there is in the army, make sure that the other soldiers who go to the army will not do the same. It's okay. [And] It's good if the Education Corps will do things that open into the inside and not outside.[44]

This apparent sinuosity between the work of Breaking the Silence and the work of the Education Corps is not, in my view, coincidental. As differently oriented as these organisations remain, their activities have common roots in the ethics of Israeli militarism and, as will be shown later, often have curiously similar consequences.

The closed theatre sessions were reduced in frequency in 2009 after a change in the personal circumstances of the convenor. However, the influence of this pedagogical approach to dealing with ethics did not cease after that. As the sessions became more popular, demand rapidly outstripped the ability of the convenor to facilitate them and a more easily distributed form of the activity was devised. This was 'dilemma theatre', which involved developing scripted sketches (written by the same convenor and based on what she had heard from soldiers), which would then be performed by the IDF's theatre troupe. Although less intensive in terms of the active involvement of combat soldiers, these sketches could be shown to much larger audiences and deployed much more flexibly. The actors were trained not only with the guidance of the convenor but also based on extensive observation at checkpoints, in order to improve their realism.

Some of the encounters depicted in these sketches are shocking but nevertheless based on actual events. In one scene, for example, soldiers at a checkpoint force a young Palestinian woman to participate

[44] Author interview.

in what they call the 'Miss Hawara'[45] beauty pageant, by getting her to lift her dress on the pretext of checking for explosives.[46] Officers were provided with copies of the scripts, as well as pre-prepared questions to facilitate discussion of the sketches afterwards. In the case of this example, and apparently because it needed underscoring, soldiers were asked how the actions depicted in the scene harmed the value of 'human dignity' in the Spirit of the IDF, as well as 'purity of arms'. The inclusion of scenes such as this demonstrates that, no matter how secretive and dismissive the IDF appears in public and in foreign media about such episodes, it has few qualms about discussing them internally if it provides an opportunity to shape soldiers as ethical subjects with a 'human image'. It is through carefully (and literally) stage-managed mechanisms such as these that the problematic political questions they raise can be neutralised through ethical work.

Conclusion: The 'Sublime Object' of Militarism

I began this chapter by exploring the questions raised by Roni Sulimani's remark that the primary function of ethical pedagogy in the IDF was to help the Israeli soldier to remain a human being. Throughout the analysis, I have continually returned to this point, showing how it reveals the fundamental priorities and contribution of military ethical pedagogy in the IDF. The aim of ethics training in the IDF is manifestly not to protect civilians or to promote a culture of accountability. Instead, the significance of this training is primarily ideological. Indeed, in its emphasis on humanity in the face of violence the teaching of military ethics conforms perfectly to the understanding of ideology developed by Slavoj Žižek:

an ideological identification exerts a true hold on us precisely when we maintain an awareness that we are not fully identical to it, that there is a rich human person beneath it: 'not all is ideology, beneath the mask, I am also a human person' is *the very form of ideology* in its 'practical efficiency'. (2008a: 21)

---

[45] Hawara is a notorious checkpoint in the North of the West Bank.
[46] Discussion of this scene is based on author interviews with the writer/convenor and on the script of the scene viewed by the author.

The achievement of this effect requires something much more elaborate than simply silencing troubling episodes or providing legitimation for every violent incident. Instead, I have shown that this ideological process is in fact stronger when it engages directly with the problematic and troubling elements serving in the IDF. To this end the IDF orchestrates the selective and carefully choreographed incitement of testimony in relation to such incidents, so that their problematic political implications can be obscured by making them the focus of ethical work.

In this sense, 'keeping a human image' should be understood as an ideological operation that produces what Žižek calls a 'sublime object', a focus of fantasy which obscures the inconsistency of the symbolic order of Israeli militarism. Military ethical pedagogy provides a plethora of ascetic activities which are designed to distract from the fundamental violence of occupation: self-examination, group discussion, multimedia, films, drama workshops, and theatre performances – all activities linked by the common thread of soldiers' testimony. These activities distract from violence not in the sense that they ignore it, but in that they turn the ethical encounter with violence into an opportunity to stage a variety of militarist fantasies, many of which also encompass a range of gendered, racial, religious, and ethno-national identifications. In the place of the difficult political questions raised by this violence, they install solipsistic projects of the self achieved through asceticism, affective work, and embodied practice.

4 'Meaningful Service': Ethics and Pedagogy at Pre-military Academies in Israel

We were gathered in a small hall at Rabin Pre-military Academy on a dark winter's evening.[1] Heavy rain was beating down on the roof of the building. Some eighty students were present and we were waiting for a class to begin. Rabin Academy, founded in 1996, is one of forty-six pre-military academies [*mekhinot kdam-tzva'iyot*] across Israel. *Mekhinot* are private educational institutions which provide a year of informal education for high-school graduates who are about to be conscripted.[2] Attendance is voluntary, and normally fee-paying, but often fiercely competitive. It is widely recognised that some of the most motivated and successful soldiers come from pre-military academies, which is why the Israel Defence Forces (IDF) grants their students a one-year deferral of military service to attend them. The class was to be taught by the head of the academy, Dani Zamir, a retired major in the paratroopers, as part of a year-long course on 'leadership and worldviews'. Although it covers a range of topics, approximately half of the course concerns military ethics. Zamir was late to the class, and while we waited for him one of the students who entered the room received a rapturous applause. He had just been selected for the infantry unit he had desperately wanted to reach.

By the time the class began, the room was excitable and it was getting late. Nevertheless, Zamir pushed ahead with his plan, which was to show a film to the students called, *To See If I'm Smiling* (directed by Tamar Yarom), as a way of continuing their ongoing discussion of the value of purity of arms. *To See If I'm Smiling* is a deeply disturbing film. It consists of the video testimonies of six Israeli women who

---

[1] The following account is based on field notes from 6 December 2012.
[2] *Mekhina* (pl. *mekhinot*) is the short-hand term used by Israelis to describe pre-military academies, which I will use throughout this chapter. Etymologically this term derives from the verb meaning 'to prepare', which underscores the academies' role as conduits for military service.

served in the IDF during the Second Intifada, interspersed with archive footage (see also Morag, 2013: 166–79).[3] The women describe episodes of repeated violence and humiliation of Palestinians, and confess their involvement and complicity. They also discuss the difficulties that women face in the IDF and how participation in masculinised violence can be a way to gain acceptance from male comrades. The film discusses the after-effects of military service and violence on these six women, which range from guilt through to difficulties in motherhood and alcoholism. The cinematic *coup de grâce* from which the film derives its title occurs in the final scene. Meirav, who served as an IDF medic in Hebron, has recounted a story from when she worked in the morgue. The body of a Palestinian man in the morgue acquired a *post mortem* erection and she asked her friend to take a photograph of her next to him. In this final scene, wracked with guilt and welling with tears, Meirav examines the photograph for the first time in years – to see if she is smiling.

Students at Rabin Academy had begun watching the film with casual interest, with many of them checking mobile phones or chatting among themselves. Occasionally they had laughed at the more light-hearted moments of the film. But by the end of the screening, the room was silent and the students were watching intently. When the lights were switched back on, the unease and discomfort in the room were palpable. Zamir began to chair a discussion with the students. Several complained that the film was politically biased, misrepresenting the reality of the occupation. Zamir responded that he didn't think the film made a political point at all. For him, the film is about how soldiers behave. He sees it as an educational opportunity to raise awareness and prepare his students to prevent similar stories from taking place during their military service. He believes the film is about ethics.

The approach of this class once again illustrates the importance of testimony for military ethical pedagogy in Israel. It shows, firstly, how testimony is a vital source of examples and discussion in attempting to encourage students to behave ethically. But, secondly, it also shows the powerful potential of using testimony to take episodes of appalling violence, to drain them of political content, and then to recycle them as opportunities for encouraging renewed military participation.

---

[3] Breaking the Silence assisted the director with the research for the film.

Responding to his students' disquiet at the film, Zamir reassured them that accepting that these events took place does not necessarily harm the image of the IDF as the most moral army in the world. Indeed, he argued that, assuming the IDF is a moral army, part of earning that reputation is being prepared to talk about such things. This logic is potentially very powerful: taken to its conclusion, it enables one to believe in the idea of the IDF as a moral army purely on the basis of its soldiers' willingness to examine themselves after committing acts of violence. It divorces this myth from political reality and guarantees its ideological efficacy on the sole basis of the affective and subjective rewards of ethical work.

The approach adopted in this class also demonstrates the importance of gender for promoting testimony and ethical activity in general. It is significant that the film chosen for this purpose should be based on women's testimonies. This suggests that the production of soldiers' testimony is often problematically coded as a feminine activity. It is also noteworthy that, in the ensuing discussion at Rabin Academy, the gender politics of the film – which consist in highlighting the masculinised violence of the IDF – were completely occluded by the concern to produce more ethical soldiers. And cultivating such an ethical soldier necessarily also involves producing a gendered subject. Dani Zamir took precisely this approach by asking his students to treat each Palestinian at a checkpoint as if they were their father, inserting ethical reflection into the always-already gendered context of familial expectations. His approach again underscores that testimony and ethical activity in the IDF are also a means of consolidating gendered identities.

* * *

Pre-military academies are a diverse set of institutions. As I will show, not all of them teach military ethics in the same way as Dani Zamir. However, in spite of this variety, ethics is a crucial dimension of the education provided at these academies and, as elsewhere, it plays an important role in the formation of their students as militarist subjects. Accordingly, pre-military academies should be understood as ascetic institutions focused on the practice of ethical self-cultivation, a process which is also bound up with the production of ethno-national, religious, and gendered identities. They should also be understood as part of the ideological apparatus of Israeli militarism that legitimates military violence. Furthermore, as private institutions, pre-military academies are one of the clearest examples of the privatisation and dispersal of pedagogy beyond the formal institutional reach of the IDF. Their rapid growth in number and size in recent years is another reflection of the influence of a neoliberal governmental rationality on Israeli militarism which favours the autonomous cultivation of ethical responsibility and ideological motivation in soldiers. Indeed, the diversity of social groups catered for by *mekhinot* underscores the strength and flexibility of this arrangement. Examining these institutions can therefore tell us something important about the changing nature of Israeli militarism, and the place of ethics within it.

The Origins and Development of Pre-military Academies

The original impetus for the creation of pre-military academies in Israel came from within the national-religious movement. Rabbi Eli Sadan founded the first *mekhina* in 1987 under the name *Bnei David* and located it in the Jewish settlement of Eli in the northern West Bank. This *mekhina* represented a new departure in the relationship between the national-religious population and the army, which had hitherto co-existed uneasily. Sadan's vision was to achieve much greater integration of the national-religious community in the IDF. Previously the most common avenue for religious soldiers to serve in the IDF was through institutions called *yeshivot hesder*. *Yeshivot hesder* allowed soldiers to combine military service and religious study at a Jewish seminary, but this involved a shortened period of active duty and was usually confined to particular units (most commonly in the armoured corps) (Cohen, 2013: 59–71). Sadan proposed a different model, which was that religious soldiers would spend a prior year studying at a seminary and preparing for military service and would then serve a full three-year period in the army throughout its ranks (Rosman-Stollman, 2014: 104–7). Graduates were encouraged to serve in combat roles and to extend their service by becoming officers and commanders.

This new model for national-religious participation in the army proved enormously successful. It drew in many students and became very attractive to the army, which thereby acquired a new pool of manpower. By 1996 five religious *mekhinot* had been established, sending hundreds of soldiers to the army each year. Indeed, for this reason pre-military academies are often portrayed primarily as institutions facilitating the entrance of national-religious soldiers into the ranks (Cohen, 2013: 11–12, 70–1, 89, 92, 104, 134 (n. 6); Levy, 2014: 277–81, 285, 287; Rosman-Stollman, 2014: 104–23). However, since its foundation the programme has expanded significantly beyond this objective. In 1996, Ze'evik Nativ received permission to found the first pre-military academy for secular students, Nachshon. This was shortly followed by Beit Yisrael (which mixes secular and religious students) and Rabin Academy. For the secular educators such as Nativ and Zamir who founded these academies, the assassination of Yitzhak Rabin was an important factor in their decision to extend the programme.[4] They perceived a crisis in the secular contribution to society, prompting a call for civic renewal which did not just include the religious.

Secular academies have also proved extremely popular and have grown steadily and exponentially ever since. In fact, in recent years the number of secular and mixed pre-military academies has outstripped that of the religious academies. From 2004 to 2012, the secular and mixed academies more than doubled their numbers from a starting point of ten. As of 2016 there were twenty-four secular and mixed academies (collectively referred to as general academies, or *mekhinot klaliyot*), as opposed to 22 'torah-based academies' (*mekhinot toraniyot*) modelled on yeshivas (see Figure 4.1). The rapid growth in the number of secular and mixed academies has also fuelled a huge increase in student numbers in recent years, a figure which recently topped 3,300 annually (Jerusalem Post, 2013; see also Figure 4.2). This makes *mekhinot* the largest pre-army education programme in the country. There is currently rough parity between the number of students at religious academies and those at secular and mixed academies, which means that the national-religious are still strongly over-represented. However, present trends suggest that this balance may continue to shift in the direction of secular and mixed academies.

In recognition of this rapid growth, the legal and budgetary framework for *mekhinot* was formalised in a Knesset law of 2008 (Knesset, 2008). Under this law *mekhinot* are formally independent from the direct control of the IDF, but are mandated to work towards military preparation and particular educational goals (including Judaism and Jewish identity, Zionism, leadership, and volunteering). They receive considerable state funding from the Education and Defence Ministries, but are also

---

[4] Author interview with Dani Zamir (Rabin Academy).

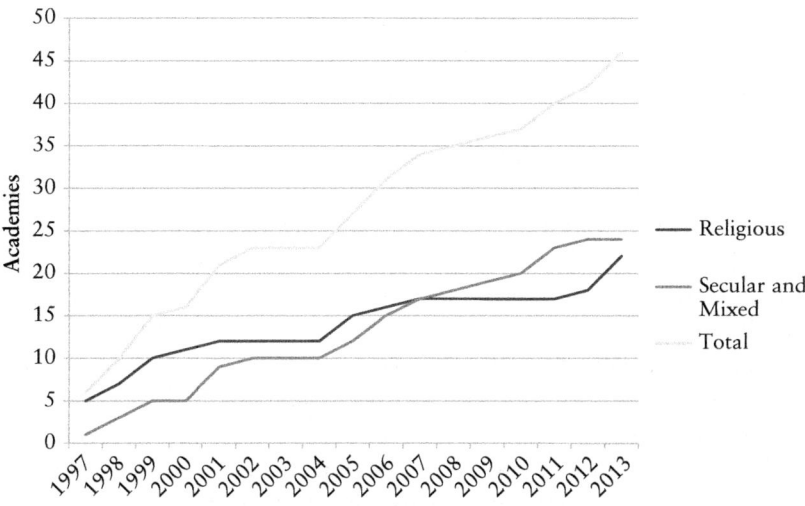

Figure 4.1 Israeli pre-military academies, 1997–2013

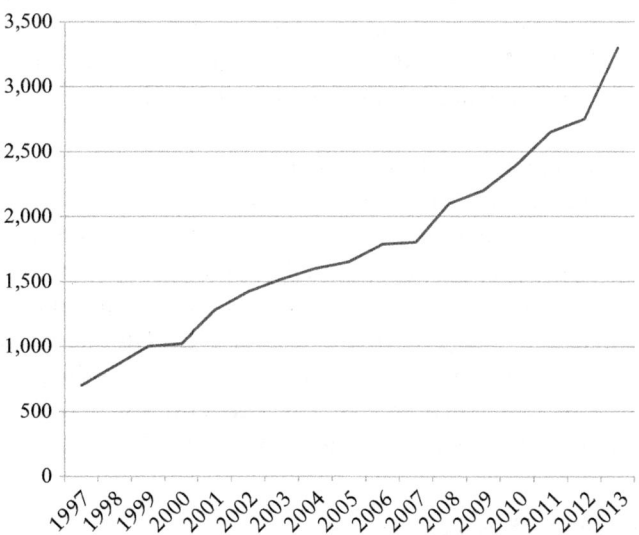

Figure 4.2 Students at Israeli pre-military academies, 1997–2013

dependent on student fees (on average about $2,500 per student) and charitable donations (Joint Council of Mekhinot, n.d.). Following the passage of the law, a Joint Council of *Mekhinot* was also established to provide strategic oversight and co-ordination in fundraising.

The growth in pre-military academies has also resulted in a more diverse student body. Some 25 per cent of students at academies now come from 'peripheral' socio-economic backgrounds (Joint Council of Mekhinot, n.d.). Even though this remains disproportionately low, a major aim of the programme is to expand its reach in these communities. This is in line with the increasing interest of the IDF in the capacity of academies to deliver extra manpower from these groups (cf. Levy, 2007: 117–25, 229–36).[5] This has also had consequences for the division between secular, mixed, and religious academies, which often blurs in pursuit of this objective. It remains true that students from national-religious backgrounds overwhelmingly gravitate towards religious academies, but religious academies also now cater to sections of Israeli society far beyond this kernel. In 2013 a new *mekhina* was established for ultra-orthodox Jews (who were until recently exempt from national service) in a settlement in the Jordan Valley. There are also religious academies which seek out students from socially disadvantaged groups who have not necessarily had a strong religious upbringing, such as Kiryat Malakhi, Tammir, or Maskiyut.[6]

Likewise, the secular and mixed academies have influence with populations far beyond affluent secular Ashkenazim. Many academy staff did confirm to me that they seek students from 'good families' and that the most prestigious academies still aim to produce an 'elite'.[7] But there are also strong efforts to expand the student body to Mizrahim, Ethiopians, and those living in poorer towns in the South, who have lower enlistment and higher dropout rates. Accordingly, a number of academies now exist which cater explicitly for disadvantaged or 'peripheral' youth, including the Jerusalemite Academy, Gal

---

[5] Author interview with Yokhanan Ben-Ya'akov.

[6] Author interview with Yokhanan Ben-Ya'akov. Compare this evidence with the assessment of Stuart Cohen: 'By definition, [religious *mekhinot* cater] exclusively to a constituency already committed to Orthodox Jewish observance' (2013: 134).

[7] Author interviews with Dani Zamir (Rabin Academy) and David Nachman (Ein Prat Academy).

Academy, Yemin Orde (which caters for immigrants, and especially for Ethiopians), Kerem-El (which is aimed at Druze students), and Asher Ruah Bo (which targets youths with a criminal record).[8] These efforts are significant because they show the important role of academies, and of the ethical project they embody, in managing and ordering the growing ethnic diversity of the IDF.

Even though the number of *mekhinot* graduates remains small compared with the overall intake of conscripts, they have still had a strong impact on the army. According to Education Ministry figures, the rate of enlistment to officer courses is 50 per cent higher across the board at pre-military academies; the rate of enlistment to 'high priority units' (principally combat units) is also 30 per cent higher (Education Ministry, 2012). Many academies, especially the oldest and most prestigious, strongly encourage their students to join elite combat units and to assume officer and commanding roles.[9] This has had a strong impact on the IDF officer corps, where *mekhinot* participants now make up 25 per cent of graduates from officer schools. This has also helped effect a sea-change in the social composition of the IDF owing to the over-representation of religious *mekhinot* graduates (Cohen, 2013: 11–12).

However, the influence of *mekhinot* on the IDF is not confined to religious academies. The available evidence suggests that secular and mixed academies can be just as influential in this respect. In data gathered by Naomi Evenshpenger from 2001 to 2004, the percentage of eligible students from academies who progressed to combat units, to junior command roles, and to the officer corps was measured and the results were published in an IDF journal (Evenshpenger, 2010: 62–9). At the time, the author was quite dismissive of the impact of *mekhinot* on the officer corps, and particularly the impact of secular *mekhinot*. This impression was primarily derived from the relatively small numbers of male graduates from secular and mixed academies (Evenshpenger, 2010: 66; cf. Cohen, 2013: 12). However, when grouped together the aggregate figures from her research indicate that there is not a wide gap between the patterns of military service of graduates of religious

[8] Author interviews with Yael Domb (Jerusalemite Academy) and Yokhanan Ben-Ya'akov.
[9] Author interview with Yokhanan Ben-Ya'akov.

Table 4.1 *Data on military service of graduates of pre-military academies, 2001–2004*

	% entering combat units	% entering junior command roles	% entering officer corps
Religious	82	43	16
Secular/mixed	73	40	25

compared with secular and mixed *mekhinot*. Table 4.1 presents the median of these figures across the years 2001–04.

Indeed, with the huge growth in secular and mixed academies since these data were gathered, it is likely that this influence will have grown significantly. Another major way in which the influence of secular and mixed academies has been felt in the army is through programmes known as 'Project Golani' and 'Project Giv'ati'.[10] The aim of such projects is to channel students from the same academy into particular units in specific brigades in order to change their character and give students from a similar educational background an opportunity to co-operate during military service.[11] Given the growth and success of the academy programme, it is worth exploring the pedagogical approach which they pursue. In keeping with the argument of this book, ethics turns out to be a central dimension of their educational philosophy.

Ascetic Institutions: Cultivating the Self

If one wishes to grasp the guiding philosophy behind education at pre-military academies (both religious and secular), the key concept is undoubtedly 'meaningful service' [*sherut mashma'uti*]. This phrase describes the desired experience which academies want their graduates to have in the IDF: military service which shapes them as individuals, has a lasting impact on their lives, and makes a positive and profound contribution to the work of the army. The concept appears on the website and prospectus of nearly every *mekhina* and is one of

[10] Golani and Giv'ati are both infantry brigades in the IDF.
[11] Author interview with Yokhanan Ben-Ya'akov. Author interview with Yael Domb (Jerusalemite Academy).

the major objectives of the entire programme. It implies a clear fusion between the activity of self-improvement and the pursuit of military goals, which become reciprocal and mutually reinforcing objectives. The pathway to effective military service is ethical self-cultivation; likewise, military service is the means to cultivate the soldier as an ethical subject.

This is as true in religious as in secular academies. When I asked a teacher at Keshet Yehuda, a religious academy, to describe what was meant by the phrase 'meaningful service', he replied with the following analogy:

One of the kids was telling me there's a game on television called 'The Golden Cage' or something. The person can go in there and while he's in there he can win prizes . . . I don't want to compare to that because it's much more than that, actually, when you realise that every minute you have in the army has great importance and meaning. And even if, you know, right now you're preparing . . . you're doing a very mundane task . . . but every task is not just an individual thing that you're doing but you're doing it for your nation, you're dedicating your time now, you know, in the most vigour you have in life, when you're young – you're giving three years of your life for your nation. Hopefully, you know, if you go on in the army – and graduates do – that's great but it makes the time much more meaningful. In other words, you take much more advantage of time. When I say meaningful: that they take advantage of the time, that they see their time there as being, you know, a very positive experience and they use it in the right means.[12]

Likewise, the response of a teacher at Lakhish Academy (a broadly secular academy) was quite similar:

I guess if you are an Israeli, one thing that I felt when I was in the army, that you wake up when you are 18 and you understand that somebody's sending you to this post in the middle of nowhere. And you understood that for the last 18 years of your life, every night, somebody froze to death on this post. Every night. And it's all around the country. And it's everywhere. And you're saying, wow, I wasn't . . . I slept fine in bed, you know, I rested. But people did that and now it's my turn. And I want [the students] to know that and I want them to do as best as they can to do that. When it's your turn, do it not whiningly and trying to get away from that and doing as little of it as you

---

[12] Author interview with Michael Cohen (Keshet Yehuda).

can – like most people do, because it's a burden. But take this burden and do it as well as you can.[13]

Both of these teachers therefore note the connection between national service and ethical effort, suggesting that a powerful link is being forged here between national, civic belonging and individual work in this military rite of passage (cf. Helman, 1997; Sasson-Levy, 2008). Academies make a great effort to facilitate 'meaningful service' by preparing their students for the army carefully. This preparation can take many forms. It might involve visits to particular units and bases to inform students about which pathways they can take in military service, or visits from serving officers and soldiers to discuss their options. Several academies organise intense physical training, whereas others hold orienteering and navigation exercises. It can also include classes on leadership, IDF battle heritage (*moreshet krav*), and military ethics.

Preparation for 'meaningful service' is not confined to these more technical aspects, however. It encompasses the entire programme of study, even where the content is not explicitly military in nature. It entails the promotion of values and a sense of identity among the students which can serve as an ideological basis for military participation. At religious academies a large part of the study programmes are modelled on that of a seminary, and includes scriptural exegesis, classes from rabbis on questions of faith and morality, collective worship, and everyday religious observance. This is combined with classes designed to deepen Jewish and Zionist identity and to provide 'spiritual' preparation for the IDF (Rosman-Stollman, 2014: 107–14; and see, for example, Bnei David Academy, n.d.). The teachings of the religious Zionist thinker, Rabbi Tzvi Yehuda Kook, are a very common inspiration for this approach.[14] This inculcates the idea that earthly pursuits, such as service in the army, can have a redemptive and spiritual function and thereby acquire the character of a religious duty (cf. Aran, 1991: 304–23). Military service is presented as an expression of faith, as an opportunity for drawing and acting on one's religious values.

This emphasis on values and identity is, however, no less present at secular academies. Although these values derive from different

---

[13] Author interview with Ohad Shamama (Lakhish Academy).
[14] Author interview with Michael Cohen (Keshet Yehuda Academy) (see also Rosman-Stollman, 2014: 110, 112).

sources and are less religious in origin, locating and deepening them is still seen as a crucial aspect of military preparation. Secular academies often borrow the military jargon, 'mental preparation' [*hakhana mentalit*], to describe this. Staff at several academies emphasised in interviews the need to reverse the influence of 'post-modernism' or 'globalisation', which they associated with a decline in the level of civic commitment and national identity in Israeli society.[15]

The programme of studies at Ein Prat, a prestigious academy which attracts religious and non-religious students, gives an example of how *mekhinot* aim to strengthen the sense of identity and values among their students. Students are immersed in the study of Western and Jewish philosophy. They read and discuss Plato and Aristotle, followed by modern existentialists such as Kierkegaard, Nietzsche, and Camus. They also study modern Zionist thinkers in-depth from Theodor Herzl to Jabotinsky, Kook, and David Ben-Gurion. The director of the academy, David Nachman, was clear about the purpose of this study:

These studies are in order to build the identity of each . . . Students are coming here because they want to understand their identity as human beings, first of all, like every other place on the planet, and as Jews and as Zionists. That's why we learn Western philosophy, which talks about life, about political philosophy. Judaism is common to all of us – it doesn't matter if you're religious or non-religious. The sources are relevant for all of us. And then Zionist thinking or Zionist thought form the basis. And then when you go to the army then you understand better why do I have to go to the army and which kind of a soldier do I have to be . . . A Jewish soldier. We are teaching how a Jewish soldier has to act.[16]

Mekhinot also build self-cultivation into everyday residential life.[17] At Rabin Academy, for example, there is a strong emphasis on what the director refers to as 'self-conduct' [*nihul 'atzmi*], which involves the students learning to manage their own behaviour and to abide by the rules and timetable of the academy. No alcohol is allowed at

---

[15] Author interviews with Yael Domb (Jerusalemite Academy), Dani Zamir (Rabin Academy), and Ohad Shamama (Lakhish Academy).

[16] Author interview with David Nachman (Ein Prat Academy).

[17] I mostly discuss secular and mixed academies below, but this is also true at religious academies. See also Rosman-Stollman (2014: 111) and below, for further discussion.

the academy, and the study day is extremely long, beginning at 7 am and lasting until as late as 11 or 12 at night. Other academies have much more relaxed rules but place a greater onus on the students themselves to manage day-to-day activities and communal living. Students at the Reform *mekhina* in Jaffa, Telem, elect weekly leaders from among themselves to organise the day-to-day running of the academy who are given authority over the other students.[18] Policies such as this often have slightly chaotic consequences. For instance, when I visited Lakhish Academy for the day lunch was delayed by several hours because the students had failed to organise it for the usual time.[19] All of these procedures are attempts to help students practise for the responsibilities they will be given during military service, and to encourage them to learn to conduct themselves.

The emphasis on self-improvement is particularly pronounced at Ein Prat Academy. The *mekhina* is located in the settlement of Kfar Adumim in the middle of the occupied West Bank. It has been very deliberately built on an outcrop overlooking the mountains of the Judean desert. Building a connection between the students and the land is an important part of this choice, but it is also designed to inspire its students and concentrate their minds. The whole academy has an isolated, cenobitic atmosphere. The classrooms and accommodation blocs also have a pre-fabricated, semi-permanent feel which is reminiscent of the homes that populate hilltop 'outpost' settlements in the West Bank. Indeed, when I visited the academy in January 2013 it was expanding the settlement by adding new classroom buildings.[20] The director of the academy, David Nachman, was adamant that the purpose of his *mekhina* is to push students as hard as possible to improve themselves:

I want to conclude all of what we do in one word – okay, what we do here is to burn something in the hard disk of everyone and what we burn is responsibility. Responsibility first of all, [for] each one's life. Take responsibility [for] your life. Live a good life in a philosophical way, okay? A good life to do good, and to work hard and to demand more and more from yourself.[21]

---

[18] Author interview with Guy Immerman (Telem Academy).
[19] Field notes, 20 January 2013.
[20] Field notes, 28 January 2013.
[21] Author interview.

The ascetic drive for constant self-improvement is also very palpable in the general atmosphere of the *mekhina*. Nachman continued: 'Our slogan here is that if one does not try all the time to climb up more and more and stays in one place, he falls down. He must all the time try to be better. All the time. This is the way of life here.'[22] Indeed, in a conversation with one student I learnt that students strongly internalise this impetus. He described to me discussions he had with fellow students about how difficult it was to know when to miss a class because of illness, since they felt it was impossible to be sure that their absence would not ultimately be down to a lack of effort.[23]

This recognisably ascetic emphasis in education at pre-military academies constitutes an augmented and intensified version of the pattern discussed in the previous chapter. Rather than simply being confined to military ethics, however, it is raised to a principle of general conduct, encouraging students into a pattern of constant personal improvement as part of their preparation for military service. Moreover, what makes this ascetic emphasis so intense is that control over conduct is not imposed externally: the students exercise it *over themselves* through intense ethical work. This ascetic drive to improve is also what underpins the belief that 'meaningful service' in the IDF can contribute to one's flourishing as a human being. This ideological function is fully compatible with the ambition of 'keeping a human image', as discussed in the previous chapter. It is also what allows several pre-military academies to claim that they are more interested in their students' development as individuals and citizens than as soldiers, even when these academies are structurally constituted to produce more combat soldiers and more officers. David Nachman emphasised precisely this aspect of the education at Ein Prat:

We don't want people to be soldiers, we want people to be human beings. And we have to be in the army and we have to defend ourselves but in my opinion [a] good soldier is at the beginning a good man. Okay? This is what we look for and this is, when you want to describe [the IDF], this is it. When you go to the best units, when you go to the officers' course, then you find that we choose the people not because they are strong or they are brave but first of all their personality, sensitivity, their ability to see [the] complexity of

---

[22] Author interview.
[23] Field notes, 28 January 2013.

things, the ability to understand the other side, that they are coming from a democratic and pluralistic environment.[24]

This emphasis on values and identity in shaping 'meaningful service' therefore creates a strong connection between the task of personal improvement and military performance. Nachman's view that 'a good soldier is in the beginning a good man', a view which was echoed by another teacher at a religious pre-military academy, also suggests that a gendered production of military masculinity takes place through this ethical work.[25] Notably, this masculine identity, rather than being primarily based on strength and courage, is once again tempered with the traits of sensitivity and empathy discussed in the previous chapter.

This attempt at ethical self-cultivation is also implicated in the production of racial hierarchies as a result of the attempt to incorporate peripheral social groups. The director of the Jerusalemite Academy, Yael Domb, described her efforts in this regard as follows:

Here in this *mechina* we try very hard to bring people from all kinds of places [. . .] They come from all different places in Israel, like the centre – the kibbutzim and the main cities – but also from the periphery, like Beer Sheva, and Kiryat Gat, and Kiryat Shmona. And in those places most of them are . . . first of all most of those places are in more danger now [from rocket fire from the Gaza Strip during Israel's assault in November 2012, ongoing at the time of the interview]. [. . .] So they come with many less humanist thoughts and even sometimes racist opinions. So it's very difficult because we can do a lesson [about military ethics] and they will say *mavet la'aravim* ['death to the Arabs'] or 'they are shooting me, so shouldn't I take revenge?' And on the other we have all kinds of people who come from the other places that bring the opinion of not going to the army and all kinds of things.[26]

Some of her students were indeed vocally racist, as I learnt in conversation with one of them and when observing lessons at the academy. What is nevertheless interesting about Yael's remarks is that preparation for the military is portrayed as a simultaneous project of moral and racial ordering, in which peripheral groups are problematised as less humane and socially ascendant groups are encouraged to bring their more liberal

---

[24] Author interview.
[25] Author interviews with David Nachman and Reuven Mass.
[26] Author interview with Yael Domb (Jerusalemite Academy).

views into the army rather than decline to serve. Again, this underscores the extent to which ethics is bound up with militarist identity formation. This is not least the case in classes specifically concerning the army and military ethics, which I shall consider in more detail next.

Teaching Military Ethics at Secular Pre-military Academies[27]

Purity of Arms

In addition to the class at Rabin Academy discussed at the opening of this chapter, I attended a similar class on purity of arms at the Jerusalemite Academy, led by Yael.[28] The class began with simple readings of extracts from the 'Spirit of the IDF' and from Asa Kasher's 'Military Ethics'. The segment chosen from Kasher's book emphasised how the value of purity of arms relates to all behaviour of a soldier, not just in battle. This interpretation makes it possible to generalise the value of purity of arms such that it becomes a constant imperative to improve one's behaviour in any circumstance. In this way the demand for 'purity of arms' becomes a generalised superego injunction to improve and fits perfectly in the wider ascetic culture of self-augmentation and self-discipline at pre-military academies. From what I encountered at this class, students do seem to internalise this. Reflecting on the formulation of the value, one student commented during the class that he approved of the use of the term 'purity': 'actually because [purity] is an extreme, it requires [the soldier] to aspire at all times to be moral [*musari*]'.

Later in the class, Yael related the value of purity of arms directly to counterinsurgency and to the concrete context of the West Bank. She did so using a soldier's testimony given to B'Tselem, the Israeli human rights organisation. It read as follows:

The common soldier is the one who makes all the decisions in the field. I have a weapon, and the person opposite me does not. That means I can decide for him what he will do. As long as he is at my checkpoint he is in

---

[27] This section analyses the teaching of military ethics at six secular and mixed pre-military academies: Nachshon Academy, Lakhish Academy, Rabin Academy, Ein Prat Academy, Telem Academy, and the Jerusalemite Academy. I will discuss the approach in religious academies in the final section of this chapter.

[28] The account is based on field notes from 28 January 2013 and copies of the hand-outs used in class.

my kingdom. I can decide if he will stand up, jump, walk, is given the run around, will bring me a bottle of coke from his car even though I haven't paid for it, everything. Even looting. I saw this kind of thing with my own eyes. [. . .] It happens all the time. I saw it myself. I once stopped a car to search it. The man had goods in the back of his car. I asked him what is in the boxes. He opened the boxes and I saw perfume bottles that cost around 300 NIS each. Then he said, 'Take ten'. I asked him 'Why, I don't want to take any', and he said, 'Take ten, what do you care, its o.k., we are used to it'. I told him that I was not going to take anything and that they could pass through. They were really surprised. They just smiled at me. They were not used to an IDF soldier addressing them and asking them how they are doing. And that an IDF soldier told them that they can go in peace – they were dumbfounded. (cf. full testimony at B'Tselem, 2003)

At first, some students reacted very suspiciously to this testimony, refusing to believe its authenticity. Several were automatically inclined to doubt anything which came from an organisation with a reputation for criticising the IDF. Yael responded to these doubts by giving a testimony of her own, based on the experience of a friend of hers from the same unit she served in who had also witnessed bribery at checkpoints. The students then seemed more inclined to accept the idea that bribery takes place and a discussion began. As with the class at Rabin discussed at the opening of the chapter, what is noticeable about this sequence is that getting students to accept that violent or exploitative behaviour takes place in the occupied West Bank is actually the precondition for encouraging ethical work. Through this pedagogical process, students abandon a more inflexible attitude to such occurrences (denying that they exist at all) and replace it with a desire to prevent them during their own military service. The unsettling political implication – that bribery and exploitation at checkpoints is widespread and actually inevitable in a situation of such power asymmetry – is thereby masked by a renewed ethical determination to improve oneself by emulating the soldier who behaved properly. This is a much more effective ideological outcome: the contradictions of seeking a moral occupation are hidden by the ascetic drive of the individual. This strategy is quite explicit. An instructor at another *mekhina* put this very clearly to me:

. . . you even take the slight chance that one of them will say, I don't want to join the army – it's too horrible. Because we show them the horrible sides of that. And there are. If you are in Hebron, it's not nice for you. [. . .] And they see everything. But we believe it will not make them not want to join the army or be part of the Jewish nation but it will help them choose the more moral way.[29]

Returning to the class at the Jerusalemite Academy, another familiar theme concerned the gendered dimension of the ethical problem. Of the many responses in the discussion, one male student commented that many soldiers might engage in such problematic behaviour to be considered a *gever*, which is a complimentary Hebrew slang term for a macho male. Again, comments such as this reveal that it is a supposedly more 'feminine' disposition which is perceived to be appropriate at checkpoints; it confirms that military ethical work also implies striving for a particular gendered identification.

Many of the above patterns can also be observed in the approach taken at Nachshon Academy.[30] Daniel, a former paratrooper, teaches a class entirely devoted to studying the 'Spirit of the IDF' document. This class is one part of three series of classes which concern 'mental preparation'. One series is taught by Ze'evik Nativ, the head of the *mekhina* and a retired colonel in the IDF, and deals with IDF battle heritage (*moreshet krav*); another is a series of occasional lectures delivered by an external military officer on the 'army and moral values' [*tsava vemusar*]; Daniel's course is much more practically orientated and focuses on concrete situations in which the ethical code is deemed relevant.

The structure of the classes is to take a separate value from the Spirit of the IDF each week and to pose dilemmas to students based on real events occurring day-to-day in the West Bank. The emphasis is on student discussion. In the introductory week, for example, students are given three hypothetical examples and asked to discuss them: one from a checkpoint where a father with a sick child wants to jump the queue; one from a situation where stones are being thrown at a military jeep in Hebron; and another from a case of targeted killing. Occasionally these examples will be well-known stories (such as the death of Madḥat Yusuf, a Druze soldier who bled to death while an effort to rescue him was delayed), which help to generate discussion.

---

[29] Author interview with Ohad Shamama (Lakhish Academy).
[30] The following discussion is based on my interview with the teacher responsible for these classes, Daniel Berkeley.

In a recognisable pattern, the emphasis is on cultivating an ethical sensibility and practising decision-making through the use of examples, with the emphasis very much on the discretion of the individual soldier:

I say to the students [*hanikhim*] all the time in the first lesson and throughout all these lessons that *Ruah Tsahal* [the Spirit of the IDF] does not give, you know, a clear answer to any question. It's not a textbook. It's not a DIY [guide]. Reality is much more complicated and every scenario has its own characteristics and challenges. And, you know, what they shouldn't expect from *Ruah Tsahal* is to know exactly what to do in the situation. So every lesson sort of ends [. . .] in the message that, you know, the *hanikhim* are going to have to try and decide themselves what they think should have been done in different cases.

Several of the examples also come directly from Daniel's experience as a soldier serving in the West Bank, which means that testimony becomes a direct part of the ethical and pedagogical experience. He used the following example to discuss the principle of purity of arms:

So when I was in commanders' course we were called to do some combat emergency stuff. And . . . It wasn't really combat. We were guarding the [. . .] Green Line, where a lot of, you know, illegal workers pass every day. Less and less now but then there was quite a lot. And what happened was we were working . . . we were there for like a week or a week and a half and it was quite hard. We were living in tents and we were eating the combat food, which is basically the worst food in the army, and we found . . . we stopped some people on their way back from illegal work and after, like, sort of checking them and writing their things down and letting them go, one of them forgot a watermelon behind. And then someone from the platoon took the watermelon back to the tent and then we had a huge discussion if we should eat this watermelon for dessert or not. And, so that's a personal example I give the kids to deal with. I, myself, think there's no reason to eat the watermelon. And I say that to the kids in the end but many of them disagree. They think eating the watermelon is fine. Soldiers are working hard and it's been forgotten anyway, it's going to just sit there and rot and whatever.

What is so striking about this example is its utter remoteness from the usual considerations of collateral damage or civilian casualties.

Indeed, it is not immediately obvious how it relates to 'purity of arms', as it is normally conceived, at all. Daniel explained:

. . . the message behind the value of purity of arms is make sure you don't turn your authority and your power in being armed into anything extra at all than the security of Israel. The minute there's anything extra, that is not necessary, that's you crossing the line and doing something that I think is immoral. So that's my explanation . . . It's a sort of silly example but I think because it's sort of silly I think it's quite good because it's sort of like taking it to the extreme.

This explanation shows not only that purity of arms can cover a wide range of activities, but also that purity of arms is at its core a value about purity of intent. Crucially, for the Palestinian who lost a watermelon, the deliberations of Israeli soldiers about whether to eat it are completely immaterial. What actually cost him the watermelon was a regime of confinement and surveillance preventing him from moving freely between home and work. Yet by converting the value of purity of arms into an extreme test of moral character, the structural violence of the Israeli occupation disappears into the background of a constant struggle for the self-cultivation of the soldier. This example shows that purity of arms is a value which is very well suited to introspection, to self-examination, and to testimony – in short, to producing an ethical subject.

Yet this example also exposes a paradox in the value of purity of arms, which we can appreciate better by taking a psychoanalytic perspective. We can think of the soldier who seeks to comply with this value also as a subject who *enjoys*, someone whose desire is structured around a fantasy. This fantasy masks the basic impossibilities of the symbolic order in which this subject finds himself – in this case, the impossibility is the impossibility of being a moral occupier. This finds expression in the anxieties surrounding counterinsurgency warfare, where the legitimate enemy never fully presents itself and the insurgent force is always mixed and contaminated with its civilian surroundings. Full enjoyment of the military encounter – direct, heroic engagement with the true adversary, as would be discussed in classes on *moreshet krav* – is never possible. The militarist ideological apparatus must therefore produce fantasies for soldiers to enjoy, ways of desiring which are capable of providing what Lacan called *surplus enjoyment* – enjoyment which is not dependent on achieving the desired outcome, but which privileges the (often failed, often irrational) gesture of striving for it.

This is why pursuing purity of arms tends to proliferate into an introspective examination of all military actions, even those mundane deeds with little to no consequence. Indeed, these mundane actions of renunciation or self-discipline can ultimately acquire greater importance, since they are far easier to approach than challenging matters of life and death. Yet there is an irony here. The value of purity of arms states that soldiers must only use their weapon and authority for the pursuit of the mission and never for any additional personal purpose. Viewed from a psychoanalytic perspective, however, purity of arms clearly breaks its own rule: in adhering to this value, the soldier *does* derive an additional benefit which is 'surplus' to the mission, which is precisely the enjoyment derived from having complied with this value. This is in fact the hidden kernel of militarism in 'purity of arms': military activity, pursued for its own sake, produces enjoyment which supersedes the purely instrumental uses of deploying force.

Anti-Military Militarists: Leadership and Authority

When discussing with Ohad Shamama, an instructor at Lakhish Academy, how he approaches issues of military ethics, I was struck by the peculiar emphasis he placed on how soldiers should conduct themselves in relation to structures of authority. He was a former student of psychology and philosophy, and therefore refers his students to several famous psychological experiments which explore human tendencies to conform and develop authority structures. In particular, he introduces them to the Milgram experiments (in which volunteers delivered simulated fatal doses of electricity to fake test subjects at the instruction of actors posing as scientists) and the Stanford Prison Experiments (in which volunteers who were randomly assigned to the role of prisoners and prison guards developed a violent and strict regime of power). The rationale behind his use of these examples is to show the potential consequences of structures of authority in the army:

... those experiments are the big ones [where] we are talking about military ethics in this way. What will happen if they put this uniform on you? What do you become? Do you become [like] people in the movies? [. . .] And what happens when you obey someone who has a uniform on? What kind of horrible things you can do by obeying those things? How far can you go?[31]

---

[31] Author interview with Ohad Shamama (Lakhish Academy).

It is not immediately obvious why it would be useful to train future soldiers to be suspicious of authority, but Ohad was clear that in fact future commanders need to develop this attitude in order to think creatively about their roles:

I'm trying to give them a way of acknowledging the power that conformity . . . that the surroundings have on you – either conformity, the group, or the commander and everything. And I want them to have the ability to think by themselves in a way. I mean, I tell them: think, don't act at the time unless it's really dangerous for somebody. But first think. Whatever you do, think. [. . .] In the army [. . .] you have commands and all day long people telling you what to do. And that becomes a part of you in a way. You do what you are told to do and you stop thinking, because of a lot of the commands are not really smart, or not important. You have to wash this and clean that and everything has to be perfect [. . .] You are not supposed to ask questions. But I want them to ask questions. And to be able to say something is wrong here because I want them to be the commanders. I want them to lead. And in the end, after they started leading, they will have to think about their commands and not just do the commands that people ordered them to do before.[32]

Developing this attitude of scepticism and independent thought is actually a part of producing a military subject. It also directly supplements the ideological model of 'keeping a human image', since it allows students to imagine that, despite their involvement in the unthinking military machine, they remain independent human beings capable of making moral choices. Ohad summarised it as follows: 'when you are in a situation which is not humane, be the humane person inside, be the human inside'.[33]

Cultivating this scepticism can actually go as far as raising questions about the entire military structure itself. At the Jerusalemite Academy, the classes on 'army and leadership' begin with a critical examination of the role of the military in Israeli society. The head of the *mekhina* described the importance of this approach in similar terms to Ohad:

. . . we are thinking about many questions like the relationship between the army and Israeli society. What does it mean that the army in Israel has such a main place in our society and that everyone must go to the army and a lot of money is spent on the army . . .? All kinds of questions. And I ask: is it

[32] Author interview.
[33] Author interview.

the way that we want our society to go? What is the effect of those things on our lives and thinking . . .? The main thing is that we are trying to develop critical thought. Sometimes they say that it's too critical and then when they need to go to the army it puts them in a bad place [. . .] But I think the main thing that helps them to understand things is that I was in the army many years, so I can be very critical . . . We can be very critical about the army but do our service and [ask] how we can do it in the best way. It means a lot when they decide where to go [in the army] and if they decide to go to the place that everyone thinks is the best or if they go to where the army needs them and where they need people like them with critical thought that can do things differently.[34]

At Rabin Academy, this encouragement of a 'critical' attitude towards the army is an extremely important part of the education on military ethics. Dani Zamir, the head of the academy, is very clear to his students that they should be willing to refuse orders which they believe are immoral.[35] There are already grounds for this in the IDF, based on the 'black flag' doctrine whereby soldiers are obliged to refuse 'manifestly illegal orders' – a doctrine which is widely taught in pre-military academies, as well as in the high-school curriculum. Zamir is especially emphatic about this point. This is based on his own experience of refusing an order during the First Intifada and consequently spending thirty days in a military jail. At the time, he had been ordered to escort a group of religious Jews who wished to visit the alleged site of Joseph's Tomb in Nablus, which would have required the curfew of the entire city. What is perhaps distinctive about this decision is that it has something of a political basis. Zamir told me that he refused on the grounds of the operation being against 'the basic rules of Zionism'. The refusal nevertheless had a strong moral component for Zamir and, indeed, this is how he teaches it to his students. In fact, he sees refusal and the challenging of authority much more as an ethical tool for the moral improvement of the IDF, than as a political statement. He explained how he presents the likely consequences of such a refusal to his students as follows:

I don't know many cases where a soldier said to his commander 'don't do it, it's not okay, you are doing something wrong' and then they took him

---

[34] Author interview with Yael Domb (Jerusalemite Academy).
[35] Author interview with Dani Zamir (Rabin Academy).

to court. What is happening is simply the opposite: a group of soldiers becomes very enthusiastic about doing something wrong and someone that [went to] *mekhinat* Rabin or some other *mekhina* or someone who has moral values by himself is saying 'Hey, what are you doing? Are you crazy? This is enough'. People, you know, will maybe laugh about him and [say] you are a sissy and this. They will not [take him to court]. This is the reality. So after 15 years I can tell you that this is exactly what is happening. In the places where my graduates serve, war crimes don't happen.[36]

This example shows that even an act as highly politicised as selective refusal can function as a facet of militarism when it is reappropriated as an ethical practice. The ideological dividend is that soldiers are able to fashion themselves as autonomous individuals whose moral commitments find expression in their military service. It is also noticeable that this model of risky speech offered to correct the behaviour of others fits very closely with Foucault's definition of *parrhesia*, the paradigmatic model for ethical behaviour in his conception of the 'care of the self'. Indeed, this encouragement of courageous speech is designed to remasculinise the maligned (effeminate) status of being a 'sissy', turning it into a demonstration of moral character.

In the above examples, therefore, refusal and criticism become corrective tools aimed at improving the work of the IDF and serve to make military participation all the more meaningful. Paradoxically this anti-military sentiment provides precisely the productive tension that militarism needs to function as an ideological system. Ohad put this point extremely well: 'The *mekhina* is like the opposite of the army, in a way. It's funny that the opposite of the army is supposed to make you a better soldier, but that's the way'.[37]

Not Teaching Ethics

One of the more interesting interviews I held with staff at pre-military academies was with Micha Shalvi, a teacher at eight different secular and mixed *mekhinot*, including Ein Prat. I had been directed to him

---

[36] Author interview.
[37] Author interview with Ohad Shamama (Lakhish Academy).

by David Nachman, the director of Ein Prat, because I had asked to speak to the person who taught military ethics. I was particularly keen to interview him because I had been told that he presents the students with literature written in the form of soldiers' testimonies, including S. Yizhar's novella *Khirbet Khizeh* and his short story 'The Prisoner' as well as Natan Alterman's poem 'About That'. All of these stories are set during the Nakba and discuss violence against Palestinians and IDF expulsions of inhabitants from villages. I wanted to investigate the ways in which these texts might be used for teaching ethics at pre-military academies.

I met with Micha at his apartment in Jerusalem and began to ask him questions about what he teaches. I soon learnt that he was unlike other teachers I had spoken with. When I pressed him on why he taught Yizhar and Alterman he seemed almost offended: 'Look, okay, so we read it. So what?' And then, in describing his use of Hebrew literature of the Nakba, he summarised his approach as follows:

When there's a story or a poem that gives the impression that there were some unethical behaviours, it cleans the majority from taking responsibility . . . Now, the way that in the IDF and in the *mekhinot* they are dealing with ethics it's as [if] the problem is out of the ordinary and we have to be . . . we have to learn them, so that we won't be like this. And I'm teaching that it wasn't out of the ordinary, it was the rule . . . And this is a state of mind that they don't know what to do with. It shocks them and they don't know how to deal with it . . . [Whether] it has any effect? I don't think so.[38]

He was also remarkably pessimistic about the contribution his teaching makes to his students and perceived of himself as being thoroughly manipulated by the *mekhinot*:

The *mekhinot* are giving all these guys an ampula of Zionism and 'we are the fine guys and we are okay . . . ah, so Micha comes and says "no, hmmm"' . . . Every year I, when I finish or in the middle, I come to my wife and tell her, look, I'm fed up of being a fig leaf [. . .] For David Nachman it's very important that I will be there, for public . . . You know, the hidden curriculum of education is more important than the curriculum. And me as a left-wing, non-religious persona, being a teacher there, makes the appearance, it

---

[38] Author interview with Micha Shalvi.

makes it look very pluralistic. 'We are single-minded? What do you mean? Micha Shalvi is teaching, he is the ethical ['*erkhi*] left-wing[er], one of the last . . .' It's very sophisticated. If I would leave, they will have just *datiyim*, just religious people, just people from the settlements, just people who talk about Judaism. They need me as a . . . and I know that they are using it. David Nachman sent you to me. I'm okay. 'Micha's dealing with it'.

When I asked him why he still bothers to teach, he fell back on its convenience as a way of making a living in later life and on his fascination with how young people respond to his approach, especially the more right-wing youth who attend Ein Prat.

Yet it was also clear that his teaching does have an impact on his students, even if it is not the one he intends. Micha reported that every year several students tell him it is important he stays at the academy and he recounted several instances in which his classes had shocked and provoked his students. Indeed, when I spoke with two of them about the classes during a fieldtrip, they told me they found the classes very interesting, even if they disagreed with many of his views, and they were able to summarise some very complex ideas from one of his classes.[39] In contrast to what Micha asserts, I would argue that the drive to maintain a pluralistic appearance at *mekhinot* is more than just cosmetic public relations. Students *do* encounter a variety of views at *mekhinot*, albeit in a highly choreographed and limited way. Its consequences are carefully managed and channelled into cultivating a 'sensitive' soldier who can think critically. Producing such a soldier, I would argue, is still a form of ascetic 'mental preparation'. Micha is a man doing his best *not* to teach military ethics but, thanks to the pedagogical pattern at pre-military academies, actually struggling to avoid it.

Graduate Soldiers' Testimony

Given the prevalence of soldiers' testimonies as examples when teaching military ethics and the close contact that continues between graduates and their academies, it is perhaps not surprising that *mekhinot* also work to produce such testimonies from their former students.

---

[39] Field notes, 10 March 2013.

Ohad, the teacher at Lakhish Academy, offered me one example of how this can take place:

I brought a guy last year, who was a student from here, a graduate, who came to ask me about ethical problems he had in Hebron with his teammates. And I brought him here, I asked him to talk to them about that. He came to me because he wanted help . . . He came to me, he told me how hard it is there, how hard it is to stay humane there and how some of his teammates are kind of losing it and how it's becoming harder and harder [. . .] It was very . . . I liked it. [The students] liked it too because that was [a student] who was here. They knew him and he comes from time to time and then he went and he told them, this is Hebron [. . .] this is what I'm going through there.[40]

In this case, the importance of testimony is elevated above the status of a pedagogical example. The practice of recounting one's experience becomes a part of the ethical work itself, a way of reaffirming the soldiers' commitment to serving in the West Bank and of preparing future soldiers for the challenges they will face.

As this remark also indicates, inviting soldiers to speak about their experiences during military service is extremely popular with students. This is as true for soldiers from outside the academy as it is with their graduates. Indeed, as I will discuss in Chapter 6, student demand is in large part responsible for the continued involvement of Breaking the Silence in *mekhinot*, despite the hostility of many academy staff. Yet student demand also generates other sources of soldiers' testimony. At another *mekhina*, Telem in Jaffa, students adopt this approach as a part of their weekly activity in the *mekhina*. This gives them an opportunity to practise testimony and self-examination outside the military context but in a way which ultimately has had a direct bearing on their conduct during military service. A counsellor at the academy explained it as follows:

. . . what happens is during the year in the *mekhina*, the students become very used to sharing, because even in a technical way they close the week with a weekly summary [*sikum shavu'a*], which means that they all share what went on with them during the week and how they feel about it, not

---

[40] Author interview with Ohad Shamama (Lakhish Academy).

just what they think, and they give the weekly administrators some critique and everything is very nice and family-like. You know, it's like a group-hug ... And then when they finish the *mekhina*, then it's all cut, like cold-turkey. They go to the army and experience tonnes of things. And, especially after a year like this, everything is just boiling up in their minds and they have nowhere to . . . to release it to. So what started happening a few years ago is they just started these Google groups . . . They send one email, I guess to everyone, and they just, every weekend, they just get home from the army and they just spill their hearts out – like pages long. And they send it to the whole group. And that way they feel like they are sharing again because they are so used to it.[41]

This kind of activity became so common at the *mekhina* that a decision was taken to make the current students aware of its existence. The emails were compiled anonymously and a booklet of testimonies was produced for use as an educational document. The purpose was to show the relevance of the ideas being discussed at the *mekhina* but also to set an example for the students to conduct similar conversations in future, so that it could act as a source of support during their military service. Revealingly, the name chosen for this booklet was *HaMekhina Shoveret Shtika* ('The Mekhina Breaks the Silence'). The counsellor was careful to emphasise that this was not a political endorsement of the organisation; rather, it represented an attempt to capitalise on the cachet of its name and to emphasise the importance of speaking to others as an ethical tool.

The clearest and best-known example of the use of soldiers' testimony at pre-military academies is at Rabin Academy. Since it is among the oldest *mekhinot*, Rabin has many graduates who continue to serve in the IDF in a variety of units and capacities. This, combined with the educational philosophy of its director, Dani Zamir, has enabled the academy to hold several events where graduates of the academy are invited back to discuss problems, especially moral issues, arising from recent military operations. In the last decade or so, they have discussed the disengagement from the Gaza Strip in 2005, the Second Lebanon War of 2006, and most famously Operation Cast Lead in 2009. Zamir believes firmly that in organising such events he is following a well-established tradition in the IDF. He described it as 'the

---

[41] Author interview with Guy Immerman (Telem Academy).

most basic tradition in the heritage, the tradition of the IDF, from the day I was a soldier, from '67, maybe from '48: you finish fighting, you speak. You speak with the soldiers, you speak with the enemy, you speak about what happened'.[42] This practice is also consciously associated with the concept of *siaḥ loḥamim* (which translates as 'soldiers' talk'), derived from an anthology of testimonies published under this title which were gathered from soldiers from *kibbutzim* across Israel who served in the Six Day War.

On Friday 13 February 2009, the academy (including parents and graduates) gathered to hear nine of its former students who had served in Operation Cast Lead in Gaza.[43] Zamir introduced the event by emphasising that he wished the conversation to focus on the moral aspects of the recent operation. He also made it very clear that the soldiers were expected to contribute:

I suggest that in the first rotation each person tells what he did, where he was exactly and whatever experience he came out with from this period. He might also say nothing happened and then I will make it difficult for him, so it's preferable that he says something. That he describes a particular experience, some particular thing, particular memory or particular impression that he has following the operation. (Rabin Academy, 2009)

What followed was a conversation which had a strong effect on the audience and which eventually would become the subject of international controversy. Two of the infantry soldiers described an episode in which an elderly Palestinian woman was shot for being in an area declared an open-fire zone as she approached a suspicious-looking youth. Several other incidents of violence and vandalism were also reported, to the extent that Zamir announced at the end the stories were 'depressing'. Zamir was so shocked by the stories that he reported them to the IDF, which rejected the claims as false. Zamir then consulted with the then Chief Education Officer, Eli Shermeister, to ask if he could publish the material, to which Shermeister indicated his approval. Within a few weeks, the transcript had made national and international news, including *Ha'aretz* and *The New York Times* (Bronner, 2009b; Harel, 2009b). Military police contacted the soldiers about their stories, and

---

[42] Author interview.
[43] The soldiers' names have been changed in the transcript but they are all male.

Zamir and his academy were pilloried in the Israeli media. The response was especially hostile from the religious right, who called for Zamir to be sacked and the academy closed. Significantly, however, Zamir also received the support of several religious academy leaders at this time, which was crucial in protecting his position.[44]

The response of the IDF was also interesting. Despite an intense media campaign on the part of the IDF to refute the allegations, privately senior army officers were more supportive. The IDF Head of Manpower and Resources, General Avi Zamir (no relation), met with Dani Zamir and reassured him that 'your soldiers are okay, I want you to tell them . . . that they did the right thing, I'm proud of them, and we, as the IDF, are not going to stop them from being commanders and officers . . . and we are very proud of *mekhinat* Rabin'.[45] Zamir was also persuaded that the testimonies of his graduates were instrumental in bringing about a wider response from the IDF. The allegations were investigated by the military police, which found (as is common in such investigations) no evidence of wrong-doing, principally because it emerged the testimonies were based on hearsay and not on eye-witness accounts (Greenberg, 2009).[46] According to Zamir, the Education Corps, under the direction of Shermeister, also increased the number of classes on the ethical code following the publication of the Rabin testimonies.[47] This response would indeed be quite typical of the IDF. In terms of criminal accountability, very little was actually implemented. Instead, the emphasis was placed on intensified ethical pedagogy. This response satisfied Zamir, who remains very proud of the whole episode despite the trouble it caused him.

However, concentrating on the public furore around this episode risks giving a misleading impression of the event itself. In fact, most of the incidents described by the students were much more quotidian forms of violence, in line with the usual fare of ethical pedagogy in pre-military academies. Indeed, according to the transcript, the stories which generated the most controversy and debate in the audience

---

[44] Author interview with Dani Zamir (Rabin Academy).
[45] Conversation as reported by Dani Zamir.
[46] Several human rights organisations expressed concern at the speed at which this investigation was concluded (Greenberg, 2009). The Goldstone Report also noted similarities between the testimonies of the graduates and those of Palestinians interviewed in the course of its investigation (UNHRC, 2009: 181).
[47] Author interview with Dani Zamir (Rabin Academy).

were not the accounts of the killings of civilians. These appear to have been met with muted shock and perplexed questions from academy staff. Instead, the most contentious questions raised by these soldiers appear to have been whether or not they should have cleaned Palestinian homes after they had expelled the inhabitants and converted them into military outposts. In the section of the protocols where this is discussed, the transcript records three moments in the space of a page when there were 'arguments', 'conversations', and even 'chaos' in the audience (Rabin Academy, 2009: 8). When Zamir heard of incidents of vandalism from the soldiers, he called it 'simply the behaviour of animals' (Rabin Academy, 2009: 7). By contrast, one soldier was keen to emphasise that his unit had cleaned the houses which they had occupied and whose inhabitants they had evicted into live firing zones:

I personally, when my platoon commander told me 'tell them to fold the blankets and put the mattresses in a pile', I didn't take it easily, there were lots of shouts, not screams at the top of your voice because you had to speak quietly, but I really didn't like this idea at the beginning. At the end of the matter, I was convinced and I understood that it's really correct and today I really respect and even admire this man – the platoon commander – for what he did there [. . .] All the soldiers in my platoon did it really without pleasure, really not in good spirits, we didn't wash it well, but we cleaned [. . .] I don't think every army, the Syrian army, the Afghan army, would clean his enemy's house, certainly not fold his blankets and return them to the cupboard. (Rabin Academy, 2009: 8)

As with the story of the watermelon analysed above, it was these relatively prosaic and inconsequential matters of military ethics, such as whether to clean this house, which most animated the discussion at Rabin Academy. Some 3,500 residential dwellings were destroyed during this operation; but the cleanliness of this one house is nevertheless a source of pride for this soldier, not to mention a mark of distinction from other armies. In this example, 'purity of arms' also takes on connotations of literal cleanliness, the concentration on objects rather than people suggesting an element of fetishisation in this fantasy. This is an ideological framing of Operation Cast Lead through testimony in which ransacked and depopulated houses in devastated urban landscapes are perfunctorily but meaningfully tidied. The effect is to mediate the violence of the operation and restore a sense of ethical purpose to the soldiers who participated in it.

Ethical Pedagogy at Religious Pre-military Academies

It is often insinuated that national-religious soldiers have fewer moral qualms about exercising violence than their secular counterparts. Especially after Operation Cast Lead, there was significant media commentary on the influence that the Military Rabbinate and the rabbis of *yeshivot hesder* and religious *mekhinot* have over the military. Evidence surfaced of rabbis having given strong encouragement to soldiers to fight before the operation. The unprecedented level of civilian casualties in that operation reinforced the impression that the influence of religious nationalists had contributed to a more relaxed attitude to civilian casualties (Breaking the Silence, 2009; Bronner, 2009a; Harel, 2009c; Lebel, 2013). Often cited was the controversial remark made by Rabbi Shlomo Aviner in a text circulated to soldiers before the operation:

When you show mercy to a cruel enemy, you are being cruel to pure and honest soldiers. This is terribly immoral. These are not games at the amusement park where sportsmanship teaches one to make concessions. This is a war on murderers. 'A la guerre comme la guerre.'(quoted in Harel, 2009c)

Yet, disturbing as such comments may be, they should not be taken as evidence of a lack of engagement with questions of military ethics among the national-religious. An analysis of pedagogy at religious pre-military academies shows that they are in fact deeply concerned with these questions, even if the approach may be different to that of more secular academies.

One major difference in the way religious pre-military academies deal with these issues relates to source material. They devote far less attention to texts such as the IDF ethical code. Instead, scripture (*halakha*) represents the main authority when discussing matters of military ethics. Until recently, the number of Jewish sources available for discussing conduct in warfare was very limited, owing to the low level of Jewish involvement in militaries before the birth of Zionism

(Cohen, 2013: 23–40). However, as Stuart Cohen has observed, the rise of national-religious soldiers in the IDF has been accompanied by a huge growth in the number and systematisation of texts by rabbis concerning military ethics which interpret Jewish law in this context (2007, 2013: 85–108). Indeed, it is striking that the main discursive innovations required to facilitate the entry of religious soldiers into the IDF have been ethical. The rabbis of religious *mekhinot* have been noticeably involved in this effort, including Rabbi Rafi Peretz (formerly of the *mekhina* in Atzmona, and current IDF Chief Rabbi), Rabbi Shlomo Aviner (principal of the Ateret Cohanim Academy in Jerusalem), and Rabbi Eyal Moshe Krim (also principal of the Ateret Cohanim Academy, and author of a four-volume work on ethics in warfare) (Cohen, 2007: 43, n. 20). Very often these texts concern how to maintain religious observance on duty, including the observance of dietary laws, keeping the Sabbath, interacting with women, and so on. Yet they also concern conduct towards other soldiers and towards the enemy.

Indeed, despite his widely publicised comments, Shlomo Aviner has been among the most actively involved in questions of morality in combat. Several of his lessons have dealt with these questions and have been published online through the Ateret Cohanim *yeshiva*, where the *mekhina* is based. In one lesson, Aviner discusses the question 'is it permissible to kill a terrorist who takes shelter behind ordinary people?' (Aviner, n.d.). Discussing concrete examples, including the assault on Jenin in 'Operation Defensive Shield', Aviner concludes that it is permissible to do so. He does so by arguing that such civilians, even though they may be innocent and without intention to harm, have the status of a *rodef*, a *halakhic* term for someone who endangers Jewish life, because he provides shelter for those trying to kill soldiers (see also Blidstein, 1996; cf. Cohen, 2007: 56–7).

When I asked a teacher at Keshet Yehuda academy about how he dealt with questions of 'collateral damage', his conclusion was no different:

If you are in battle and terrorists are hiding in a house behind a civilian population, even children, and they are shooting at our soldiers and they're being wounded, what would the right reaction be? So some soldiers will tell you we can't shoot because we're going to damage civilians, even children. Is that the right approach or not? So that's a very big decision that has, you know . . . it's a dilemma, and it depends on obviously the reality in the field.

If you can do it in any other way, you should attempt any other way but harming innocent children and civilians, but in reality there's a very basic moral question here. Whose children are more important? Are their children more important, or my children more important? Because those soldiers fighting are our children [. . .] And I think any sane human being, when his house is being threatened or his children are being threatened, is going to prefer saving his own children.[48]

Disagreeable as we might find this conclusion, it is also clear that it is based on ethical reflection. Indeed, it is not dissimilar to the logic of secular Israeli military ethicists, who have argued that the IDF has higher obligations to its soldiers than to civilians not under its 'effective control' (Kasher and Yadlin, 2005).

Another purpose of teaching military ethics at religious *mekhinot* is to pre-empt and confront the potential difficulties soldiers may have during their military service. In the face of problems of conscience, teachers encourage soldiers to concentrate on the ethical purpose of what they are doing. The teacher at Keshet Yehuda Academy described to me how he would do this in class:

So in the *beit midrash* [study hall] I can talk to them about . . . how it can be that [there] are very good people who are moral people who may be amongst the population of our enemy. But when they're in battle and they're facing off these enemies they have to be able to know that . . . you know, their reactions cannot be dulled by that understanding . . . When you're facing off a terrorist and he's about to kill you or your friend, you don't try and look for the points of merit within him: you shoot.[49]

In another of his lessons, Shlomo Aviner also emphasises the importance of taking ethical pride in one's actions in combat:

A soldier kills a terrorist and afterwards feels bad that he killed a person. Is this bad feeling a sign of a gentleness or imperviousness? Certainly it is a sign of imperviousness . . . Moral people fight to destroy evil . . . [The soldier] must be very joyful that he kept this religious duty [*mitsva*]. (Aviner, 2012; my translation)

---

[48] Author interview with Michael Cohen (Keshet Yehuda Academy).
[49] Author interview with Michael Cohen (Keshet Yehuda Academy).

This clarification of the moral purpose of military activity helps to prevent the potential problems of motivation and conscience and fortifies ethical conviction in battle.

These examples also illustrate some of the key differences with the approach of secular academies. The examples used are more abstract, dwelling far less on the actual details and consequences of violence. Insofar as it is broached, the violence is presented as a battle between good and evil, or a struggle against vilified 'terrorism'. The moral ambiguities are therefore less pronounced than at secular academies and equivocation is usually rejected as a sign of weakness. However, the positions of religious *mekhinot* on military ethics should not be reduced to their views on the question of harming civilians. As I have argued throughout this book, the role of ethics in Israeli militarism should primarily be considered from the broader perspective of subject formation. When this approach is taken, some tentative comparisons suggest that asceticism and ideas of 'purity' are also themes of pedagogy at religious *mekhinot*, even if they are articulated in different ways.

To begin with, the emphasis on ascetic self-cultivation is just as evident at religious academies. The teacher at Keshet Yehuda, for example, was keen to emphasise to me that being ethical was a crucial part of being an effective soldier:

. . . one of our goals is to push them into being officers and higher level positions in the army. How do we do that? The first idea . . . is focusing on the importance of being in the army, of having the right people in the army, and the national service that goes along with it. In other words, they are doing a great service to their nation by being, you know, good, strong, ethical soldiers, representing the nation of Israel in a positive way. And this is considered to us to be a *mitsva* [religious duty].[50]

He further explained that there is a complex relationship between ascetic self-maximisation and the pursuit of 'meaningful service':

. . . the understanding is I'm not going to the army to be a macho individual, in order to prove my worth [. . .] That totally shifts when I see meaningful service as also part of it. I'm not going there to reach my maximum potential.

---

[50] Author interview.

Along the way I may do that. I'm going there to do a service. What's pushing me forward is an ideology and that ideology means I'm going to see my service in a different way [. . .] And that's going to mean a totally different approach from someone who's a macho gung-ho guy.[51]

In this vision, military service is pursued rigorously for its own sake, but nevertheless rewards the individual precisely because of his sense of ascetic discipline in pursuit of the mission. This conforms to the pattern of 'surplus enjoyment' discussed earlier. Indeed, it is notable that this effect is explicitly identified as a product of ideology. Furthermore, there is once again a clearly gendered dynamic to this ethical process. The 'macho' masculinity of the soldier must be carefully restrained and modified in order to make a more useful military contribution.

One of the main ways in which this sense of ascetic striving for improvement is achieved is through practices of self-examination. Questions of personal morality are often discussed in the light of the eighteenth-century text *Messilat Yesharim* ('Path of the Upright') by Rabbi Moshe Haim Luzzatto, which is widely taught in religious *mekhinot*, including at Keshet Yehuda, Bnei David, and Ateret Cohanim.[52] This text describes the key traits of righteousness and how to acquire them. Notably 'watchfulness' [*hizaharut*] is the first of these qualities to be discussed, and the text explicitly encourages self-examination (Luzzatto, 1966: 35–80). Such practices are not merely taught but also institutionalised at religious academies. At Keshet Yehuda, for example, a regular slot is allocated in the timetable to personal accountability [*heshbon nefesh*] where students are encouraged to review and evaluate their past actions in consultation with rabbis in order to improve.[53] As the teacher there commented:

heshbon nefesh means personal accountability, right? I go through my behaviour and I see, do I hold the standards I expect of myself? In other words if I believe that speaking badly of other people is negative, I shouldn't bad mouth people and speak negatively. Have I done that or not? If I've done that then what can I do to correct that behaviour? And . . . many

---

[51] Author interview.
[52] Author interview with Michael Cohen (Keshet Yehuda Academy).
[53] Author interview with Michael Cohen (Keshet Yehuda Academy).

different standards . . . again, those type of things where we try and bring a person to a higher level of accountability and ethical standing.[54]

It is also common for soldiers to consult with their teachers and rabbis from their *mekhina* during their military service as part of this culture of self-examination (Rosman-Stollman, 2014: 174–9). Rabbis frequently issue *responsa* based on these enquiries for all students to follow. Indeed, Cohen has noticed that information technology has permitted this practice to become extremely common through the use of SMS messaging and online forums (2007: 43). During Operation Protective Edge, for example, Rabbi Shlomo Aviner from Ateret Cohanim academy posted several rounds of SMS questions and answers on his website, with topics ranging from dietary matters and fasting, to prayer, to the ethics of killing civilians (e.g. Aviner, 2014). These activities then become an opportunity for constant supervision of one's actions in consultation with an authority.

Although more diffuse and private than the forms of testimony at more secular academies, I would suggest that such encounters perform a similar function in maintaining ideological motivation to serve in the military. Indeed, these interactions have often proved crucial. One exception to the tendency of religious academies to minimise moral ambiguities was their response to the difficulties faced by national-religious soldiers during the disengagement from settlements in the Gaza Strip in 2005. Dalsheim has analysed the discussions taking place among the wider national-religious community at this time, observing that doubt and uncertainty were just as much a feature as resolve and determination (2011: 69–90). At that time, religious pre-military academies also held very intensive discussions about the morality of evicting Jewish settlers from land they viewed as theirs by divine inheritance (Rosman-Stollman, 2014: 148–62).[55] In the end, all religious academies instructed their students to obey orders and continue to serve the IDF; but careful deliberation over the dilemmas it posed was an important part of this process. It is of course notable that it was the question of evacuating Jewish settlements, not violence

---

[54] Author interview.
[55] Author interviews with Michael Cohen (Keshet Yehuda Academy) and Yokhanan Ben-Ya'akov.

against Palestinians, which provoked this process; but the centrality of ethical deliberation is once again recognisable.

Additional comparisons regarding the theme of 'purity' might also be drawn. Similarly to the invocation of 'purity of arms' at more secular academies, the idea of 'purity' as an extreme zero-point is common at religious academies and is often used for describing soldierly virtue. In one lesson entitled 'Purity [*nekiut*] and the Victory of the Army in War', Rabbi Eliazar Castiel of Bnei David academy cites Psalm 18, in which King David attributes his military victory to the 'cleanliness of my hands' and 'according to my righteousness' in the eyes of God (Castiel, n.d.). Castiel argues that military effectiveness depends on soldiers being 'cleaner, purer, more precise' [*yoter nekiyim, yoter tehuriyim, yoter medakdakiyim*] in order to maintain their motivation and the belief that they are doing 'the work of God'. Although the more secular value of 'purity of arms' is rarely invoked, it is possible to see how this emphasis reproduces a similar kind of surplus enjoyment through an ascetic superegoic drive to improve.

Following the death of Hadar Goldin, a graduate of Bnei David Academy, in Operation Protective Edge, a speaker at his memorial service praised him precisely for this quality of 'purity':

Our dear Hadar, you know what you were fighting for: not for quiet skies over the South and not for an iron dome [*kipat barzel*] or some agreement or another. You were fighting the war of the yarmulke of faith [*kipat ha'emuna*], the dome of heaven [*kipat shamayim*], the powers of purity [*tahara*] against the tunnel dwellers, the cave diggers who do not know the sun's light, who sit in silence and are considered as nothingness. (Bnei David Academy, 2014)

By eulogising Goldin in this way, military participation in Operation Protective Edge – in which over 2,200 Palestinians were killed, many of them in the bombardment of Rafah which took place in the frantic search for Goldin – is constructed as a demonstration of ethical character.[56] Moreover, the trait of purity is almost explicitly racialised in

---

[56] See the report by Amnesty International (2015) for a detailed account of this incident. One striking possibility is that Goldin was in fact killed by Israeli fire as a result of the so-called 'Hannibal Directive'. If this is the case, it would mean that Goldin was effectively killed on the orders of another graduate of Bnei David Academy, Colonel Ofer Winter, who was the commander who invoked the directive.

these remarks, through the direct comparison with Hamas fighters in tunnels. This ethical value, pursued through ascetic self-cultivation, thereby comes to constitute an ethnic and national marker, cementing the ideological belief in the IDF as a moral army.

Undeniably there are important differences in the way this theme of purity, and its accompanying ethnic and national significance, is broached at secular and religious academies. In religious academies, the 'purity' of the soldier is achieved primarily before battle as a way of deepening faith and resolve, and is axiomatically contrasted with the perfidiousness of the enemy. Conversely, in secular academies this contrast is more complex, arising from a messier encounter between the soldier and the enemy population. Purity is therefore usually demonstrated during and after battle through acts designed to distinguish Israeli soldiers from the enemy population (in, for example, refusing to eat a watermelon or insisting on cleaning a house). In each case, however, it is around this theme of purity that the ascetic emphasis on self-cultivation and the ideological emphasis on military ethics are able to coalesce.

Conclusion: Militarism as a 'Test of the Self'

In his closing lectures on 'The Hermeneutics of the Subject', Foucault emphasises the importance in Stoic ethics of 'life as a test of the self', in which one's conduct becomes the yardstick for the success of the ethical work undertaken through study, self-mastery, and self-examination (Foucault, 2005: 486). At Israeli pre-military academies military service is treated precisely as the experience which forms the proper basis for this test. Militarism inheres in the fact that it is participation in war which becomes the most crucial indicator of ethical character. As in the previous chapter, testimony is the foremost activity through which this testing of the self is conducted. This involves the contemplation of others' experiences as an exercise in ethical decision-making, the practice of self-examination through reflection on past deeds, and the use of such narratives for the ideological legitimation of structural violence. Soldiers' testimony in all its various guises is a common element of this ethical pedagogy, ranging from communal, public, and even ritualised events for recounting experience to more private, but no less far-reaching, consultations between soldiers and rabbis.

The shared focus on military ethics at pre-military academies certainly has a key role to play here. It reflects a common belief among *mekhinot* that the education they offer contributes to the morality of the IDF. This is also effective at producing a sense of shared purpose between religious and secular academies, despite their often deep political and ideological differences. Dani Zamir, director of the secular Rabin Academy and chairman of the Joint Council of *Mekhinot*, was adamant about this in interview:

To tell the truth, I think that the Orthodox *mekhinot* that are very extreme in their view, their political view, of the political solutions, are doing excellent work in the ethical education of their students. For example, there is no one who graduated from Orthodox *mekhinot* or from secular *mekhinot* who have done war crimes or refused to do something. I mean, it's a very successful programme [. . .] There is more lack of understanding between secular soldiers who went to *mekhinot* and those that went straight from school [. . .] than between soldiers from secular and Orthodox *mekhinot*.[57]

Whatever the truth of his claims about 'war crimes', what is striking is Zamir's conviction that the shared focus on the ethical preparations for warfare is what unites religious and secular academies. This ideological belief in the IDF as a moral army does not simply appear as a convenience, nor simply derive from a narrow focus on the traditional topics of military ethics *tout court*. This belief must also be produced through constant ethical work rooted in the everyday experience of soldiers, much of which concerns a much wider project of personal self-improvement.

Accordingly, in this chapter I have shown how the wider culture of 'meaningful service' in pre-military academies contributes to the ethics of Israeli militarism. Although different kinds of *mekhinot* attach differing significance to military service, they all emphasise it as an opportunity for self-realisation. They also pursue similar strategies of preparation for their students, which broadly take the ascetic form of mental and spiritual preparation. The sources for these exercises can be diverse, ranging from cinema to esoteric Jewish philosophy, from the 'Spirit of the IDF' to scripture, but the ethical subject produced is in many ways comparable and often encourages similarly gendered,

---

[57] Author interview.

ethno-national, and civic identifications. The aim is to produce a more fully rounded individual capable of self-discipline, leadership, and initiative, but also to ground these qualities in military experience such that they become inseparable from the exercise of violence.

Deepening my psychoanalytic critique of militarist ideology, I have also emphasised the importance of the theme of 'purity' as a shared *telos* of ethical work. Notwithstanding important differences in the way this theme appears at secular and religious academies, in both cases the emphasis on purity functions very effectively as a form of fantasy. This fantasy produces surplus enjoyment for the individual subject but also obscures the structural violence of war and occupation in favour of cosmetic moral change or religious self-affirmation. Through the cultivation of such fantasies, pedagogy at pre-military academies helps to consolidate a sense of the ethical purpose of military service and the identity of the IDF as a moral army. Ethical pedagogy is aimed at constructing, preserving, and restoring military service as a meaningful and therefore worthwhile activity.

5 | Between Guilt and Anxiety: Collecting Testimony in Breaking the Silence

In that first [operation] I had to drag, I don't know, an 11–12 year old kid from his bed in the middle of the night at gunpoint. And the look on his face, his eyes, it's crazy. When he looked at me, you know, so scared, when I pull[ed] him from his bed – I've got, you know, my vest from the army and weapon and everything and my face all painted – and he was so scared and I said, okay, what I'm doing can't be really involved with keeping my country safe like they told me. No it's . . . it doesn't have a chance to do that. And I thought to myself, okay, what can I do, what can I do, what can I do? So okay, I will be the good soldier, I will argue a lot, I will talk a lot with my teammates. And we did that, you know, we talked a lot. But in the back of my head was like, okay, there is that organisation Breaking the Silence. I know about that organisation. And I was in the Naḥal brigade. You know, Breaking the Silence is from the Naḥal brigade.[1]

As we sat in his Tel Aviv apartment Nadav described to me his decision to testify to the organisation Breaking the Silence. He highlighted this early episode from his military service to explain the feelings which had eventually prompted him to do so. As these remarks show, his initial response to this episode was fully consistent with the ethics of Israeli militarism described in previous chapters. His instinct was to engage in discussions with his fellow soldiers to work towards moral improvement: 'I thought, like almost every one of us in Breaking the Silence, that I could make the change from inside, that I could be the good soldier, the good occupier, the moral occupier, call it how you want.' However, his continued exposure to the violence of occupation – such as that of the encounter described above – gradually made a mockery of this idea. It aroused strong feelings of complicity within him. It made him question his motivations for serving in the

---

[1] Author interview with Nadav Weiman.

155

military, despite his loyalty to comrades in his unit. The impulse to talk about his experience slowly gravitated elsewhere, beyond the military.

Yet while he had often thought about Breaking the Silence during his military service, it was several years after he left the army before he decided to approach the organisation. This was partly because of the stigma attached to it. He anticipated (correctly) that giving a testimony would arouse the strong opposition of his family, which was proud of its military heritage. He was also concerned about incriminating his comrades in his testimony. But his reluctance was also bound up with feelings of uneasiness about what giving testimony would entail confronting. It would mean making his political commitments explicit, but also revisiting the violence of his time in the military. Nadav had been made acutely aware of this when watching the film *Waltz with Bashir* at the cinema during his military service. The film, now internationally famous, charts the director Ari Folman's attempts to come to terms with his involvement in the Sabra and Shatila massacres in the First Lebanon War.[2] During one scene in the film, a therapist tells the director that film and photography are a common means through which people attempt to create a screen between themselves and reality. For Nadav, a keen amateur photographer during his military service, this struck a disturbing chord. He recognised that several of his own photographs of military violence were an attempt to aestheticise and neutralise his feelings of moral ambiguity. Troubled, he initially put this thought to the back of his mind. But eventually he went to see a lecture by Breaking the Silence and the thought of testifying returned.

Even when he did decide to testify, Nadav experienced a great degree of nervousness and emotional turmoil:

It was like breaking a really, really big taboo in my life. I thought about my family, what I'm going to say about it with my friends [. . .] I was really, really stressed about it. Not because of what I just did and [because] they are going to use my testimony. Because, you know, I'd woken up a lot of memories that I didn't want to remember again.

---

[2] Several hundred Palestinians were killed in this massacre by the Phalangist militia. The IDF allowed the militia access to the Sabra and Shatila refugee camps and facilitated the massacre by launching flares. For a critique of the way the film serves to soothe the Israeli conscience regarding this episode, see Kaufman (2010).

Nadav's experience of coming to testify to Breaking the Silence placed him in the predicament described in the title of this chapter: he was caught between feelings of guilt and anxiety. On the one hand, he felt the urge to do something to change and resist the reality he had witnessed as a soldier; on the other, he feared the personal consequences of exploring his past involvement in violence. As Nadav himself recognised, this is a common experience for members of Breaking the Silence, and it relates something important about the work of the organisation and its relationship with patterns of militarism and ethics in Israeli society.

Breaking the Silence is one of the best-known anti-occupation organisations in Israel. As discussed in the Introduction, it is also a successor to a long tradition of Israeli soldiers speaking out about their military service. Yet it is also a product of the regime of militarist ethics I have been exploring in this book. Indeed, despite its political orientation, I conceive of the work of Breaking the Silence first and foremost as an ethical activity, one which bears the marks of the broader pedagogical and ideological regime I have already analysed. The ethics of guilt and anxiety evident in Nadav's experience are the principal way in which this is manifested in Breaking the Silence, both in the process of giving testimony (explored in this chapter) and in its public activism (explored in the next). But a closer examination of the organisation not only reveals that the ethical work of the organisation is shaped by these wider patterns of militarism. It also shows that ethical pedagogy in the Israel Defence Forces (IDF) and the activities of Breaking the Silence in fact work together, though in different capacities, to produce and perpetuate this militarism.

The Emergence of Breaking the Silence

Breaking the Silence was born in Hebron. It was founded by members of the 50th battalion of the Naḥal brigade, a unit which is regularly stationed in the city and which saw lengthy periods of active service there during the Second Intifada. Hebron is in many ways a unique city with regard to its position in the occupation. It is the only Palestinian city in the West Bank which has Israeli settlers living directly at its heart, which has resulted in a very severe regime of separation and sterilisation being applied to it. Palestinians no longer have access to its commercial centre, which is under varying degrees of curfew and traffic restrictions. This regime of military control began as a response to the disturbances following the massacre of twenty-nine Palestinian worshippers by the radical settler Baruch Goldstein in 1994 and has been steadily tightened since. The city was the site of violent confrontations during the Second Intifada and experiences constant bouts of tensions and violence up to this day.

It was the experience of implementing this violent regime of military control which prompted members of the 50th Naḥal battalion to reflect on the morality of what they were doing. The Naḥal brigade is distinctive in that it makes arrangements for its soldiers to combine their military service with volunteering activities. Many of the soldiers who served in Hebron at that time were therefore involved in charitable work, youth movements, the Israeli scouts, or other educational projects. They tended to be left-leaning, though some also came from right-wing families, and to be strong believers in Zionism and the idea of the IDF as a moral army. It was this combination of ideologically motivated soldiers and the extreme violence of the Intifada which produced Breaking the Silence. One former activist who was present in Hebron during those early days described the beginning of the moral response as follows:

It starts with the small daily decisions that you take when you're there in the platoon on the street in Hebron, for example . . . And then it kind of becomes bigger and you start discussing those things with your friends, with your commanders if possible. For example, you know that a certain patrol of the day goes through a school – a Palestinian school – and you fucking hate it. Just the shame . . . as an educator, as a person who sees himself as an educating figure, standing with a gun in front of a class, standing with a gun and a metal jacket, going into schools and seeing the hate in the kids' eyes after educating kids for two years. And you don't want to be there. And you know that the patrol goes to the school at a certain time of the day, so you try to do a different task in the platoon. You try to be on the watchtower instead of on the patrol. You try to be on the vehicle patrol instead of the foot patrol, so that you won't have to go through school, for example. And then you realise that [others] don't want to be on the patrol as well . . . And that's in the very early stage. And then the discussions come up . . . You actually talk about it. 'I don't want to be on the patrol that goes to the school. I feel really bad. I can't believe I'm doing this, 7–8 months after teaching kids about recycling and stuff, going into class with a gun'.[3]

[3] Author interview with Ilan Fathi.

Following these efforts to avoid the most difficult duties with their like-minded friends, however, a further realisation took place. They feared that those who would replace them in these duties would be less conscientious and perhaps more violent. In particular, they began to notice that those who had come from the more right-wing nationalist youth movements were beginning to take on these tasks:

I think in this time, when we understood that we cannot just say we're not going to do it and these guys started doing it – we knew exactly what they are doing, which is bad obviously, that's where our sense of responsibility was created in us. We understood that avoiding was not a solution. This is where our activism was pretty much coming to life, let's say – for me. And then you find yourself doing the opposite thing. You find yourself asking the commander to be in the school.[4]

The soldiers were therefore re-motivated to take on these duties by a classic feature of the ethics of Israeli militarism, which is the idea that good soldiers can make even the most violent of military activities more moral. In usual circumstances, as previous chapters have sought to show, it is quite possible to get this ideological mechanism to work. In the conditions of Hebron in the Second Intifada with members of the 50th battalion of the Naḥal brigade, however, this was much more difficult. One of the founding members of Breaking the Silence described the process whereby the fantasy of a moral occupation began to disappear:

I mean, you stand at a checkpoint. You've got 800 people going through. And the first one . . . you know, I was a scout, I thought: I can be professional, I can be courteous here. We can make this a moral occupation. We can even hand out candies. We can be the most courteous . . . and explain. The first hundred people I tried to explain. I'd say, you know, 'I'm sorry sir, there's a curfew' or 'my orders say the checkpoint's closed today, try again tomorrow maybe, maybe my orders will be different'. And after 100 people I got a little tired and like . . . 'sorry, curfew today – go home now'. And after three or four hundred people, you know, you're standing there 8 hours at a time, 400 people go through. You're going to get a few hundred people a day, especially if you're in Hebron, back then . . . it was a busy, busy market. After four hundred people you say, 'you know what? fuck off, it's closed, go away'. . . . [A]fter 800 people, you say, you know what I'm going to handcuff

[4] Author interview with Ilan Fathi.

you, I'm going to blindfold you, you're going to sit here for six hours, you're going to learn your lesson, I don't want to see you breaking curfew ever again. Because we can. You know, one red line at a time.[5]

This recognisable process of attrition (or *shḥika*, as soldiers term it) is certainly not unique to Hebron in 2001–04. Indeed, Erella Grassiani has documented the widespread phenomenon of Israeli soldier's gradually becoming numb to their prior moral concerns during the long, difficult routine of military service (2013: 73–89). Typical responses for many Israeli soldiers are apathy and fatalism, or the use of justificatory discourses such as having no alternative (2013: 102–30). Yet in the more extreme circumstances of Hebron, and with soldiers who cared deeply about their ideological commitments and identities, these coping strategies were not adequate. Two different kinds of ethical response in particular became common for those early members of Breaking the Silence: guilt and anxiety.

Feelings of both guilt and anxiety reflected a deep discomfort with what the soldiers were doing in Hebron; but whereas guilt focuses attention on the soldier's own individual moral behaviour, anxiety is the outcome of questioning the whole system of values and meanings underpinning an individual's subjectivity. For some, the emphasis was clearly on guilt. When I asked one of the founding members of the organisation why he had wanted to establish it, he responded simply: 'I felt guilty'.[6] Suggestions are also made that the leading figure in founding the organisation, Yehuda Shaul, had similar feelings. In an early video interview about the founding of the movement, revealingly entitled 'Burning Conscience', one activist commented: 'Breaking the Silence was founded because one day Yehuda Shaul could no longer look himself in the mirror' (Alternate Focus, 2006).

Very often, this feeling of guilt coincides with a continued belief in the reality, or possibility, of a moral army. The same founding member of the organisation who openly admitted to feeling guilty about what he had done, also professed his belief that the IDF remains a moral army – and he offered me several examples from his continued military service to attempt to prove the point.[7] Likewise, the activist

---

[5] Author interview with Micha Kurz.
[6] Author interview with anonymous founding member of Breaking the Silence.
[7] Author interview.

Noam Chayut records in his memoir that in the early stages of his involvement with Breaking the Silence he still believed in the idea of a moral army (2013: 174). Some soldiers took their earlier pattern of behaviour even further. As well as deliberately taking on the more difficult duties and attempting to do them in what they considered a more moral way, they also sought to enter commanding roles and to influence the behaviour of other soldiers.[8] The idea was to redouble their efforts and take it upon themselves to attempt to make the occupation more moral. In this framework of guilt, where the symbolic order of Israeli militarism remains intact, the soldier is more likely to question his own behaviour, to wonder whether he is a 'rotten apple', and to experience an associated sense of dejection.

Yet feelings of anxiety – of concern that the symbolic order of Israeli militarism was collapsing around them, that what they used to believe about the IDF and even Israel as a whole may no longer be coherent or true – were also a large and growing component of the responses of the early Breaking the Silence activists. Some of this anxiety began to develop in Hebron itself, as a natural escalation of the conversations the soldiers had among themselves about what they were doing:

Then these questions start rising consciously. I mean it goes a further step, where you don't just say to your friend 'I really don't want to be on the patrol tomorrow, let's find a way to be on the watch.' It turns to 'I really don't understand why Israeli soldiers have to go into a Palestinian school.' It goes a second . . . another step. 'I don't understand why we are [occupying] civilians. What's the goal, what's the point of doing this?' And from there the sense of responsibility starts building up.[9]

Interactions with the more violent settlers inside Hebron also contributed to this process. Many of the soldiers from a secular, more liberal background began to have difficulty identifying with the Israelis they were asked to protect. As one testifier described it, this had a serious effect on the soldier's identity as Jewish Israelis:

. . . on the one hand you say to yourself fuck it, I'm supposed to guard the Jews that are here. On the other hand these Jews don't behave with the

---

[8] Author interview with Ilan Fathi.
[9] Author interview with Ilan Fathi.

same morality or values I was raised on. I reached a point in Hebron where I didn't know who the enemy was any more: whether it's the Jew who's going crazy and I need to protect the Arabs from him, or whether I need to protect the Jew from the Arabs who are supposedly attacking . . . (Breaking the Silence, 2005; cf. Grassiani, 2013: 94–6)

This experience of anxiety about their identity and role was therefore already developing in Hebron itself. However, it was the experience of taking their experiences from internal monologues and personal conversations to recorded, publicly available testimony which accelerated this process.

The first major step was the decision taken by the early activists, and especially Yehuda Shaul, that they should develop their experiences in Hebron into an exhibition. On being released from the army, they used the discharge money they had been given to record each other's testimonies and collect new ones from friends, to collate their pictures of serving in Hebron, and to rent gallery space to display it all.[10] The soldiers had exhausted all possible avenues to improve the morality of what they were doing within the existing political and military structure. The aim was now to show Israeli society what the military occupation of the West Bank entailed and to reveal its moral price. This message had some political content, but at this early stage it was still inchoate:

We said there is no political objective. Our message was very clear: this is not political. This is about soldiers . . . because a soldier in Israeli society is like the purest voice: (a) we all know they're young children but (b) they're the consensus. We're all in a consensus around soldiers. So if soldiers would come out and say something . . . It was non-political. The point was that there's no education, preparation to the army that can make this a more moral situation. This is the reality. This is what it means. Controlling men, women, children, old folk, there's no way around it.[11]

A familiar trope surrounded this ambition, which was the belief that Israeli society does not sufficiently know what is entailed in occupation and that soldiers and the public do not want to speak about it.

---

[10] Author interview with Micha Kurz.
[11] Author interview with Micha Kurz.

Very frequently, this impression came from the soldiers' own difficulty in communicating with their families about their experience of military service:

Nobody wants to talk about this stuff. And it became very obvious . . . that people need to know. I needed my mother to understand, I needed my father to understand what was going on. People didn't understand settler expansion and how our job wasn't just to protect Israelis or protect the settlers: it was to support and enable their expansion. Without us they wouldn't have succeeded . . . And I needed my mother to understand what it meant for us to be . . . you know, what does it mean to give a kid a gun and tell him to go and patrol a civilian operation. We noticed how people were going crazy.[12]

In keeping with a well-established theme in the historical production of soldiers' testimony, therefore, the organisation took aim at this perceived societal silence and hence acquired its name.

The exhibition in Tel Aviv created a media frenzy, attracting interest from journalists and politicians as well as members of the public. Following its initial success the exhibition travelled to Haifa and even briefly to the Knesset at the invitation of the then education minister (something which would be unthinkable today). The activists began meeting with more experienced political campaigners, including the photojournalist Miki Kratzman and the documentary film-maker Avi Mograbi, who encouraged them to expand the project and collect more testimonies. The soldiers made more connections with like-minded individuals from other units and a strong drive began to gather a larger collection of testimonies. They also began to appear frequently in the media and developed a very active public relations campaign.[13] Meanwhile, however, the questions which this huge media exposure generated among the individual activists began to mount. Micha Kurz, one of the founding members of the organisation, described his growing sense of anxiety:

I was the most confused kid you've ever seen. I really didn't have a clue what was going on around . . . Because the more we talked, the more people we

---

[12] Author interview with Micha Kurz.
[13] I discuss the formalisation of Breaking the Silence's approach as an NGO in more detail in the next chapter.

met, the more questions we asked . . . there were no answers. The ground was falling apart. I thought we were this kind of state. Democracy . . . Turns out we're not a democracy, turns out that being Israeli isn't that cool, turns out that there was a Nakba, turns out that this was unjustified . . .[14]

For some, like Micha, this experience of anxiety rapidly became too much. He ceased to be an activist with the organisation and arranged to leave the country without returning for six years. Micha is no longer a Zionist and now works with a grassroots activism project in Sheikh Jarrah, Jerusalem. Other activists have experienced this anxiety to different degrees and with different consequences. Noam Chayut joined Breaking the Silence very soon after its establishment and also experienced a process of political transformation through his involvement with the organisation. He abandoned his Zionism but remained a Breaking the Silence activist. By contrast, many other activists – probably a majority – consider Zionism entirely compatible with their involvement with the organisation. For the founding member mentioned above who still believes in the IDF as a moral army, however, the organisation quickly became too radical. He left the organisation and pursued a career in Jerusalem municipal politics.[15]

In short, all manner of political trajectories are made possible through participation in the organisation and the anxiety to which this can give rise. It remains very difficult to generalise about the political consensus among its members, both at senior and junior levels. Yet while there is no uniform or stable experience, a minimal set of shared tenets among all activists did emerge. Over time, these would be refined into a clearer, if still limited, political message. One activist summarised the basic insight to me in Hebrew as follows: *hakibush mashhit*, the occupation corrupts. There is no way for an occupation to be moral, no matter how hard one tries.[16] Regardless of their personal political commitments, all Breaking the Silence activists share this view.

For practically every combat soldier in the IDF, arriving at this view requires going through at least a minimum degree of anxiety. As previous

[14] Author interview with Micha Kurz.
[15] Author interview with anonymous founding member of Breaking the Silence.
[16] Author interview with Ilan Fathi.

chapters have shown, Israeli militarism enshrines the possibility and desirability of a moral occupation. It produces ethical subjects who attempt to embody this ideal and who shape and prepare themselves to do so. Yet for a limited number, usually from a certain background and in certain conditions, their encounter with the military reality of occupation renders this ideological belief problematic. Some will experience this as a form of guilt, as a further impetus to improve their behaviour and the conduct of others in order to bring the uncomfortable reality closer to the ideal. Others, however, experience this as anxiety, as an unsettling experience of doubt in the consistency of the symbolic order of militarism itself. This may occur as their initial reaction, especially if they have prior political commitments. It may also be as a consequence of trying and failing to improve the situation through a guilt-response. But, finally, it may also happen through confronting this experience after military service, especially in a framework such as giving testimony to Breaking the Silence.

'Psychological Shit': The Testimony Process

Since its establishment, over one thousand soldiers from all areas of the IDF have testified to Breaking the Silence. While these testifiers are usually aware of the message of the organisation, not all of them fully support it. To an even greater degree than the leading activists in the organisation, their motivations for agreeing to give testimony are diverse and complex. They are rarely straightforward volunteers who approach the organisation without any prompting and with a clear aim in mind. Nevertheless, an ethics of guilt and anxiety is just as central to the production of testimony beyond the activist core, as a closer examination of the process of collecting testimony reveals.

Testimony collectors constantly attempt to recruit new testifiers by soliciting phone numbers at lectures or tours or by asking existing testifiers to suggest the names of friends or acquaintances they know who might be willing. The testimony collector will then call the soldier directly. Eran Efrati, who conducted up to 150 interviews over two years, estimated that roughly nine out of ten people whom he contacted in this way would refuse to give testimony. Approximately half of those who refuse to give testimony will do so almost straightaway on principle when they hear the suggestion, either because they do not like the organisation or they do not feel comfortable sharing the information. The other half refuse either because it proves difficult to build rapport and trust with them or because they do not yet feel prepared to but might in the future.[17] Only a small minority of those who are contacted therefore go on to give a testimony.

There is no typical testifier profile, but it is possible to discern some trends and categories. The largest group represented among the testifiers is secular, Ashkenazi, and relatively wealthy, usually from a left-leaning or liberal Zionist background.[18] Testifiers are overwhelmingly male; women testifiers are under-represented even compared with the proportion who served in some capacity in the occupied territories. Particular units are also over-represented, especially the Naḥal 50th Battalion because of the origins of Breaking the Silence in this unit. However, practically all groups in Jewish Israeli society are represented among the testifiers, including national-religious, Mizrahi, and even settler soldiers. The organisation also has testimonies from all major army units.

The personal motivations of the testifiers can be further broken down into groups. Avichai Stollar, the head of the testimonies project, who has interviewed upwards of 150 soldiers, identified five major groups to me.[19] The first group are those with political motivations, which is a very common reason to testify. These soldiers sympathise with the goals of Breaking the Silence and oppose the occupation of the West Bank and Gaza.[20] Many of these will be politically active in some capacity already or are looking for some way to become politically active on the left. Indeed, most of the activists I interviewed fell into this category, including Avichai himself.[21]

Just as common, however, is a second group: those with a guilty conscience. Avichai described these soldiers as 'people who feel like shit about either things they did or participated in or witnessed; and they do this to get some kind of . . . you know, like the Catholic "forgive me father for I have sinned" shit'. In other words, a large number of testifiers treat it as some kind of opportunity for confession. Although this group is

[17] Author interview with Eran Efrati.
[18] Author interview with Noam Chayut.
[19] The observations that follow are drawn from my interview with Avichai Stollar, unless otherwise indicated.
[20] Author interview with Noam Chayut.
[21] Author interviews with Nadav Weiman and Hillel Cohen; fieldnotes, 11 December 2012.

large, it is unlikely to constitute an overall majority of testifiers.[22] The distinction between these first and second groups turns to a large extent on the difference between anxiety and guilt I have already identified. Whereas the former group has embraced the experience of anxiety about the fantasy of a moral occupation and a moral army, many retain these beliefs and often feel guilt as a response, placing them in the second group. Together these first two groups constitute the vast bulk of testifiers.

A third group are those that believe in the importance of truth and public information. These are usually people who do not have a problem with what they did, either personally or politically, and therefore do not feel any compunction in talking about it. Occasionally these soldiers are actually proud of what they did and are trying to confound Breaking the Silence by bringing what they consider more positive stories about the occupation. Soldiers with more right-wing politics and even settlers fit into this group. A smaller subset of this group might have a particular episode or issue which concerns them but would fundamentally remain believers in the morality of the occupation. They approach Breaking the Silence in order to expose what they consider a localised problem to the public.[23] Some of this third group are therefore also exhibiting a guilt-based response. A fourth group are those that testify out of a sense of obligation, usually because they have some kind of personal connection to a member of Breaking the Silence and they do not have any real objections to it. A final fifth group are those whose motivations remain mysterious and who in some cases appear not to have understood what the aims of Breaking the Silence are at all. This group will sometimes tell what they think are impressive war stories or racist jokes about Palestinians.

Having secured the willingness of the testifier, the interviewer will then fix a time and a location. The length of the interview is flexible but usually takes two hours or more. The locations at which the testimony takes place range from private homes to cafes, universities, bus stations, and even military bases.[24] Generally, the interviewers I spoke with preferred to conduct the interviews at the soldier's home in order to encourage a more informal atmosphere; but they would

[22] Author interview with Ilan Fathi (see also Chayut, 2013: 180–1).
[23] Author interview with Noam Chayut (see also Chayut, 2013: 179).
[24] Author interviews with Avichai Stollar and Eran Efrati.

be prepared to meet them wherever they wanted. Interestingly, Eran noted that it was very rare for a soldier to be willing to be interviewed at their family home, usually because of the stigma attached to the organisation and a sense of embarrassment: 'They understand they are doing something they are not supposed to.'[25]

The interviewer begins the meeting by informing the testifier about Breaking the Silence and its aims, followed by reassurances about anonymity and the legal and journalistic protections under which the testimonies are collected. The interviewer also emphasises that he is interested not just in sensational stories but in the routine practices of service in the occupied territories. Interviews are tape-recorded from beginning to end. All of the interviewers I spoke with started the interviews in a similar way, by asking if the soldier had any particular stories he wanted to share.[26] Often, and especially among those who have strong feelings of guilt, testifiers will have prepared one or two of the more remarkable stories from their military service. The initial discussion about such incidents can go on for a while, even up to an hour. Interviewers seemed to interpret the rationale for this opening strategy differently. For some, it was a way to generate talking points and make the soldier more comfortable; for others, the idea was to get this story out of the way, allowing them to direct the testifier towards those things they were less inclined to mention or prepared to discuss.

After this point, the interviewer will then lead the testifier through his service chronologically, beginning with basic training and then through all of their deployments and missions. This structure has two purposes. The first is mnemonic, helping the soldier to recall details and arrange his recollections. The second is more analytic, helping the interviewer to find details and stories of interest. Since Breaking the Silence now has a very large database of testimonies, it may even be possible to use the interview to verify stories they had previously heard or to augment the picture of a particular area or particular time of interest. In general, the preference is for the soldier to formulate his memories as particular stories located in a time and place, since these are more powerful to read than dry analysis or scattered remarks. Occasionally, the interviewer will also interject with a question asking for clarification or attempting to solicit particular details.

---

[25] Author interview with Eran Efrati.
[26] Author interviews Avichai Stollar and Eran Efrati (see also Chayut, 2013: 180).

These procedural aspects of the testimony process change very little from interviewer to interviewer. However, one major area of difference in the practice of taking testimony has concerned the role of emotions both in the interview itself and in the content of the testimony. On this question there has been some considerable disagreement within the organisation. For most testimony collectors, the aim is to minimise the role of emotions and to concentrate on extracting information. Yet this is often difficult to achieve in practice. Expressing this majority view, Avichai described his interview technique as follows:

I try to minimise my interference in what he is saying. I would never stop him in the middle of a sentence unless he is talking about something which is completely irrelevant . . . Even there, unless he got carried away with it then I wouldn't stop him because the intention is to make it as informal as possible, to make him feel that it's a conversation and not like an interview. That's one of the reasons why I never touch the recording device, not to remind him . . . And it's also about the feeling that you give him. That you're not judgemental, no matter how horrible the stories that he's telling you. It's not a poker face, because a poker face would give him the feeling he's being interviewed. Even if I . . . deep inside do feel resentment to what he's saying or the way that he's presenting what he's saying . . . the general feeling in general in Breaking the Silence is to make him feel that his story is not just his own personal story, but it's a bigger story. And when he's telling something, it's usually the case that there are a million people, or a hundred people, or five hundred people telling the same story. Sometimes I would even say that 'yeah, it's amazing, you know I did the same thing five years before you'. And when he's telling a joke I would laugh, even if the joke is inappropriate or even a bit racist sometimes. That's the art of interviewing. Making the person who's being interviewed feel comfortable is the most important thing that you can do. But in Breaking the Silence it's even more important because you're already touching something that for many Israelis is very sensitive in many, many aspects, both in the personal sense and in the guilt sense. A lot of people feel like when they are doing this they are snitching out or . . . from the complete opposite [point of view], they feel awful about the things that they did. They feel genuinely bad and guilty about the things that they did and then it's also important to give them the feeling you know, that . . . keep talking, it's all of us. And that reassures people and gives them the confidence and the ability to speak freely, or the willingness to be more accurate.[27]

---

[27] Author interview with Avichai Stollar.

While Avichai starts by stating his intention to minimise his involvement in what the solider is saying, by the end of his comments it is clear that producing the desired kind of testimony requires carefully managed interventions in the emotional and psychological situation of the soldier. Even a purely extractive approach to generating testimony which is unconcerned with the soldier himself must nevertheless engage with these questions, and this is where the unavoidable influence of the affects of guilt and anxiety is felt.

Officially, Breaking the Silence is not interested in intervening in soldiers' lives, either politically or otherwise. Instead, its objective is to record and publish as many soldiers' testimonies as possible in order to document its claim that the occupation is immoral. The aim is to change public discourse in Israel, not to change the behaviour and attitude of soldiers. 'We are after the information . . . In a way we don't really care about the interviewee,' activist Noam Chayut put it to me. 'I shouldn't put it that way but we kind of use them, as journalists.'[28] This attitude partly emerges from the conclusion that the occupation is in itself immoral and that, no matter how hard they try, individual soldiers cannot change this. Yet it is also driven by other concerns, which derive from the organisation's awareness of its history in the tradition of soldiers' testimony in Israel. Breaking the Silence wants to avoid indulging in 'shooting and crying' (*yorim vebokhim*) and facilitating a discourse of victimhood among Israeli soldiers. Avichai was the most straightforward about his distaste for this kind of discourse:

. . . it re-empowers the feeling of people like my family who want to be moral and live comfortably with the fact that . . . yeah, you know it's such a horrible reality in which we have to shoot and then cry. You know, in the words of Golda [Meir], I will forgive them for killing our children but I will never forgive them for making us to kill their children. Fuck that! That's bullshit. That is bullshit. That's horrible. If you want to understand how to be really moral then you need to understand those that are oppressed . . . and those who are oppressed are not the soldiers, those that are oppressed are the Palestinians. They don't care about the psychological shit when it comes to the Palestinians. They only care about it when it comes to their own soldiers and they're getting it from all possible directions.[29]

---

[28] Author interview with Noam Chayut.
[29] Author interview with Avichai Stollar.

Avichai's discomfort with soldiers' 'psychological shit' is a common attitude in Breaking the Silence. Noam Chayut – who recorded the video testimonies given to Breaking the Silence – also stressed his wish to avoid turning soldiers into victims by allowing them an outlet for their feelings of guilt:

> . . . we don't want to be these Catholic priests. For example, in the video testimonies . . . I did not agree to have any kind of victimhood in this project. And there was a soldier from Hebron that, in each and every story . . . I made a mistake as the interviewer and let him understand that I don't like his victimhood and he went and put it in all the stories in a way that it would be difficult to edit. And some stories didn't go in because he felt that he is a victim, that his comrades [and] friends are victims, [that his] commander is a victim of a system, of a militaristic society.[30]

The difficulty is, as the resistance of Noam's testifier shows perfectly, that testimonies depend on experiences such as guilt and victimhood in order to come about in the first place. Moreover, emotions have an important mnemonic and interlocutory function in extracting precise and important information from soldiers. Not only this, those testimonies which contain an emotional component are also those most likely to have an impact on the reader or viewer. Avichai acknowledged this, with reference to his own personal testimony:

> If you watch the last video testimony that I gave I'm talking about what I did but the deepest thing that comes out of it is, you know, the part where I am saying that I am a sadistic shit. It's the most powerful part of the testimony. More powerful than what I'm telling about how an entire battalion was beating the shit out of a Palestinian. I understand that and it has its place and it's inevitable and I'm completely okay with that . . . I'm well aware in the political war the importance that emotions have. I'm just saying we shouldn't place our focus on that just because it's somehow convenient and many would say it's almost expected . . .[31]

There is, however, an alternative strand of thinking in Breaking the Silence, which is less well represented today but which was especially

---

[30] Author interview with Noam Chayut.
[31] Author interview with Avichai Stollar.

clear during 2008–10. This was the period when Eran Efrati was one of those responsible for interviewing soldiers. Eran believes in the necessity and importance of the emotional element of the interview. Not only does he recognise that this is inevitable, he actively attempts to encourage it. This is partly because he believes that emotions are an effective way to trigger the memory and extract better information. Eran would regularly intervene with questions about how the soldier felt at the time of the events he was describing, including by asking about seemingly unrelated matters such as the soldier's relationship with his girlfriend or family. However, Eran's principal motivation for introducing a more emotional element into the interviews was as a means of intervening in the ethical, political, and psychological development of the soldier. Unlike the majority in Breaking the Silence, Eran saw it as his responsibility to bring about a transformation in the soldier and if possible to radicalise his political perspective.

In Eran's view, refusing to allow the soldier an opportunity to come to terms with what he did was reflective of a wider attitude in the organisation that soldiers do not deserve such redemption. Indeed, his interpretation was that some activists in Breaking the Silence – many of whom remain close friends of his – deny this opportunity to testifiers precisely because they also deny it to themselves as a form of 'self-punishment' for what they did during their military service. Eran felt that this approach was politically counterproductive, or at the very least was passing up an important political opportunity to recruit new activists:

I didn't want to punish them. I wanted them to understand they are one of a million. It's not them, it's a system, it's a society, it's a country. Also, I wanted them to be active. I hope all through the years with my testimony that all of the guys I took testimony from will be active. I really hoped. It's an illusion but I think a large number of them became somehow involved in the process.[32]

Eran's approach was therefore to amplify the tendency already latent in Breaking the Silence (which Avichai also refers to above) to show the soldier that his actions were part of a larger context which itself is corrupted. In other words, Eran was accelerating the transition from feelings of guilt towards feelings of anxiety. Rather than simply

---

[32] Author interview with Eran Efrati.

suggesting that the occupation was the problem, however, Eran would also often begin to connect the occupation with wider and deeper questions about the nature of Israeli society. He would talk with the soldiers about the history of the conflict, about Zionism, about racial politics and particularly about the role of Mizrahim in Israeli society. This last point was especially important for him as a Mizrahi Jew in an organisation dominated by Ashkenazi, often 'Anglo', activists.[33] After a certain point in his own process of radicalisation, he even began encouraging the soldiers he interviewed to refuse to serve in the IDF, which caused controversy in the organisation. He would combine such questions and probing with more emotional questions, asking them about their current feelings about what they did or asking if their families and friends knew whether they were testifying to Breaking the Silence. Eran often stayed in close personal contact with those he interviewed, hoping to encourage their transformation from occupying soliders to anti-occupation activists. At the time of interview, he estimated that he was still in contact with 50–60 of them on a regular basis, despite having now left the country.

Eran's perspective was also derived from another area of contention concerning the testimony process, which is its relationship to the soldier's experience of trauma and possible psychological damage. Despite the often harrowing details which emerge from testimonies, and the fact that some soldiers do experience some kind of trauma, Breaking the Silence does not train its testifiers in dealing with such issues and still has not developed a clear protocol for this. Certain informal institutional links have been established. Eran used to recommend that his testifiers visit the organisation 'Psycho-Active', a left-wing Israeli NGO run by psychologists who oppose the occupation and who offer subsidised treatment to activists. More recently, Avichai has begun to attempt to co-ordinate with Physicians for Human Rights and to try to act as a bridge for soldiers to seek treatment. However, these efforts have not matured and it remains a source of concern for Avichai: 'I really don't feel comfortable with the fact that a lot – I don't know if it's a lot – that some of our testifiers, you know . . . [say] "goodbye, I'll carry on with my life" and he's basically fucked.'[34]

---

[33] 'Anglo' refers to Jewish Israelis with a personal or family history in an Anglophone country, usually the US or UK.

[34] Author interview with Avichai Stollar.

This is another reason why Avichai has tried to reduce the emotional element of the interview process to a minimum. Indeed, his view was that Eran's approach was likely to aggravate psychological problems. Yet Eran retains his view that this was unavoidable and that failing to engage with these issues, albeit in an amateur way, was likely to lead to more, not less, harm:

If you're opening a conversation with a guy who saw the body of a Palestinian child . . . and decided to take a picture with it and now you are trying to open this story to use it, the trauma is already there. Now, you've got two choices: to try to . . . get him to a place where he understands what he did but you can be somehow forgiven; or you can just leave him like that, dazed and confused. [. . .] Most people will never take [the] opportunity and go to speak with someone else. You are their shot. They are coming for you, this is it, this is what they are doing with their life. And if you are there enough at that moment realising that, you can take them and make them go through a process. Even if you just start pushing and then let go and see what happens. It's not like I'm calling every one of my guys and asking 'Are you still doing veteran service, you motherfucker?' If someone didn't do the journey, I let it go [. . .] It's dangerous. It's dangerous to play with someone, with his memory, with his feelings, with his trauma. But it's more dangerous to open that and then leave. I still believe in that.[35]

Eran clearly associates a political transformation with a process of psychological healing. This is not the same as a process of 'shooting and crying', even though in some cases that may still be what soldiers use the testimony process for. Eran was not trying to reconstitute the soldier as a military subject with a clear conscience and greater esteem for himself and his mission: 'I didn't really want them to feel good about themselves. I wanted them to feel like they are not the problem, they are not the issue.'[36] Eran believes that the testimony process can be a beneficial and politically productive experience precisely insofar as it does not seek to marginalise or ignore its irreducibly emotional (and subjective) aspect. He refers explicitly to his own personal political trajectory as an example of this. Eran feels that engaging with his experience through testimony allowed him to become the activist he is today, moving from

---

[35] Author interview.
[36] Author interview.

the heart of the Zionist consensus to being a strong supporter of the Boycott, Divestment, Sanctions (BDS) movement outside Israel:

I think my process is a lot healthier. I think my process helped me continue my life as an activist and understand the occupation is not narrow, it's very wide. And it helped me realise I need to fight something bigger and I'm a better activist right now because I learned to . . . I don't know if forgive myself, it's not a forgiveness thing . . . I just learned to live with the idea that it's not something I did, it's a situation I was brought into and if you can understand that, then you can be a really good activist. You can say, okay, let's stop this situation from happening, not just take the story after it happens. Let's dismantle this project, let's dismantle this idea. And maybe [others] will not get to this point because they really want their process to be cold, like they feel they deserve.

What remains to be seen, however, is whether Eran's experience can be generalised to the wider population of testifiers.

Melancholy Politics

When I interviewed Nadav, he showed me the collection of photographs he had taken during his military service. Several of them depicted house invasions, demonstrations, or sniper outposts. Yet one photograph struck me in particular (see Figure 5.1). He had taken it using a

Figure 5.1 Me, the soldier, looking with envy at me, the civilian
[Photo courtesy of Nadav Weiman, reproduced with permission]

long exposure which had allowed him to capture himself sitting in two different positions on his sofa. On the right hand side, he sat in civilian clothes reading the newspaper, *Ha'aretz*; on the left hand side, he sat in military uniform holding his rifle and looking at his civilian counterpart. He captioned it: 'Me, the soldier, looking with envy at me, the civilian.'

The long exposure also means that neither of Nadav's two selves appears fully in the picture, but rather as translucent ghosts. The soldier-subject in this photo is neither fully the man in uniform, nor fully the man reading the newspaper (nor, indeed, the man behind the camera). Instead, the subject is expressed in the relationship between all three positions. Taking this photograph as a starting point, it is possible to think more theoretically about the structure of subjectivity, and particularly the role of guilt and anxiety, in the ethics of soldiers' testimony to Breaking the Silence. It also provides a diagram for thinking about the likely efficacy of the political transformation Eran tried to bring about.

In the terms provided by Lacanian psychoanalysis, this photograph represents the struggle of the soldier-subject to find consistency in the symbolic order of Israeli militarism. Confronted with the Real of the violent military encounter, the desire of the Nadav-the-soldier to uphold the professed values of the Nadav-the-civilian for a moral occupation proves impossible. There is an irreducible gap between the two subject positions, such that the desiring soldier will never fully overlap with the civilian ego-ideal. The soldier-subject is therefore a *split* subject who remains alienated from the symbolic order of Israeli militarism. Moreover, this symbolic order remains inconsistent, demanding unachievable and hopelessly contradictory things from the soldier. It seeks to mask this inconsistency by producing fantasies, some of which (such as 'keeping a human image' and 'purity of arms') I have discussed in previous chapters. These fantasies incite guilt in the soldier who (inevitably) fails to fulfil the expectations placed upon him by the symbolic order and who therefore finds the fault within himself. This guilt operates to prevent the much more dangerous experience of anxiety, in which the subject starts to manage to *separate* himself from the militarist 'Big Other'[37] and not merely alienate himself in it. Žižek has rendered these important distinctions as follows:

---

[37] The 'Big Other' is the Lacanian term for the impersonal figure which represents the demands of the symbolic order on the subject.

In terms of affects, the difference between alienation and separation equals the difference between *guilt* and *anxiety*: the subject experiences guilt before the Big Other, while anxiety is a sign that the Other itself is lacking, impotent – in short, *guilt masks anxiety*. In psychoanalysis, guilt is therefore a category which ultimately *deceives* – no less than its opposite, innocence. (Žižek, 2000a: 255)

Many Breaking the Silence activists have managed to achieve this separation through anxiety. Indeed, both Eran and Avichai described their own personal experience in this respect in strikingly similar ways, drawing on the same distinction between their military and civilian selves. For Avichai, this meant abandoning his soldier self after his discharge by insisting that people no longer use his army nickname, Stollar: 'No, no, no, you don't call me Stollar. My name is Avichai. I buried Stollar in the military base where you get discharged. I told them Stollar does not exist any more.'[38] In an even more surprising case, Eran began to effect this separation in dramatic fashion during the period of his military service:

I understood that I was doing something really, really bad from the beginning. And I had these fantasies that I was protesting against myself, like against the army . . . After 3–4 years in the army I started going to Bil'in every Friday.[39] So, I would leave the army, take the uniform, put it in a bag, have my civilian clothes on me, the bag was on my back, and I was set with guys in Tel Aviv, and we would drive together to Bil'in. And nobody there knew I'm a soldier.[40]

Testimony plays an important role in this process of separation through anxiety. In a fascinating Masters thesis written at the Hebrew University of Jerusalem, Efrat Even-Tzur analyses this question precisely from a Lacanian perspective (Even-Tzur, 2011). Based on nine depth interviews with soldiers who testified to Breaking the Silence, she draws comparisons between the process of giving testimony and the ethical consequences of psychoanalytic treatment (Lacan, 2007a: 645–70, 2007b).

---

[38] Author interview with Avichai Stollar.
[39] Bil'in is a famous site for weekly protests in the West Bank where local Palestinian villagers demonstrate against their separation from their farmlands by the construction of the separation barrier around the settlement of Mod'in Illit.
[40] Author interview with Eran Efrati.

She notes that in many cases soldiers who testified did so in the classic framework of 'shooting and crying', using the testimony as an opportunity for confession. In Lacanian terms, the ethical process these soldiers underwent remained at the level of the Imaginary. Testimony for them meant indulging in a kind of 'ego psychology' reminiscent of the American psychoanalytic school, which Lacan had criticised for being principally concerned with restoring the individual to an ordinary way of life without effecting serious change (Lacan, 2007a: 197–268). However, in a few cases, Even-Tzur also notices that some testifiers engage in what Alenka Zupančič has termed an 'ethics of the Real' (2006), an ethical process in which the soldier confronts through testimony the way in which his subjectivity has been shaped by his military participation. She observes 'the choice that was made by some of the participants to expose themselves in their testimony, standing openly behind the truth it reveals, and presenting their own vulnerability' (Even-Tzur, 2011: 7).

This confrontation with the Real allows the testifier to locate his subjective constitution not primarily in his individual deeds but instead as a response to wider social, political, and military structures. This does not involve absolving the soldier of responsibility or forgiving him. Rather, it involves connecting the soldier's individual responsibility with this larger context and thereby identifying how the soldier as a subject came to be in this order. This is consistent with the Freudian dictum, championed by Lacan, of 'Wo es war, soll ich werden' – 'Where it was, there I shall become'. In this phrase, 'it' refers to the unconscious object which constitutes the fundamental fantasy of the subject and orders his experience of reality (Lacan, 2007a: 334–63, 2007b: 51–86). In the psychoanalytic process, as Freud conceives it, the aim is to make the analysand consciously assume this unconscious desire so that it no longer exercises the terrifying power it once did. Eran, without even knowing it, articulated precisely such an ambition in the account of his own political radicalisation quoted above: 'I just learned to live with the idea that it's not something I did, *it's a situation I was brought into.*'[41] In Lacan's famous phrase, by making this discovery the subject succeeds in 'traversing the fantasy', in coming to terms with the impossible desire which made him who he is. To refer

---

[41] Author interview with Eran Efrati, emphasis added.

back to Nadav's photograph, the subjective movement which takes place in such a testimony process is represented by the shift in gaze that the photograph effects. Nadav no longer gazes at himself as a soldier looking at his civilian ego-Ideal: from behind the camera, he now gazes at himself gazing at himself. His gaze is no longer guilty and envious, it is anxious.

In many ways, one could therefore consider this model of giving testimony a potentially positive political tool, one which helps the soldier to escape the confines of a de-politicised and militarised ethics. However, there are several problems with the ethics of giving testimony in Breaking the Silence which raise doubts about the reliability and efficacy of the transition from guilt to anxiety through testimony.

Uneven and Incidental Occurrence

Firstly, as already mentioned, the personal and political transformation of the soldier is not the primary aim of Breaking the Silence. Privately, some activists expressed a hope to me that testimony might still serve such a purpose.[42] Many also showed a clear awareness that guilt was not a politically useful affect and made efforts not to encourage it when taking testimonies.[43] However, the extraction of information remains the principal goal of the testimony process; any other consequences it has for the soldier are simply 'by-products'.[44] In addition, many testifiers are not interested in this side of giving testimony. As Avichai remarked: 'Some of the testifiers, many of the testifiers, give a testimony and they want you to leave them alone. You know, that's for their catharsis or whatever. They want to break their silence and get it over with and really leave their military service behind them.'[45]

Eran's approach therefore represents only a minority of the testimonies conducted, and this proportion will have diminished even further since he left the organisation. Moreover, even when, as in Eran's interviews, personal and political transformation does assume a more important role in the testimony, this transition from alienation to separation through anxiety is still very difficult and time-consuming to

[42] Author interview with Noam Chayut.
[43] Author interview with Nadav Bigelman.
[44] Author interview with Noam Chayut.
[45] Author interview with Avichai Stollar.

achieve. One sign of this is that many soldiers who testify to Breaking the Silence continue to serve in the IDF, either in reserves or (less commonly) in mandatory service. This was one of the reasons why Eran gradually began to consider his activism in Breaking the Silence a relatively inefficient way to achieve political change:

I think that was one of my breaking points. When I understood that a lot of the people I'm talking to . . . seeing them just giving the interview and we're staying in touch but continue going to the occupied territories, maybe going to be officers and commanders – I think that was the time when I understood that I can't wait for the Israeli public to understand why it's a problem. Because we don't have this time – either the Palestinians don't have this time, or us as Israelis don't have this time – and that was the point I understood I need to go and try to pressure Israel from outside, I think.[46]

The question of whether testifiers continue to do military service is one of the most vexed issues in Breaking the Silence. Privately, many activists have found ways to avoid further military service. The most usual way for this to take place is so-called 'grey refusal', where soldiers are exempted either from service as a whole or from service in the occupied territories through informal arrangements or deception. However, many activists (especially relatively new members of the organisation) do continue to serve in the occupied territories. During my fieldwork I spoke with three Breaking the Silence activists who had all received emergency call-ups during Operation Pillar of Defence in November 2012.[47] Two of the three soldiers had previously attempted to come to informal arrangements to exempt themselves from service in the occupied territories. Although for each of them it was not an easy decision, they had all been deployed to the border with their units. They primarily attributed their decisions to accept the call-up to loyalty to their units and the national mood in support of the operation.

Among the wider population of testifiers, the proportion who continue to do military service is even higher and probably amounts to the

---

[46] Author interview with Eran Efrati.
[47] Author interviews with three Breaking the Silence activists. During this eight-day operation, 167 Palestinians in Gaza and four Israeli civilians were killed. The operation concluded without a large-scale ground invasion by Israeli regular forces.

majority of those who give testimony.[48] However, it is difficult to be certain about the precise number because of partial information and because some soldiers may have changed their minds since giving testimony. Breaking the Silence did attempt to gather some statistics on this question based on the testimonies of 625 testifiers (roughly two-thirds of the total at the time of writing).[49] Of those who gave a definite response in their testimony, 109 were still serving in reserves and fifty-eight were not. However, there is no information on precisely why those fifty-eight were not serving, which makes it even more difficult to determine whether their non-service was a consequence of refusal, grey, or otherwise. It is also not clear what influence, if any, giving testimony to Breaking the Silence has on testifiers' decision to refuse or continue serving. For some activists, testimony has clearly been an important step in their political radicalisation and decision to refuse to serve. However, for most testifiers the decision to refuse is a product of a much wider set of considerations. The most that can be said with confidence, therefore, is that testifying to Breaking the Silence is fully compatible with continuing to serve in the IDF. This should serve as further confirmation of the point that, whether it is intended to or not, testimony to Breaking the Silence has only an unreliable and incidental tendency to bring about political change within the soldier.

The Return to Guilt through Melancholia

The second problem with the ethics of giving testimony is that the experience of anxiety it gives rise to can still relapse into politically unhelpful forms of guilt. This occurs even in cases where the experience of separation through anxiety, and the consequent radicalisation of the soldier, is at its most intense. To demonstrate this point, I will take the example of Noam Chayut, a long-standing activist in Breaking the Silence who recently published a memoir of his political transformation since his service in the IDF, including his activism with the group. The memoir is entitled *The Girl Who Stole My Holocaust* (*Ganevet HaSho'a Sheli*, in Hebrew), which refers to the encounter from which Noam dates the beginning of his journey from IDF soldier to anti-Zionist activist (Chayut, 2010, 2013).

---

[48] Author interviews with Avichai Stollar and Noam Chayut.
[49] Email communication from Avichai Stollar, 28 March 2013.

During his service in the occupied territories, Noam remembers
smiling at a group of children playing a game in a village in the West
Bank. The aim of his smile was to show 'I am sensitive but also masculine and strong' (Chayut, 2013: 58). But the children did not return the
smile and one girl in particular looked back at him with a stare of hor-
ror. This moment had a profound effect on Noam, who subsequently
began to lose his belief in the Zionist and militaristic narrative which
had equipped him with the ideological justification for serving in the
IDF. Noam describes this narrative as his 'Holocaust', wrapped up as
it was in the memory of the extermination of European Jewry and the
concomitant belief in the necessity for a state to protect Jews. The look
he received from the Palestinian girl undid this narrative:

I only understood much later what that scrawny girl in light-coloured clothes
had taken from me: she took away my belief that there is absolute evil in
the world. She took from me the belief that I was avenging my people's
destruction by absolute evil, that I was fighting absolute evil. For that
girl, I embodied absolute evil . . . As soon as I realised the fact that in her
eyes I myself was absolute evil, the absolute evil that had governed me until
then began to disintegrate. And ever since I have been without my Holocaust.
Ever since, everything in my life has taken on new meaning: the sense of
belonging is blurred, pride has gone missing, belief has weakened, regret has
grown strong, forgiveness has been born. (Chayut, 2013: 63)

What Noam is describing here is the clearest and best-documented
example of the process of separation through anxiety that I have been
describing in this chapter. The encounter with the Palestinian girl
(retroactively) marks the moment at which Noam traverses the fundamental fantasy of Israeli militarism. The moral justification for his
military participation begins to evaporate and the symbolic order of
Israeli militarism loses its apparent consistency. This provoked a wor-
risome series of questions for Noam, who over time lost his belief in
the IDF as a moral army and in Zionism. This personal crisis was more
than simply moral, however. It is also deeply bound up with questions
of identity and belonging, including not only national but gendered
identifications ('I am sensitive but also masculine and strong'). Noam's
position as a subject among the signifiers of Israeli militarism becomes
unclear: 'This process was slow at first, but after a while I felt I was
sliding down a slope, losing grip on my sense of self. I lost more and
more components of my previous identity, mostly based on what I no
longer believed in' (Chayut, 2013: 163).

Through his experience in Breaking the Silence and his investigations into the history and landscape of the conflict, Noam gradually reconstructs his worldview. He makes connections between his individual responsibility as a soldier with a wider social picture of racism, colonialism, and militarism. He also comes to understand the profound role which the Holocaust and its commemoration in Israel played in shaping him as a subject, and the way in which – despite its 'theft' from him – the empty place where his Holocaust once stood still structures his experience of reality. Yet what is interesting about this process of separation from the militarist and Zionist 'Big Other' is that, in Noam's experience, guilt has not completely disappeared. Indeed, Noam is remarkable for his brazen insistence that he must still be punished for what he did as a soldier. In explaining why he chooses to remain in Israel and campaign with Breaking the Silence rather than leaving the country, Noam writes:

At this phase of my life, I still owe a heavy debt to Israeli society and to Palestinian society. I was among the brainwashed who committed crimes in the occupied territories, and the quiet struggle over public opinion that Breaking the Silence is conducting is also a kind of penance [*kaparat aṿonot*] for me. (Chayut, 2013: 210, cf. 2010: 192)

When translated into the English word 'penance' the term *kaparat aṿonot* loses some of its potency, since its literal rendering is 'atoning for sins', which refers directly to the rituals religious Jews perform on Yom Kippur ('The Day of Atonement'). During our interview, I asked Noam about what exactly he meant by 'atoning for sins':

In a different political situation I would mean jail for years. For the violence that I carried out, for the crimes that we carried out. Now, like British soldiers nowadays, like American soldiers nowadays, like strong societies, we don't pay for our violence [. . .] I do feel that the only way I can try to pay for what we did, for what I did (let's be more harsh with myself) is by letting people know what we did, which are crimes, and I really believe people should pay for them and be responsible for them . . . And there's nothing else we can do.[50]

Noam makes clear in this statement that, for him, there is still a strong connection between truth-telling and atoning for sins, bringing

---

[50] Author interview with Noam Chayut.

the model of testimony much closer to confession. This is despite the fact that Noam fully accepts the criticism that confession, and the use of the testimony process as conscience-clearing, is a problematic feature of what Breaking the Silence does. But how is it possible for someone such as Noam, who has experienced separation through anxiety and traversed his fantasy, to nevertheless return to the experience of guilt?

The answer, I would argue, lies in the phenomenon of melancholia. Freud first defined melancholia in psychoanalytic terms in his essay 'Mourning and Melancholia'. He distinguishes melancholia from mourning on several grounds, the most important being that the loss felt during mourning is a loss of a real object (typically the death of a loved one), whereas the loss felt during melancholia is the loss of an unconscious object (Freud, 2001: 245). This unconscious object lost during melancholia need not imply the actual loss of a real loved object but the loss of what it was *in* that object that the subject formerly loved (Žižek, 2000b: 659–63). The Lacanian term for this quality *in* something which causes our desire for it is the *objet a*, which is also the object of fantasy. What melancholia describes, therefore, is a condition in which the subject's fantasy disintegrates, in which a love object fails to excite the response it once used to. For Noam, his fundamental fantasy has been damaged in precisely such a way. The theft of his Holocaust is not a real loss – the Holocaust is of course still there – but rather the loss of what it was *in* the Holocaust that used to motivate him to serve in the IDF.

The other major difference from mourning lies in how the subject responds to the loss of the unconscious object. Freud observed a tendency for melancholics to engage in intensive self-abasement and self-punishment and to consider themselves as worthless:

In mourning it is the world which has become poor and empty; in melancholia it is the ego itself. The patient represents his ego to us as worthless, incapable of any achievement and morally despicable; he reproaches himself, vilifies himself and expects to be cast out and punished. (Freud, 2001: 246)

Freud's explanation is that melancholics displace their libido from the lost object onto the ego itself as a way of refusing this loss:

An object-choice, an attachment of the libido to a particular person, had at one time existed; then, owing to a real slight or disappointment coming from this loved person, the object-relationship was shattered. The result was not the normal one of withdrawal of the libido from this object and displacement of it on to a new one, but something different, for whose coming-about various conditions seem to be necessary. The object-cathexis proved to have little power of resistance, and was brought to an end. But the free libido was not displaced on to another object; it was withdrawn into the ego. There, however, it was not employed in any unspecified way, but served to establish an *identification* of the ego with the abandoned object. Thus the shadow of the object fell upon the ego, so that the latter could henceforth be judged by a special agency as though it were an object, the forsaken object. In this an object-loss became transformed into an ego-loss, and the conflict between the ego and the loved person transformed into a cleavage between the criticising activity of the ego and the ego as altered by the identification. (Freud, 2001: 248–9)

As Judith Butler has argued, what Freud develops here is an account of how melancholia produces the effect of self-punishment and hence power over the subject (Butler, 1996: 167–200). As a way of forestalling the loss of the love-object, the subject transforms the relationship he used to have into topographical mutation of the ego in which one part, standing in for the lost object, is criticised and berated by another. This 'criticising activity of the ego' is none other than the superego, the part of the subject responsible for producing guilt. The reason why this formerly loving relationship mysteriously develops into a wrathful urge to punish is the most difficult to grasp element of Freud's hypothesis. Freud elsewhere observes the tendency for love to acquire sadistic elements; in the case of melancholia, this seems to happen because the subject feels anger towards the lost object for disappearing:

If one listens patiently to a melancholic's many and various self-accusations, one cannot in the end avoid the impression that often the most violent of them are hardly applicable to the patient himself, but that with insignificant modifications they do fit someone else, some person whom the patient loves or has loved or should love. (Freud, 2001: 248)

My suggestion is that Noam's experience of losing his Holocaust can be understood as a melancholic process, which explains the re-emergence of guilt in the ethics of his political activism. Other features of his experience also conform to melancholia. The fact that Noam's memoirs are written to the girl who stole his Holocaust betrays the tendency of the melancholic to reproach the lost object, even though this is usually introjected as self-reproach. Yet the clearest indication is the desire for self-punishment Freud identifies. This is first evident in the 900 km hike across Palestine that Noam put himself through immediately after his army service. He undertook this almost completely alone and often without talking to anyone for days on end. His mother called it a 'purification journey'. 'Why was I tormenting myself like this?' Noam asked along the way (Chayut, 2013: 111–12). Further indications of this tendency are the schedule and rules that Noam imposed on himself for three months when he returned to Israel after his post-army service travels, which included strict limitations on calorific intake, alcohol consumption, smoking, and even masturbation (Chayut, 2013: 165–7).

Yet this tendency for self-punishment also appears to drive his activism. Noam is very clear that he should be tried for war crimes and, failing that, that he should at least pay some kind of price to repay the debt he owes to Palestinians. During our interview, he was very open about the emotional importance to him of at least doing something to pay for what he did:

Every evening that I walk with my dog I collect clothes from the garbage around houses in my neighbourhood. People leave their nice clothes that they don't want any more and nice handbags. And I collect them and every week I bring them to my mother, which goes every two or three weeks to a village in the West Bank and somebody sells it. And [these are] things that I do in order to feel better and every Israeli should do. But the one thing I should do and can do to really deal with my crimes . . . [is letting people know what we did]. And, you know, I'm a party pooper in the pride parade of macho-Israelis, that's I think the price to be paid. And it's party-poopering: I'm destroying my party as well . . .[51]

Indeed, at certain points Noam also suggested that his activism was a kind of compulsion:

You know, it's not a question. I mean, I cannot not do it. Actually Yehuda [the co-founder of Breaking the Silence] and I asked ourselves this question here in this restaurant just . . . three or four months ago. We were sitting and

---

[51] Author interview with Noam Chayut.

talking about something and he came over and we had a conversation: why are we doing [this]? And you know, we just answered ourselves as friends that we have no other choice [. . .] because we both understand that we have to do it.[52]

Other Breaking the Silence activists seemed to confirm this picture. One former education director appeared to concur that it was affective investment, and not necessarily political efficacy, that drove Breaking the Silence to continue: 'You fail to reach your goals, so you just start documenting. Why? Because the EU funds it. Why? Because that's the only thing you can do. Why? Because you cannot quit. You have to do something.'[53]

Of course, the fact that activists have strong affective investments in a certain political activity does not necessarily discredit it. Political campaigning which relies on individuals' sense of guilt or obligation can still be effective. It is in the next chapter that I will evaluate in more detail the successes and failures of Breaking the Silence's campaigning. However, for my present purposes, the important point to be made is that there is a risk that individuals' affective commitments might begin to instrumentalise activism, displacing political efficacy with affective reward as the criteria for success. There are signs that, for Noam at least, this is beginning to take place, since he seems not to believe that what he is doing will lead to serious political change: 'You know why it's *kaparat avonot* [atoning for sins]? Because it won't make a difference. Because this place is going to hell anyway . . . I've nothing else to do, so that's what I'm doing. Can I do more? Maybe. Probably not.'[54]

In this context, it should not be forgotten that the concept of melancholia has been of immense interest to political theory. Indeed, the political phenomenon which Wendy Brown has termed 'left melancholy' can provide us with an excellent model for understanding the ethical dimensions of testimony and activism in Breaking the Silence. In her essay 'Resisting Left Melancholy', Brown engages in criticism of the contemporary Left for an attachment to defeat (1999). This attachment takes a melancholic form, according to Brown, because the Left

[52] Author interview.
[53] Author interview with Ilan Fathi.
[54] Author interview with Noam Chayut.

has transformed the lost object of its desire – revolution – into a form of endless self-criticism for failure. Rather than truly engaging with that loss and its consequences through renewed political engagement, she argues, the Left has continued to cling to it indirectly through this melancholic disposition (Brown, 1999: 23–7). Jodi Dean has recently re-evaluated Brown's argument, agreeing with Brown that the Left remains addicted to failure but disagreeing that this is because of its refusal to abandon a hopeless orthodoxy (2012: 157–206). Dean reverses this position and claims that it is the Left's failure fully to pursue its desire for revolution which has generated this melancholia. She accuses the Left of having given up on its desire, in the Lacanian phrase (2012: 169–76).

The most interesting dimension to Dean's critique, however, is that she then directly attacks the turn to 'the drive' as a political strategy on the Lacanian Left (2012: 173–5). Lacan famously distinguished between desire and drive, arguing that whereas desire is aimed at a lacking object, drive is invested in the very gesture and movement towards that object. For Žižek, and other Lacanians, the corollary of 'traversing the fantasy' is supplanting impossible desire with drive. The subject realises that the object of its fantasy is inherently unreachable and ceases to be oppressed by the search for impossible consistency in the symbolic order. However, this desire, being unconscious, cannot simply be abandoned, since that would imply the disintegration of the subject. Instead, the subject must now find a way to come to terms with this desire through the drive; one must learn to 'enjoy the symptom', assuming it consciously and deriving satisfaction from a repeated movement towards the empty place where the object once resided (Žižek, 1991: 130–41; Zupančič, 2006: esp. 238–59; see also Bosteels, 2011: 72). Drive, in other words, is the only way to safely enjoy one's desire without giving up on it. Dean, however, is not satisfied with this resolution, arguing that it is the Left's very turn to the drive which has given rise to its melancholy:

For such a Left, enjoyment comes from its withdrawal from responsibility, its sublimation of goals and responsibilities into the branching, fragmented practices of micropolitics, self-care, and issue awareness. Perpetually slighted, harmed, and undone, this Left remains stuck in repetition, unable to break out the circuits of drive in which it is caught, unable because it enjoys them. (2012: 174–5)

The relevance of these theoretical insights for understanding Breaking the Silence is that it shows the limits of the political and ethical transformations that testimony can effect. Even if some activists succeed in 'traversing the fantasy' through confrontation with the violent Real of their actions in testimony, there is a danger that the vicissitudes of the drive can then produce melancholia. Noam's desire for penance is only one individual case of this. Eran felt that this was a general tendency in the organisation, even in himself, that was reflected in the way testimonies were conducted:

I think every one of us has a way of self-punishment . . . but it's all very different. For [some], it's like: 'I want you to confront what you did' because this is what they want from themselves. So they say, 'I want you to be confronted with what you did, feel bad about it, look in me in the eyes, understand what you did, and then you can go away.' And I feel like I was always trying to . . . I don't know . . . it was still a self-punishment, I think, for me but it was more as a . . . how can I say it? Trying to forgive myself, trying to understand why I sat frozen in all of these situations, start[ing] to comfort myself, stuff like that. And that's why we were so different, every interviewer was so different.[55]

What Eran has identified very well here is the constant oscillation between guilt and anxiety in Breaking the Silence. Even in cases where separation through anxiety is achieved, melancholia allows for the return of guilt and self-punishment, impulses which can then colonise and divert activism away from the most politically effective paths.

The Blocked Path to Courage and Justice

The third and final problem with the ethics of giving testimony in Breaking the Silence follows directly from these diverted impulses, in that they tend to obscure political possibilities and strategies for wider structural change. One interesting aspect of the self-reproaches Noam directs at himself in his memoirs is the tentative accusation of cowardice:

For I – you must have already understood this from my previous stories – am not especially fond of taking risks. I am not one to rush ahead and get beaten up at a demonstration, not one to march, head held high, off to a military or

---

[55] Author interview with Eran Efrati.

any other kind of jail. I decided long ago not to violate any law. If the law becomes unbearable, then I will exchange my old dream of a little house in my home village . . . for a new dream of a little house abroad with the same beloved wife and four imaginary children. Some would say this is cowardice, but as far as I am concerned, it is a simple order of priorities: laws are geographic. Man isn't . . . And still, perhaps 'cowardice' is the concise, precise definition for a life philosophy of this sort? (Chayut, 2013: 210–11)

Partly, Noam justifies his aversion to risk-taking in political activism by reference to simple pragmatism:

I don't go and breathe tear gas in Bil'in. I think it's . . . I mean I adore these people that do it. I don't do it . . . Now, seriously, politically speaking it wouldn't make any difference if I would make this night a night in [jail] or have dinner with someone . . . if all of us, a few millions of us would go to a checkpoint and say 'arrest us', we'd cross [. . .] the occupation would end tomorrow. But these people around us don't even understand what the fuck is wrong and I don't have the guts to be in jail [. . .] That's the fact. And I do admit in the book that you can call it whatever you want to call it but that's the way I act . . .[56]

However, Noam also seemed to acknowledge that his level of willingness to risk himself in activism had diminished since he left the army and he acquired his new political identity:

A nationalist would go and fight for the flag forever and he would die for the flag, as I would do when I was 21. You know, I won't fight to the end today . . . I would be happy to say I would but it would be a lie. I wouldn't . . . You can call it cowardice. You can call it just being a coward and not fighting for others. And I would agree probably.[57]

Elsewhere in her analysis of 'left melancholy', Jodi Dean suggests that the guilt that leftists often feel comes from the sense of having given up on their true political desire, substituting it with 'criticism and interpretation, small projects and local actions, particular issues and legislative victories, art, technology, procedures, and process' (2012: 174). Foolish as demonstrations, marches, and getting arrested may seem to Noam, his remarks nevertheless betray a respect for such

---

[56] Author interview with Noam Chayut.
[57] Author interview.

actions and a belief that ultimately they would have to form the basis of real political change.

The accusation of cowardice is particularly notable because of what its opposite – courage – suggests about the ethical basis of such alternative political activities. The philosopher Alain Badiou has devoted considerable attention to the ethical approach required to achieve emancipatory political change. In his early work, *Theory of the Subject*, he offers a typology of four ethical concepts (2009: 277–332). The first two are extrapolated from Lacan, anxiety and superego, whereas the latter, courage and justice, are Badiou's own additions (Badiou, 2009: 144–7, 277–303). He codes each of these pairings Ψ (anxiety-superego) and α (courage-justice). My claim is that the ethics of testimony in *Breaking the Silence* remains confined to the Ψ strand, trapped in a constant movement between affects of anxiety on the one hand and guilt produced by the superego on the other, and that this is a key source of its political limitations.

As I have done above, Badiou describes anxiety as occurring when the symbolic order disintegrates and its inconsistency is exposed to the subject (2009: 291–2). Superego, by contrast, is the conservative impulse to restore a previous order, which takes the form of a terrifying and senseless reassertion of the law. Badiou argues that anxiety, which is a potentially radical moment where new political possibilities become thinkable, will often be followed by an encounter with the superego because of the unbearable and disorientating extremity of anxiety: 'Hence anxiety calls upon the superego. Anxiety is that inevitable side of subjectivisation which, caught in the web of the dead order, makes an appeal to the reinforced sustenance of the law. Here the Freudians will mention the anxious practice of self-punishment' (Badiou, 2009: 292). Badiou's point is that these two poles of ethical experience are insufficient to produce revolutionary change. Unsupported, anxiety will degenerate into superego, guilt, and self-punishment. As Bruno Bosteels puts it:

Between anxiety and the superego, a subject only oscillates in painful alternation, without the event of true novelty, just as the insufferable experience of formlessness without a law provokes in turn the reinforcement of the law's excessive form. At best, these two subjective figures thus indicate the point where the existing order of things becomes open to a fatal division, but without allowing a new order to come into being. (2011: 89)

Badiou therefore appeals to the concepts of courage and justice as a pathway out of this tendency: courage forces the 'dead order' to disappear, even at the risk of losing oneself in this gesture; justice reconstitutes a new order, which exists not as law for the sake of law (as in the superego) but as law tested against the requirements of the cause (2009: 294–6).

Without the addition of these ethical components of courage and justice, Breaking the Silence remains contained between anxiety and guilt and therefore limited in its contribution to political change. Occasionally, Breaking the Silence does successfully 'indicate the point where the existing order of things becomes open to a fatal division'. However, there is little in the corresponding ethics which encourages a genuine confrontation with this order or a creative moment of political novelty. In fact, the melancholic tendency appears to militate against these possibilities, creating affective investments in modes of self-punishment and criticism which obstruct alternative approaches. This is something which several activists appeared to have realised, especially those who have now left the organisation, who were even more forthright in suggesting that Breaking the Silence was diverting energies towards less effective activities. Micha Kurz, the co-founder of the organisation who now works for a grassroots activist network, remarked:

[Unless we are] building capacity within communities to overcome their oppression and human rights violations, or just development goals, then we are wasting our time. If we are not doing that, if Breaking the Silence doesn't find a way to do that, they become irrelevant . . . they are just putting another bandage or documenting the wound, but it's not healing anything.[58]

Conclusion: Militarism as 'Cruel Optimism'

Lauren Berlant has described 'cruel optimism' as 'a relation . . . when something you desire is actually an obstacle to your flourishing' (2011: 1), 'a relation of attachment to compromised conditions of possibility' (2006: 21). She explicitly distinguishes this experience from melancholia, 'which is enacted in the subject's desire to temporise an experience of the loss of an object/scene with which she has identified

---

[58] Author interview with Micha Kurz.

her ego continuity' (Berlant, 2006: 21). By contrast, cruel optimism is 'the condition of maintaining an attachment to a problematic object *in advance* of its loss' (2006: 21, emphasis in original). However, the analysis presented above suggests a more complicated, even recursive, relationship between these two phenomena. The ethics of Israeli militarism, as explored in earlier chapters, can be conceived as a kind of cruel optimism, in that it instils desires and creates fantasies which motivate soldiers to participate in an inevitably compromised and violent military project of occupation. However, when soldiers encounter, perhaps through testimony, the utter inadequacy of such claims, the loss of these relations of attachment can be experienced as melancholia. In Noam Chayut's case, what was formerly an optimistic attachment to Zionism and Israeli militarism translates into a merciless and pessimistic attachment to 'atoning for sins'.

Yet the possibility of cruel optimism does not cease here. Although this melancholic experience does not return the anxious soldier to his former position and opinions, it does have significant consequences for the kind of activism it subsequently encourages. A recursive transition from guilt to anxiety and back may create cruelly optimistic investments in modes of politics not best suited to achieving desired outcomes.[59] Specifically, the ethics of testimony in Breaking the Silence may foreclose a more disruptive politics governed by the imperatives of courage and justice, one in which more is risked but more is potentially gained. In the next chapter, I will provide a much fuller analysis of how in practice the campaigning activity of Breaking the Silence is self-limiting in this way. For now, it suffices to note how the ethics of testimony creates affective attachments to the deficient approaches, and hence compromised conditions of possibility, I will discuss next.

Before moving on, however, it is also worth glancing back at the way in which this outcome has been constituted by the ethics of Israeli militarism. What is notable about the soldiers who founded Breaking the Silence, and indeed about its activists more generally, is that prior to their involvement with the organisation they tended to be among the most ideologically committed soldiers and citizens. Although they came typically (but not exclusively) from secular and left-wing backgrounds, the fact remains that they were frequently

---

[59] For an exemplary application of Berlant's ideas to the impasses of activism and political apathy in Israel, see Natanel (2016).

members of major Zionist youth movements, participants in the 'year of service' IDF volunteering programme, and even in some cases graduates of *mekhinot*. They were those for whom the idea of a moral army, and concepts such as purity of arms, tended to mean the most. This not only amplified the common sense of guilt at being unable to realise these values in practice. It also made the experience of anxiety all the more disorientating (and therefore likely to lead toward melancholia). In short, it is important to see that the predominance of guilt and anxiety as ethical responses in Breaking the Silence are a *product*, and not merely an anomaly, of Israeli militarism. Indeed, insofar as these responses produce the political limitations that I will discuss in the coming chapter, they must also be seen as part of its disciplining effects.

6 | 'Creating a Moral Conversation': The Public Activism of Breaking the Silence

We arrived in the desert near Nitzana at mid-morning, just as the December day was beginning to warm up.[1] I was travelling with a group of Breaking the Silence activists for an educational activity they had planned in the Negev desert. Every year, hundreds of high-school graduates from the kibbutz movement cycle a route around this area, stopping along the way to hear lectures and talks from various Israeli civil society organisations. Alongside other left-wing groups such as Combatants for Peace and Machsom Watch, Breaking the Silence runs a station where the youths can meet and talk with former and serving soldiers who oppose the occupation. The plan was to arrive early, set up the stalls and tents, and then wait for the youths to arrive. There were ten of us present, including two women.

I looked around. The place immediately struck me as an odd location for an educational activity. A sign on the side of the road we had stopped on read, 'Danger! Firing zone.' A large tank was parked a few hundred yards away and a couple of soldiers were standing nearby. The only distant building visible on the landscape was the (supposedly secret) nuclear reactor at Dimona. A surveillance balloon floated ominously above it. Everyone referred to it simply as *ha kur* [the reactor]. The team began to assemble the tents and stalls on the left-hand side of the road, directly beside the firing zone sign. A couple of minutes after we had set to work, an army jeep pulled up and told us to move to the other side, where the ground was less even. Ayal protested that he had set up camp in the same spot on the left-hand side at last year's event. But the soldiers would not back down, so we wearily began to dismantle things and move them over the road. 'Why does everything have to be on the right in this country?' joked Nadav.

---

[1] Field notes, Tuesday 11 December 2012.

The wind had begun to pick up, which made the task of erecting the tents, stringing up signs, and preventing testimony booklets from blowing away quite a challenge. We stretched out the canopy material and attempted to hoist it onto the stilts. Desperate to appear helpful, I grabbed a corner and tried to assist the process. However, my tent-assembling Hebrew was not very proficient (I was better with words like 'battalion', 'grenade', and 'curfew') and, compared with soldiers who had plenty of experience putting up tents, it became clear that I was being more of a hindrance than a help. I helped tie up a sign instead. After a struggle, the rudimentary camp was more or less complete.

We sat down to eat the large picnic breakfast which Ayal had brought for us. The activists ate hungrily while he briefed them on the day's work. Many of those in attendance were relatively new to the organisation and had little experience giving public talks. Ayal, Avner, and Shachar were the most experienced, followed by Nadav and Yoni. Others were there to watch and learn, and perhaps to speak informally with individuals on the sidelines. Neither of the women would be presenting. Ayal stressed that today would be tough: the kids would only be staying for a few minutes each and many would be coming and going throughout proceedings. They would be tired after the long ride and levels of prior knowledge about the occupation would be quite low. Ayal advised them to stick to giving and reading testimonies as much as possible. He warned them not to get into conversations about political solutions to the occupation, repeating that the goal of Breaking the Silence was simply to highlight the problem. He further made clear that the official line of Breaking the Silence on whether to refuse army service was that this matter was a personal choice. Finally, he added: 'We don't use the word "Nakba" and we don't use the word "Apartheid".'

* * *

Breaking the Silence is no longer a small Israeli NGO, though neither is it particularly large. In 2015, it reported income of 4,937,792 NIS (New Israeli Shekels), which equated to roughly £850,000 (Breaking the Silence, 2016b: 9).[2] Breaking the Silence receives donations from,

---

[2] By way of comparison, in their most recent financial reports, B'Tselem, probably the most renowned Israeli human rights observatory, had a budget of 9,318,169 NIS (roughly £1.5 million) in 2015 (B'Tselem, 2016: 4); Yesh Din, another human rights organisation working on legal accountability, had a budget of 6,045,236 NIS (roughly £1 million) in 2014 (Yesh Din, 2015: 4).

among others, the European Union, the Spanish and Norwegian governments, UNICEF, the Irish Catholic Church, Oxfam, Christian Aid, and the New Israel Fund. It is, in short, a medium-sized but prestigious NGO attracting a lot of confidence from foreign donors in a crowded marketplace of potential grantees.

What grounds this confidence is the ability, and willingness, of Breaking the Silence to engage a much larger section of Israeli civil society than many other NGOs. This derives primarily from the identity of its activists as soldiers, which gives them an instantly higher level of credibility in the eyes of most Israelis. It has been the use of this soldier's voice which has consistently propelled Breaking the Silence into the national consciousness. Avichai Stollar, the head of the testimonies project, divided the enhanced credibility that soldiers have in Israeli society into two aspects, factual and social.[3] From the point of view of facts, soldiers appear more credible because they were eye-witnesses and participants in the events they describe.[4] Not only this, as soldiers they are able to offer insights into the logic behind the military occupation. They also have access to information which would be difficult for researchers, especially Palestinian researchers, to obtain. This insight gives soldiers a certain kind of epistemic authority. As Avichai put it, 'You cannot say that we are naïve and do not understand the reality because we were the implementers of the reality.'[5]

Yet the social credibility accorded to soldiers in Israeli society is, if anything, stronger than the claim to epistemic authority. Serving the nation through military participation still holds high symbolic rewards in Israel, especially when it includes service in combat units (Levy, 2007: 11–15). A culture of national sacrifice sanctifies the military contribution of citizens, especially those who risk death, injury, or capture (Handelman and Shamgar-Handelman, 1997; Zerubavel, 2006). The military functions as the avatar of the nation and its soldiers are often imagined to speak in some sense on behalf of all citizens (Benziman, 2010). Moreover, a lengthy history of soldiers' testimony about the ethics of war has generated a heightened receptivity to the voice of the morally sensitive soldier. The figure of the idealised speaking soldier tends to occupy a privileged place in Israeli social hierarchies: his body

[3] Author interview with Avichai Stollar.
[4] Author interview with Dana Golan.
[5] Author interview with Avichai Stollar.

is identified as male; he is normally affluent and well-educated; he is usually of European descent (Sasson-Levy, 2002, 2003a; Weiss, 2002; Sasson-Levy and Levy, 2008). Testifiers to Breaking the Silence tend overwhelmingly to inhabit the privileged position afforded by these social trends: they have usually served in combat units and are usually from relatively wealthy secular Ashkenazi families.[6] The number of women and Mizrahi activists is disproportionately low.[7]

Breaking the Silence activists are aware of the advantages that their position affords them, as well as its problems. Acknowledging the criticism that Breaking the Silence participates in societal militarism, Avichai responded as follows:

I do agree in some ways that we are empowering . . . a discourse in which those who were combat soldiers have more ownership over what's true and what's really reality and who should be listened to and who should be heard. But I think in this sense you really need to define your aims. Are you doing it in order to reconstruct Israeli society or are you doing it in order to end a specific well-defined political reality? And we decided that we are doing the second thing. We decided that our aim is to end the military occupation of the Palestinian territories, and in this sense what we're doing is the most effective thing because you can say that we're riding on the Achilles heel of Israeli society which is [that] the fact that you wore the helmet and carried the gun gives you some kind of a card to the heart of the Israeli mainstream society. And if you're trying to influence the mainstream [of] Israeli society then you need to the find the means to do so. And I would argue that even when it comes to the greater cause, which I support, making a society which is not militarised and is not based on all these concepts, then that's a process and we cannot continue on the next step until we end the occupation.[8]

Breaking the Silence has therefore made a very explicit calculation that participating in societal militarism is a worthy price to pay for access and credibility with a wider range of people. This calculation is based on the conviction that the message which Breaking the Silence has crafted is sufficiently effective and disruptive to provoke a serious shift in Israeli public opinion about the occupation, and perhaps even to pose a significant challenge to militarism in the longer term. The

[6] Author interview with Noam Chayut.
[7] Author interviews with Eran Efrati and Gil Hillel.
[8] Author interview with Avichai Stollar.

question of whether Breaking the Silence helps to reproduce or disrupt Israeli militarism therefore turns on much more than simply its use of the privileged voice of the soldier and the perpetuation of the attendant class, race, and gender hierarchies that this implies. Any answer to this question must also take the effectiveness of this message and the campaigns used to disseminate it into account. Only then will it be clear whether the other political costs incurred have been worthwhile.

The Political Strategy of Breaking the Silence

We waited several hours at our camp for the youths to arrive.[9] During this time we sat and talked among ourselves. Nadav mentioned his plan to gather together all of the soldiers from his twelve-man unit and record a conversation with them about their experiences serving in the West Bank, in conscious imitation of *Siaḥ Loḥamim*. 'That would be great,' replied Avner, and others readily agreed. As boredom set in, Nadav began to construct a makeshift catapult out of spare materials from the camp. The atmosphere was quite jocular but masculine, with plenty of coarse language.

During this period we were only approached by a few people. A man arrived on a bicycle who introduced himself as the co-ordinator of the *Garʿin Tsabar* project, which brings Jewish volunteers from America to serve in the IDF and live on a kibbutz in co-ordination with the Israeli scouts. He seemed very interested in Breaking the Silence and began asking Ayal a series of questions. Most of all, he wanted to know exactly where and in which units each of the soldiers had served. He pointed to each person in turn to find out, including to me ('the ginger', as he called me), and seemed disappointed to learn that I had not served. At another point, the two serving soldiers walked up from the tank further down the road and asked for copies of the testimony booklets. They seemed interested.

Several members of the group, mostly relative newcomers, then started a conversation about why Breaking the Silence does not organise demonstrations. They seemed keen to pursue this kind of activism further. In response, Avner and Ayal stressed that they were in favour of demonstrations in the abstract but that the main tool of Breaking

---

[9] Field notes, Tuesday 11 December 2012, afternoon.

the Silence was educating the public rather than organising protests. It was a question of tactics rather than principle, as Avner put it.

Finally, the youths began to arrive, gradually at first and then building up to a steady stream. The leader who had been guiding them on their cycle ride announced the station to those who were stopping. He told them that this station was a joint station with two parts. This took me somewhat by surprise because I was not aware of another nearby. He then explained that the other half of the station was in fact the tank further down the road, where there were soldiers who would explain possible pathways through military service. On later inspection, it turned out that there was also a hands-on experience with a machine gun and a noticeboard covered with stories from soldiers who had served in different parts of the IDF. To these young kibbutzniks, service in the IDF and testifying to Breaking the Silence were somehow being presented as a seamless whole, as fully compatible with each other.

* * *

Breaking the Silence has a simple, primary claim to make, which is that the occupation is immoral by nature and that there is no way for it to become moral without ending.[10] As I have argued, arriving at this conclusion in the first place was the outcome of a shift from guilt to anxiety, in which the ethical experience of soldiers as voiced in testimony prompted the realisation that the immorality they perceived was a structural condition and not a product of individual failings. The message which follows from this, which has been refined over several years, is that the only way for the immorality of the occupation to end is for the occupation itself to end.[11] This moral approach is certainly distinctive among left-wing Israeli NGOs, most of which develop a critique of the occupation based on international law and human rights.

Breaking the Silence uses soldiers' testimony to persuade its audience of its viewpoint, using something like a two-stage process. The first stage is to elicit an instinctive moral response from the reader or listener. This requires testimonies which show soldiers describing the moral difficulties which they themselves faced: 'what the soldier did,

[10] Throughout this chapter I will use the terms 'immoral' or 'immorality' descriptively, rather than normatively, to indicate the view of Breaking the Silence.
[11] Author interviews with Dana Golan and Avichai Stollar.

what the soldier saw . . . something that describes what was going on in a soldier's mind because that's what most touches people'.[12] In this, the social position of the soldier as a respectable, moral voice of the nation is particularly helpful. Furthermore, the role of emotions, as explored in the previous chapter, has its most powerful part to play here. Occasionally, although less commonly, it is sometimes the lack of moral reflection which stands out when soldiers report instances of violence as if they were unremarkable or justified features of their everyday world (e.g. Breaking the Silence, 2010: 56–7, 72–3).

The second stage is to show that this immoral condition is structural and that individual soldiers cannot change the fundamental pattern of violence that the occupation projects. This is usually achieved through the simple accumulation of evidence of immorality, which is why Breaking the Silence is constantly seeking to expand the number of soldiers who have testified.[13] Another strategy is to show the structural limits imposed on individual soldiers. Very often, testimony will show soldiers struggling to improve the morality of the occupation by changing their behaviour or encouraging others to do so, with the inevitable result that the fundamental problems remain unresolved. In its more sophisticated forms, this has involved editing testimonies in such a way as to reveal these structural dimensions. In the largest collection of testimonies released by Breaking the Silence, published in English as the book *Our Harsh Logic*, the aim is precisely this (Breaking the Silence, 2013). The material is subdivided into four sections analysing different terms used to describe the purpose of the military regime governing the West Bank: prevention, separation, the fabric of life, and law enforcement.

The focus on morality in the public advocacy of Breaking the Silence is a deliberate, strategic choice. Ayal Kantz, the former educational director of the organisation, explained the rationale behind this decision to me, arguing that it forces arguments away from the usual discussions about plausible political solutions or the presence or lack of a 'partner for peace' to a discussion about the fundamental problem of the occupation and its immorality. The idea is to change the discourse surrounding the occupation, moving it away from typical discussions about security and diplomacy: 'my job, or Breaking the Silence's job,

---

[12] Author interview with Ayal Kantz.
[13] Author interviews with Dana Golan and Noam Chayut.

is to implement a new discourse, that point of view that we're not so used to, that point of view we're not usually talking about [at] Friday [night] dinners: the point of view of testimonies'. This requires constantly diverting from a political discussion, in which everyone has opinions and authority, towards a conversation about the morality of what Israeli soldiers are doing, in which Breaking the Silence is best placed to succeed:

I'm not an expert in the two-state solution. I cannot contribute anything as Breaking the Silence towards the two-state solution and I would probably lose that discussion . . . And also we would miss our target . . . First of all, you would find yourself on the defensive; and second of all, you wouldn't have a lot of tools to defend with. Now, as long you're speaking Breaking the Silence, as long as you're speaking testimony, you're on the offensive side and you have a lot of tools to be on that side.[14]

Avichai Stollar concurred with this assessment of the discursive strategy, emphasising the importance of adding a moral supplement to public discussions about the occupation:

When it's purely political, your ability to convince people is much more limited . . . I mean, 'moral', at least for our audiences, is supposed to be a common ground. When you're saying something is immoral that's what we're trying to convince them [of] because we want the discourse to start from there. In this reality within Israel the discourse when it comes to the conflict is highly polarised. It's polarised because – and not only polarised, it's leaning to the right when comes to the general opinion – it's because the discourse completely ignores the implications of the occupation. It's about our security needs, it's about our historical right, it's about the intention of the other side, it's about the fragments of a possible peace agreement, eviction of settlements, right of return. It deals with the things that terrify Israelis – suicide bombing, the existence of a new country West of the Jordan River. But as long as this is the discourse you can never win . . . [T]he right-wing would always have the upper hand because it will always have the security card. But we're coming from a point that we believe that at least, again, within our audience, that we believe that the majority of Israelis do accept the . . . this mantra here that we do have the most moral army in the world. It's not just a PR stunt. It's a genuine belief and a genuine desire of the Israeli public. We want to be moral, we truly do. And we believe that if this is the starting point, or if this could be the starting point, then there is a chance to fundamentally change the discourse regarding it.[15]

It is therefore precisely insofar as the ethics of Israeli militarism produces the belief that the IDF is 'the most moral army in the world' that Breaking the Silence believe they have the opportunity to change public discourse about the occupation. By arguing that the only way to be a moral army is to cease the occupation, rather than through pedagogical improvements to the conduct of individual soldiers, Breaking the Silence believes that this moral critique can acquire political force. Indeed, it is the strong conviction among activists that this moral message, generic though it might be, is a political statement: 'We are political because saying that occupation is immoral is a political statement.'[16] Activists also argue that this sets them apart from other NGOs in Israel, because Breaking the Silence takes a normative stance and calls for the occupation to end, rather than simply documenting human rights abuses: 'we are a political organisation because when you are saying that the only way out is by ending the occupation that is political per definition'.[17]

Valid though these points may be, they overlook the trajectory of the ethical process explored in the previous chapter, which entails the possibility that anxiety can relapse into guilt. By focusing on a message with primarily moral content and by delivering it in the ethical form of testimony, the public campaigning of Breaking the Silence remains exposed to this prospect. Its target remains one of moral improvement achieved through a process of ethical work in listening to testimony. In this sense, it remains isomorphic with the pedagogical tendencies I have explored previously, even when it is directed towards an ostensibly political goal. As I will illustrate below, it is relatively easy for militarism to strip away this political element, especially when it so inchoate, and to reinstate testimony as a military ethico-pedagogical tool.

This process is made much easier by the tendency of Breaking the Silence to frame the discussion in purely moral and even pedagogical terms, even when wider political issues are pressing. For example,

---

[15] Author interview with Avichai Stollar.
[16] Author interview with Ayal Kantz.
[17] Author interview with Avichai Stollar.

following Operation Protective Edge, the new executive director of Breaking the Silence wrote in *The Guardian* that she was concerned that the values of the IDF she had served in as an air force officer were being undermined:

> I was made commander of a course for air force officers. I taught cadets how to take responsibility for their actions as officers. We studied the lessons of previous air force operations. I taught them that the IDF is the most moral army in the world, and that the air force is the most moral corps within the IDF . . . I believed with all my heart that we were doing what needed to be done. If there were casualties, they were a necessary evil. If there were mistakes, they would be investigated. Things have changed, and now I can no longer have that certainty. (Novak, 2014b)

The continuities evident here between military ethical pedagogy and political activism also extend to the way in which Breaking the Silence distributes its materials. Following the publication in 2009 of a booklet of testimonies concerning violence towards Palestinian children, Breaking the Silence set up stalls outside high schools in Haifa, Tel Aviv, and Jerusalem and handed them out to students. The rhetorical point was that, if Palestinian children were old enough to be killed by the IDF, then Israeli children were certainly old enough to read about it. Yet when I discussed the reasoning for targeting this social group with the executive director, there were signs of the continuing temptation to frame Breaking the Silence's contribution as pedagogical:

> We believe people should know as fast, as soon as possible. And then you give it to them before they join the army. So at first it might shape their idea. And maybe they choose to join the army or not to join the army . . . so maybe you managed to give them one moment to think about it and maybe it will prevent them from becoming those abuser soldiers at the checkpoints. Of course, for us, as long as the occupation is there it does not make a difference whether you have . . . The checkpoint is the story, it's not the soldier. So long as there are soldiers standing at checkpoints the problem is not solved. But for us of course we prefer that the soldiers that are standing at checkpoints will be the ones that are not abusing Palestinians and so on . . . So maybe if I give them time to read that or think about it . . . maybe I will contribute something [to] changing the reality as well.[18]

[18] Author interview with Dana Golan.

These comments illustrate the extremely delicate balance between a political critique couched in moral terms and a straightforward case of military ethical pedagogy. It is possible to see how the constant oscillation between guilt and anxiety produces this ambiguity. Whereas the focus on the behaviour of individuals within the army derives from the affect of guilt, anxiety produces a more thoroughgoing critique of the entire political and military apparatus of the occupation. It is usually clear in the minds of Breaking the Silence activists that there is an important difference between these two approaches. Yet, as I will describe, this difference is far from reliably absorbed by the Israeli audience targeted by these campaigns. Indeed, the tendency of anxiety to relapse into guilt I have noted is increased when these discourses approach more closely the ethical forms of pedagogy described earlier in this book. The shrewdest of Breaking the Silence activists are usually quite aware of this danger. As Noam Chayut put it to me, 'The strength is that it's a moral organisation, rather than just a political one. And the weakness is that it's a moral organisation, rather than just a political one.'[19] The hope is that this strategic awareness can prevent the weaknesses from overtaking the strengths; in practice, this outcome seems far from secure.

'Bringing Our Parents to Hebron': Tours and Lectures

The activists split themselves up and began giving individual talks to small groups of youths.[20] I circulated among the talks trying to hear each of them in turn. I started with Avner, who is probably the most polished of the presenters. He began by introducing himself and the organisation, but he wasted no time in getting into details: 'My name is Avner, I served in the paratroopers. I am a member of Breaking the Silence, a group of soldiers who talk about the things they did when they served in the territories. Things like straw widows. Do you know what a straw widow is?' A straw widow is a military term for a house occupation, which involves turning a Palestinian home into a temporary military base. They can last for a few days, during which time the family are confined to one room, or for as long as several years, necessitating a full eviction of the family.

[19] Author interview with Noam Chayut.
[20] Field notes, Tuesday 11 December 2012, afternoon.

As I circulated around the talks, it turned out that straw widows
were a very common topic of conversation. Both Shachar and Avner
emphasised that they did not feel at all 'professional' after conducting a straw widow, but rather embarrassed at what they had done.
Shachar remembered the mud his soldiers traipsed into the house during winter and how dirty they had left it. Nadav told the story of his
first straw widow, when he dragged an 11-year-old child from his bed;
he said the image of the child's face would stay with him forever. All
of the activists worked very hard to emphasise that these stories were
not simply individual failings but part of a bigger picture of the reality
of military rule. 'I couldn't have done anything more,' Shachar said,
stressing that it is impossible to be 'nice' all the time, day after day,
when serving in the West Bank.

During the post-talk questions, one of the youths asked Avner
whether he thought that soldiers should stop going into houses. Avner
said that it wasn't as simple as this, since straw widows were only one
part of a system of military rule. Countering the questioner's impulse
to find ways to improve the IDF's performance, Avner pushed the
youths to question the whole logic of military rule, and not just the
soldiers' tactics. Both Avner and Shachar also referred to the upcoming
elections, remarking that many of the youths would have a vote and
could possibly help change the political reality. However, they resisted
requests to give recommendations about who to vote for. Shachar
instead asked the youths to make a decision 'based on knowledge',
even if they disagreed with Breaking the Silence, or even if they were
to decide that Israel had 'no choice' but to continue the occupation.

* * *

Breaking the Silence have been leading tours to Hebron since the
organisation was established. In a common refrain, the activists often
say that they realised after the success of the first exhibition that it
would not be enough to bring Hebron to Tel Aviv: they would also
need to bring Tel Aviv to Hebron. In the more telling formulation of
one activist, this meant 'bringing our parents to Hebron' and showing
them what their children had been asked to do in the name of Israeli
society.[21] At first the tours were loosely organised.[22] A group of activ-

---

[21] Field notes, 29 October 2012.
[22] Author interview with Ilan Fathi.

ists hired a bus between themselves and walked sporadically around the centre of Hebron, pointing out features of interest and explaining what they had done while serving there.[23] They would bring friends, family, journalists, and tourists with them. The tours soon began to generate controversy among the settlers living in the city centre. This often degenerated into disorder when settlers shouted over the tour guide and threw things at the group. As a result of these disturbances, Breaking the Silence faced several struggles with the IDF and the High Court to gain permission to run tours in the city. However, as the years have progressed – and despite continued disruptions and attempts by settlers to block them – Breaking the Silence tours to Hebron have become routine.

The route, timings, and content have been steadily regularised.[24] The tours around the city follow a clear path of stations, which is adjusted according to the preference of individual guides and time constraints. After an introductory lecture about the history of Hebron and Breaking the Silence on the coach journey from Jerusalem, the tour first stops in Kiryat Arba, a settlement to the north of Hebron. There the group visits the grave of Baruch Goldstein,[25] still honoured by local residents, before moving on to the 'H2' area of the city under direct Israeli control.[26] Beginning at the Ibrahimi Mosque/Tomb of the Patriarchs complex, the tour walks down Shuhada Street, formerly the main shopping district in Hebron but now completely closed to Palestinian pedestrians and shopkeepers. Along this main street, the tour makes several stops – at the entrance to the Palestinian Casbah, at the site of the murder of two Jewish settlers, at the settlements of Avraham Avinu, Beit Romano, Beit Hadassah, and Tel Rumeida, at the military base on the site of the old bus station, at the main checkpoint between H1 and H2, and at the permanently closed chicken and

---

[23] Some indication of the nature of these early tours is available in a video produced by the organisation (Breaking the Silence, 2011b).

[24] Author interview with Ilan Fathi.

[25] Baruch Goldstein was a religious settler who murdered twenty-nine Palestinians in a massacre at the Ibrhami Mosque in 1994. He was eventually subdued and killed by surviving worshippers.

[26] Under the agreement signed in 1997, security deployments in Hebron were divided between the Palestinian Authority (H1) and Israel (H2). The IDF retains a constant presence in H2 but has largely withdrawn from the rest of the city. Regular incursions into H1 still take place and the whole city remains under Israeli military control.

gold markets. The tour usually concludes with a talk at a Palestinian grassroots activist centre called 'Youth Against Settlements' on the hill above the city.

This itinerary has become completely routine over the years. Rarely does a week go by when there is not a tour running in either Hebrew or English; during most weeks there is more than one. Having several tours on a single day is not uncommon. The tours have therefore in some sense become part of the fabric of the city. Since the area which the tours explore is under constant curfew, the inhabitants can easily recognise them as they progress around the streets. The few remaining Palestinian shopkeepers left in central Hebron are on friendly terms with the activists; street peddlers selling bracelets rely on the tours as a source of income; the settlers observe the tours and frequently approach them to contribute their opinions, usually in a civil but slightly intimidating fashion; soldiers on duty often watch over the tours from their posts, occasionally listening in but usually appearing unmoved; European volunteers from the Temporary International Presence in Hebron (TIPH) observatory regularly pass on their encouragement.

Although there are frequently violent clashes in Hebron, the tours usually remain unaffected by this. Occasionally, demonstrations in the 'H1' zone are audible, punctuated by the boom of sound grenades. Soldiers sometimes warn the tours away from certain areas, citing the threat of stone throwing from the Casbah. One tour I attended received a dose of teargas when the wind carried it back from the checkpoint where it had been fired. But such events are uncommon. For the most part, the violence of the occupation in Hebron is a slow violence which is not immediately obvious. Hints of the coercive regime in action emerge here and there: arrested Palestinians walking with a patrol of soldiers; Palestinian children warned away from forbidden areas; and small arguments at checkpoints. Yet the coercion must generally be inferred from the landscape, with its empty streets, shop doors welded shut, barricades, caged windows, and soldiers moving across the rooftops above. The area is bleak, uncanny, and depressing.

Intersections between war and tourism are not uncommon. The consumption of danger and insecurity is often a powerful attraction for the traveller's gaze (cf. Lisle, 2000). Yet Hebron must surely rank among the most extreme examples of tourism directed at a conflict which is ongoing, rather than simply memorialised, and where visitors consume the violence as it unfolds before their eyes. Activism has a curious role to play in this war/tourism dynamic. For foreign visitors, activist political commitments often feed into the desire to visit a site of conflict (Landy, 2008). One former Breaking the Silence tour guide was quite cynical about their presence on tours for this reason:

> . . . every day there would be a bunch of 40 Dutch, lefty 19-year-old girls, 45 extreme left-wing British guys, 25-year-olds, 35 Protestant Priests for Peace. And they're there and it doesn't matter what you're going to say. So they're left wing, they think Israel should get out the West Bank, they think Israel is a war criminal . . . blah, blah . . . they think all the regular lefty things that they think . . . I felt that the group is not interested in what I had to say . . . They wanted to go back home and tell their Dutch, British friends that they were in Hebron with Breaking the Silence. It became a brand . . . I was very disappointed by it.[27]

These days, however, the majority of tours are run for Israelis in Hebrew, even though the English tours remain very popular. There has been a very deliberate attempt to target the Israeli audience, in part due to the feeling that tours for foreign visitors are often a case of preaching to the converted.

When Israelis join Breaking the Silence tours the activist–tourist dynamic is less obvious than in the case of foreign visitors, but it is still possible to discern. In the first place this is because the tours take place alongside the arrival of coach-loads of religious tourists who have come to visit the holy sites. Mostly, however, it is because Hebron is still being *consumed* on Breaking the Silence tours, even when this process remains largely detached from the political economy of leisure and travel. The tours make use of the built environment and the people who live there as tools for advocacy and education. Moreover, since access to the space of Hebron is unequally distributed, in that it is forbidden to Palestinians, the tours participate in a political economy of gaze, circulation, and association which is fully implicated in the colonisation of the West Bank (Weizman, 2007: 111–38; Ophir et al., 2009; Collins, 2012: esp. 79–108). When former soldiers and reservists lead civilians, some of whom may also be reservists or even future soldiers, on tours around Hebron to view the realities of military rule and to assess its morality, it

---

[27] Author interview with Ilan Fathi.

is difficult not to see this as an example of the Israeli occupation watching itself happen. One might even say that in this movement of gazes a certain elementary structure of ethical subjectivity is being produced in which a critical faculty of the ego looks back upon itself.

The crucial question is what *kind* of ethical subject this is. Is it driven primarily by anxiety or guilt, by structural political critique or moral self-examination? Breaking the Silence activists remain convinced that it is primarily the former. Indeed, the tours are considered the most powerful educational tool available to the organisation. In the words of the former executive director:

I know that if I bring 3000 people to Hebron every year, it does something. It's difficult for me to say what it does, but I know because I hear people talking about the tours in Hebron four years after it took place and . . . pointing at this point as a turning point in the shaping of their political views or their perceptions of the situation.[28]

This hoped-for process of political transformation is understood as affective as well as merely informative. On this point it is worth comparing the tours in Hebron with another tour that Breaking the Silence operates to the South Hebron Hills. Far fewer activists in Breaking the Silence have experience serving as soldiers in this area. Moreover, the area is much larger and more complicated than Hebron. Whereas there are clear signs of division and military rule in Hebron itself, in the South Hebron Hills the military presence is far less concentrated. In this area, the occupation works through legalistic mechanisms, including the confiscation of farmland as 'state land', the use of 'closed military zones' and nature reserves to restrict movement, planning regulations, and the *post factum* justification of temporary settlement outposts (Weizman, 2007: 87–110; Gordon, 2008: 116–46). In many ways, this area is a far more appropriate place to explain the violence of the occupation, since it is more typical of wider trends. However, fewer tours go there, simply because it is harder to make as emotive a point about it. Ayal described the relationship between the two tours:

In some way, the tour in Hebron hits you much more than the tour in South Hebron. It's much more vivid, and it's personal – you see the place. But I

[28] Author interview with Dana Golan.

think for everyone who did the South Hebron tour after they did the Hebron tour, the South Hebron tour was much more troubling because then you understand the mechanism and you understand that it's not only Hebron, it's not only a certain place – it's a whole mechanism. But at the end of the day, what bothers you are the pictures of Hebron . . . You need to understand that this testimony is not a single testimony, it's a part of a mechanism, it's part of a bigger thing . . . but what I believe is that you can talk about the mechanism until tomorrow, what people go home with is that testimony that made them feel 'oh my God'. . .[29]

The relationship between moral outrage and a political critique of 'the mechanism' is complex. Ideally, the trajectory leads from the former to the latter, from guilt to anxiety. However, it is the initial and emotional moral reaction which often leaves a more lasting impression. As Ayal indicates, additional work is needed to ensure that this response is contextualised as a political reaction to a feature of a wider system. The difficulty that Breaking the Silence faces is that it is precisely on political grounds that many Israelis are prepared to accept the 'moral price' of the occupation. Without any engagement with this side of the question, it is very easy for a supposedly distinct sphere of morality to remain cordoned off from the wider debate. It is also very easy to reinsert the moral content of testimonies back into a militarised ethical process.

On one of the tours of Hebron I observed, which was organised for students of the Hebrew University, these issues of the distinction between morality and politics were raised quite sharply.[30] The group was standing underneath a stone archway near the entrance to the Casbah and the Avraham Avinu settlement. Usually the tour remains in the courtyard further from the settlement. However, this time the soldier stationed there had asked us to move under the archway and closer to the settlement. He was concerned about stones being thrown from the Casbah. Shachar, who was leading the tour, commented wryly that the settlers might also throw stones at us if we moved any closer. As we shuffled under the archway, he began taking questions from the group. One student commented that, although the lack of morality of the situation in Hebron might be evident, there was still a political discussion to be had about the Israeli presence there. Shachar agreed that

[29] Author interview with Ayal Kantz.
[30] The following account is derived from field notes dated 14 November 2012.

there was an important political discussion to be had, but stressed that it was not the role of Breaking the Silence to participate in it. Instead, he said, their place was to encourage a moral conversation.

We walked further along the route of the tour, and I tried to catch the attention of Ayal and Yuli, the new executive director, to ask for their thoughts on this exchange. They were deep in conversation. When I finally spoke with Yuli, it emerged they had already been discussing this question between themselves. She asked me why I was interested in the exchange, and I mentioned the distinction that Shachar had drawn between morality and politics. It was clear from her slightly frustrated expression that she recognised the problem I was getting at. She replied that it was important to be 'strategic'. 'You need to understand the discourse here,' she told me. We stopped at another station where Shachar discussed the moral difficulties presented by protecting the settler community in Hebron given that it was located in the heart of a Palestinian city. He argued that the moral cost of defending the settlement, which required curfews, street closures, and strict control of Palestinian movement, was the main issue, not the ideology of the settlers. Breaking the Silence does not really have a political argument with the settlers, he said, just as it does not really have a political argument with the army. In his view, the settlers had already done an 'accounting of their souls' [heshbon nefesh] and were comfortable with the moral costs of being in Hebron. He said that Breaking the Silence instead wanted to have a moral conversation with the wider majority of Israeli society and to get them to go through the same process of self-examination.

Clearly, however, there are political limits to the use of this ethical process of self-examination, especially when it is an approach that is commonly used as a technique of military ethical pedagogy. These limits were readily apparent at the lectures organised by Breaking the Silence at the Hebrew University itself, where students from settlements in the West Bank frequently attend.[31] At one lecture I observed, a settler directly challenged Ayal to be more explicit about his political aims.[32] The settler distinguished very clearly between two levels of activity – one of which was aimed at improving the conduct of the IDF, the other of which was aimed at ending the occupation. He said

[31] Field notes, 8 January 2013.
[32] Field notes, 5 December 2012.

that he could agree to the former but not to the latter. Furthermore, he claimed it was fundamentally dishonest to argue that withdrawing from the occupied territories was a moral issue when it has fundamentally political dimensions. It is indeed a common criticism from the Right that Breaking the Silence hide their politics behind a moral discussion.

Another lecture at the university was presented by Dana Golan, the outgoing executive director. The right-wing organisation *Im Tirtzu*[33] has a number of activists among the student body who regularly attend the lectures and events organised by Breaking the Silence in order to argue with the lecturers. The *Im Tirtzu* activists left leaflets on every chair in the lecture room describing Breaking the Silence as liars who try to delegitimise Israel. Dana introduced the organisation and described her own experience of conducting a house search in Hebron. As she opened for questions, she asked if anyone else had served in Hebron; two of the *Im Tirtzu* activists raised their hands. They argued continuously with her throughout the questions, trying to coax her into declaring her political preferences. Dana refused and continuously tried to stick to what she had described in her opening remarks as 'creating a moral conversation' [*le'orer diun musari*] about the occupation. After several minutes of arguing, she conceded that if the *Im Tirtzu* activists did not see a moral problem in the occupation, then she could have no further argument with them.

I had seen one of the *Im Tirtzu* activists before, while observing a Breaking the Silence information booth on campus. *Im Tirtzu* had established their own directly next door.[34] I introduced myself to him and asked for his opinion on the work of Breaking the Silence. He said that they didn't tell the whole picture, only a part of it; he effectively reprised the 'rotten apple' thesis that incidents of violence are attributable to individual failings, not structural problems. What was most interesting about his response, however, was that he used a testimony of his own to make his point. He told me about his time during the army, when he had been an officer in the armoured corps. During one

---

[33] *Im Tirtzu* is a right-wing organisation which calls for a 'second Zionist revolution', aimed mainly at defending and promoting Israel's name and Jewish character both at home and abroad. It has more recently been associated with increasingly public and vicious attacks on Breaking the Silence.

[34] Field notes, 28 November 2012.

arrest operation he told his soldiers that they were only supposed to arrest and not to do anything else. However, one of his soldiers put plastic handcuffs very tightly and painfully around the wrists of the Palestinian in order to cause him discomfort. The activist was proud to tell me that he reported the incident and that the soldier spent twenty days in jail and was denied leave because of it. He said that if an army is imposing an occupation there will always be moments of transgression, just as in any large organisation there will always be problems and individuals who do wrong. But he said Breaking the Silence elevate these inevitable occurrences to the status of the norm, which was not a fair picture.

Despite these interventions and questions, there was no doubting that each of these events – the tour, the lecture, the information stall – went well from the point of view of Breaking the Silence. They were well attended and generated a lot of interest from the audience. Indeed, for Ayal, a sign that the work that Breaking the Silence does is effective is that audiences exhibit at least some emotional reaction:

After every lecture that you go to, you feel like 'wow, that's important' because the people I met, the majority of them, even if it was hard for them to accept me, they more or less realise that there is something wrong and many times you get very, very good reactions . . . Even if the majority were irritated by you, it touches them. You feel that you touched the people. You feel that we really want to be different. The problem is people don't know about the situation and people don't know what to do . . . when I'm giving a lecture I'm much more concerned [if] people tell me, 'ah, okay, so what?' but it never happens. It's either people are . . . very irritated, some people are . . . very shocked, but it touches them.[35]

These signals can also be misleading, however. As Lauren Berlant has written of ethics in the service of politics:

Self-transforming compassionate recognition and its cognate forms of solidarity *are* necessary for making political movements thrive contentiously against all sorts of privilege, but they have also provided a means for making minor structural adjustments seem like major events, because the theatre of compassion is emotionally intense. (Berlant, 2011: 182)

---

[35] Author interview with Ayal Kantz.

In Berlant's view, attention to the affective rewards of ethical activity can reveal its political shortcomings: activism which *feels* worthy and important does not necessarily translate into effective political change. Indeed, it might actually distract from it in favour of the pursuit of minor, cosmetic, or phantasmic improvements. For several of the critics of Breaking the Silence described above, working *within* the military to make moral improvements is a more worthy approach than public critique of the occupation as a whole. This seems to be the principal lesson they draw from their campaigns. For all the professions of the importance of understanding the occupation as a mechanism which is structurally and irredeemably immoral, then, at a certain point the 'cruel optimism' of Breaking the Silence activism begins to converge with more conventional forms of the ethics of Israeli militarism. This convergence of ethical responses becomes more palpable the closer one gets to the military apparatus itself, as I will show next.

* * *

We left the site in the late afternoon and headed back to Beer Sheva, from where we were travelling our separate ways.[36] Ayal invited me to join them for the debriefing at a local Indian restaurant, and I gladly accepted. The general feeling was that the day had gone very well. Something like 600 youths had passed through the station, Ayal estimated, though I thought this number rather optimistic. Yoni remarked that high-school kids were much easier to talk to than students or adults, who often prove difficult to persuade.

Ayal invited the activists to evaluate their performances and began with himself. The most difficult part of the day for him was an exchange with a youth who had asked him to talk about possible political solutions to the occupation. This, as Ayal had indicated earlier, is a very common but difficult question. This is principally because Breaking the Silence has no real answer to it – only ways to avoid it. The youth had continued to ask 'what do you propose?' [*ma 'ata matsi'a*] over and over again; and Ayal had lamented that he had allowed himself to get stuck in this 'loop', leaving not enough time to read testimonies.

Others remarked that this was indeed the most common and difficult question. Shachar estimated that 90 per cent of the questions he had received were either 'what is the solution?' or 'should I or others

---

[36] Field notes, Tuesday 11 December 2012, evening.

refuse to do army service?' Many of the activists seemed dissatisfied with the answers Breaking the Silence gives to this question, and much of the conversation revolved around effective strategies for drawing discussion away from 'solutions' and towards testimonies. Ayal also tried to argue that arguing that the occupation has to end is a concrete enough proposal to serve as a solution.

Avner remarked that, however satisfied people were with that as a solution, the main contribution that Breaking the Silence could make was to get people to talk about 'the occupation' in the first place. It was important, he thought, 'not to be afraid of' this term and to try and let it enter public consciousness. Yoni remarked that he often likes to begin by talking about 'military control' [*shliṭa tsva'it*] and gradually work his way towards the term 'occupation' [*kibush*].

The group then turned to me, and asked for my impressions of the day. Not wanting to sound too downcast, I remarked that I was struck by how little variation there was in the content of both the lectures and the audience questions. I had been attending Breaking the Silence events for some time by this point, so it is true that very little sounded new to me; but, particularly on that day, I had seen several talks arrive precisely at the 'loop' Ayal described. Even among what could be described as one of the most sympathetic audiences possible for Breaking the Silence, the question of 'the solution' and political action remained unanswered. Instead, following the talks, the youths had picked up their bikes, cycled down the road, and gone to see the tank.

'Bringing Our PTSD into the *mekhina*': Breaking the Silence at Pre-military Academies

We sat in a small circle on the patch of grass in front of the Ibrahimi Mosque in Hebron, an area which is forbidden to Muslims, who must enter the complex from the rear.[37] Avner was about to introduce his tour of Hebron to the students of Ein Prat pre-military academy, a mixed academy of religious and secular students located in the West Bank. Like many pre-military academies, the students of Ein Prat visit Hebron every year. The night before they had stayed with settlers in

---

[37] Fieldnotes, 10 March 2013, afternoon.

the heart of Hebron; this afternoon they were going to meet Breaking the Silence and hear an alternative perspective.

Avner began in dramatic fashion. Without introducing himself, he read directly from the first testimony booklet Breaking the Silence produced. One student was not comfortable with this and attempted to disrupt the reading: 'Excuse me? Who are you?' Avner was not deterred. He finished reading the passage and then told them who he was. He explained that he grew up in a religious family and that he attended yeshiva when he was young. He told them of his relations living in Kfar Adumim in the West Bank, where the pre-military academy is located. He said that he did a year of volunteering before joining the paratroopers and that he had always tried to be a moral and professional soldier. Then he told the story of his first straw widow operation, and how – despite the disruption it had caused the family living in the house – it had only been a practice run. He said that the biggest question the occupation raises is a moral question. He was careful to emphasise that he understood the settlers and the religious significance of Hebron; but he also referred to the importance of keeping *mitsvot* [religious duties] and observing 'moral limits'.

In the typical fashion of Breaking the Silence, Avner was attempting to hold a moral conversation with the students about the occupation. The reaction was mixed. Some students raised the issue of the foreign funding that Breaking the Silence receives and criticised the organisation for giving Israel a bad name abroad. Others seemed more receptive but were looking for ideas on how to improve things. As usual, Avner demurred from offering political solutions. Likewise, he stated emphatically that Breaking the Silence was not interested in making the IDF more moral in the situation it was in, but rather in changing an immoral situation.

The students were intelligent and quite knowledgeable. When Avner raised the topic of the 'neighbour procedure' (under which the IDF uses Palestinians as human shields when entering suspicious houses), one of them countered with the observation that the Supreme Court had made this practice illegal. Avner responded by saying that he himself had used the 'neighbour procedure' when he was a soldier in 2006, one year after it was made illegal. At the time, he had no idea that it was a forbidden practice, he said. The students were quite shocked by this revelation and pressed him for more details.

What stuck in my mind most from this introductory talk, however, was not the content of the discussion but what was taking place in the background. At a certain moment, Avner remarked on the fact that the area we were sitting in was closed off to Muslims. He said that the Palestinian children currently playing on it were liable to be removed at any moment. The discussion then continued and moved on to other issues. But sure enough, as Avner predicted, two soldiers soon walked over to the children, who were no older than ten, and shouted at them, ordering them to leave. The children did not listen and continued to play. One of the soldiers then marched towards them and pushed one of the boys, before grabbing him and dragging him out of the area. I had been coming to Hebron for months by this point but I had never seen such direct violence against children. The students from Ein Prat, however, barely turned their heads. They were too interested in what Avner had to say.

* * *

Breaking the Silence has been active at pre-military academies since at least 2009.[38] The education director at that time, Ilan Fathi, approached them as part of an attempt to reach mainstream Israeli society, rather than simply the growing crowd of foreign media interested in the organisation. His personal motivations for doing so were a mixture of sympathy for the future soldiers and a hope that he might persuade them to refuse army service:

> . . . *mekhinot* are usually the salt of the earth. Very good kids, well educated, good families, volunteering. And they would go to the best combat units in the IDF, which means they're going to see the hideous things and do the worst things and not have any chance to take the easy way out. I don't know if the original idea was that I feel bad for them, that someone should tell them what they're going to do[. . .] I don't know what was stronger: the feeling bad for them thing, or the political activism of telling people before they recruit what they're going to do, hoping their going to refuse to serve the IDF.

Officially, Breaking the Silence never calls on soldiers to refuse to serve. Privately, a number of activists hope for this outcome without being able to say it. The most common answer I received when I asked

---

[38] Author interview with Ilan Fathi.

for the justification for speaking with *mekhinot* was that they are an effective way to reach students who have ambitions to enter leadership roles in society, either in education, social work, or politics. The fact of their impending army service was downplayed as coincidental.[39]

Getting access to the *mekhinot* was very difficult in the first instance. Only a few academies allowed them to come, and then only in tightly controlled circumstances. Ilan recognised that this limited exposure to Breaking the Silence was quite ineffective, and perhaps even harmful:

One of us would go talk for an hour and a half and go and that's it. Without us controlling the discussion afterwards, without making sure that it's being held within a context. And you have no idea what's the discourse around your talk. In the religious *mekhinot*, in the beginning, we would come after the teachers in the *mekhina* for 45 minutes would tell them, don't take anything they say for granted, they are a bunch of liars, they are a bunch of traitors, they're ruining their country . . . And it would be easier for me to talk to those kids . . . because there was a certain context, because they expect something, because they are trying to understand this within a certain frame: rotten apples in the military, traitors. They are trying to understand somehow. But in *mekhinat* Rabin these guys were shocked, really really shocked. I mean, we brought our PTSD into the *mekhina*, put it there and left.

In fact, for this reason, it was initially much harder for Breaking the Silence to get access to left-leaning academies. The more right-wing academies were confident in their ability to portray the organisation as unreliable and unpatriotic, whereas the left-wing academies feared that their discourse would be subversive once it was accepted as plausible.[40] This trend was only reversed when Rabin Academy, one of the earliest academies to invite Breaking the Silence to speak, held its widely publicised and controversial event in which veterans from Operation Cast Lead spoke about their experiences.[41] After this point, students from *mekhinot* across Israel began to ask for Breaking the Silence to visit. This upsurge in interest in the organisation took place at a time when opinion around it was polarising, especially as a result of the release of its testimonies about Operation Cast Lead and the publication of the Goldstone Report, which drew on them as

[39] Author interviews with Ayal Kantz and Dana Golan.
[40] Author interview with Ayal Kantz.
[41] I analysed this event in detail in Chapter 4.

evidence. Religious academies gradually stopped inviting the organisation, to the extent that it is almost unheard of for Breaking the Silence to visit them today. The result of all these developments has been that Breaking the Silence became a regular fixture at secular and mixed pre-military academies, and for a period they had some form of interaction with almost all of them each year.

This is not to say that their presence in pre-military academies remains uncontroversial among the staff of *mekhinot*. Erez Eshel, the founder of Ein Prat Academy and a senior figure in the leadership of the *mekhinot*, has tried very hard to prevent them visiting. Ayal, the education director during the period of my fieldwork, claimed to have received abusive phone calls from Eshel about their work in academies. He also said that some academy staff refuse to allow Breaking the Silence to visit, citing heavy pressure from Eshel as their reason.[42] For the most part, however, the main impact of this pressure has been to constrain rather than prevent the work of Breaking the Silence:

I think what's hard is not to get us in, it's to get us in the way we want . . . what started happening this year – very, very much from the managers – is to limit our meetings, so . . . what we're trying to do is a tour but not a meeting before, and not a five-hour tour but a two-and-a-half-hour tour.[43]

The consequence of this pressure has been that, although Breaking the Silence remains highly active in pre-military academies, they do so decreasingly on their own terms.

The first lecture by Breaking the Silence that I witnessed at a pre-military academy took place at Telem Academy in Jaffa, a mixed academy associated with the Reform movement.[44] It was 8:30 am and most of the students had just woken up. Many of them sat with bowls of cereal in the small lecture room while the talk took place. Nadav, the lecturer on that day, began by emphasising very clearly that Breaking the Silence was not interested in helping the students be better soldiers but rather in talking with them about the occupation. He gave several testimonies from his own experience, including a straw widow

---

[42] Author interview with Ayal Kantz.
[43] Author interview with Ayal Kantz.
[44] The following description is from my field notes of 29 November 2012.

operation and a house mapping exercise.[45] In each case he stressed how he had made an effort to be polite and to clean up after entering a house but that it still felt wrong. 'We gave candies to the children and then arrested their dads,' he said. He then played the students a video from Hawara checkpoint. This video is commonly used by Breaking the Silence at its educational events (see Breaking the Silence, 2011a). It depicts the daily drudgery of passing through the checkpoint, showing long queues of Palestinians waiting at the ramshackle barriers while soldiers shout at them to maintain order. On several occasions in the video we witness violence from soldiers towards civilians. At one point, a man is beaten and detained in front of his wife and small children.

The most astonishing thing about this video, however, is not the content but its source: it was filmed by the IDF Education Corps and then subsequently leaked. The purpose of the video appears to be to document the problems that soldiers might face when on duty at a checkpoint. It features several interviews with the soldiers who acted violently, in which they discuss their difficulties. One soldier who punched a Palestinian even acknowledges that what he did was wrong and would be punished if discovered by his superiors. Although there is no way of knowing how this video was in fact used for educational purposes, such an approach seems commensurate with the pedagogical strategies discussed in Chapter 3. Indeed, even if the material was not used, it gives a good indication of what was being sought. Breaking the Silence is therefore making use of a testimonial video first designed to improve the ethical performance of soldiers at checkpoints in order to make the political point that such improvements are meaningless without an end to the occupation. The ethical form of this claim seems to run at cross-purposes to its content.

This tension between medium and message, between guilt and anxiety, was exposed very clearly in the ensuing discussion. The teacher responsible for the session, Guy, concluded by telling the students not to be discouraged by the video they had seen. He recounted his own experience of being a commander at Hawara checkpoint, saying that

---

[45] 'House mapping' refers to an operation in which the IDF enters a civilian home, usually at random during the night, and logs the identity of each of the inhabitants. The intelligence gathered from these operations is rarely used and they are more commonly aimed at 'demonstrating the presence' of the army.

with good soldiers and officers it was possible to avoid problems such as those in the video. He argued that the video, in spite or perhaps because of its shocking nature, should in fact encourage the students to seek out positions in the army which were less socially respected (compared with elite combat units) but which made all the more difference in the field. He said that he wanted to encourage the students to join precisely those units doing difficult work at checkpoints, to become commanders, and to act as leaders who took the initiative in challenging situations. He also conceded that it was possible to make a difference outside the army, such as by joining Breaking the Silence. In one short speech, therefore, Guy managed to turn a presentation aimed at outlining a political critique of the occupation into an opportunity to encourage the students to engage in ethical self-cultivation through military service.

It is this pattern – whereby a political critique, however carefully framed, loses its potency through its reliance on the ethical form of testimony and its contextualisation in a programme of ethical self-cultivation – that I observed repeatedly in my conversations and exchanges with staff and students at pre-military academies. Most academies accept that there is an element of truth to what Breaking the Silence say, but they do not like that the organisation does not want to work with the IDF in order to improve the morality of the occupation. Dani Zamir, the head of Rabin Academy, criticised Breaking the Silence for engaging in 'confession' [*vidui*] rather than in a constructive effort to change the IDF for the better:

when they come here to give a lecture at the *mekhina*, I say to the students that, for me, they are not doing the right thing. The right thing is: the moment something happens, you have to speak. Not two days after. Not to be a civilian for ten years and then say: 'well, when I was a soldier I was doing this and this and this . . .' It's okay but it's a little cowardly.[46]

Zamir's remarks are interesting because they echo Foucault's critique of confession. Zamir prefers the model of *parrhesia*, risky truthtelling aimed at moral improvement. Of course, Breaking the Silence would reject the idea that their activity is primarily confessional. In many ways, they too aim at a kind of public *parrhesia* directed at

---

[46] Author interview with Dani Zamir.

civil society. Indeed, several scholars have analysed the organisation sympathetically as a clear example of political *parrhesia* (Shavit and Katriel, 2011, 2013; Morag, 2013: 180–210). The problem is that this is all too easily subsumed in the pedagogical aims of pre-military academies, which restrict the use of *parrhesia* to a technique of moral improvement in a culture of military asceticism.

David Nachman, the director of Ein Prat Academy, adopts a similar approach to Breaking the Silence. He argues that, even though he disagrees vehemently with the organisation, it is important to hear their views because 'every opinion has truth inside' and it is important for students to know how to respond to their arguments. Nachman believes that Breaking the Silence reveal the occasional moral difficulties that soldiers face and thereby show the importance of ethical activity:

I say every time after they come here what the points of truth they have to say are but also when and where we don't agree with them and their way and why – and deeply . . . The important thing [that Breaking the Silence show] is that sometimes IDF soldiers do not act as we expect a Jewish soldier to act. As I said [earlier in the conversation], a Jewish soldier must be sensitive [. . .] The problem with Breaking the Silence – and it's a very, very, very big problem – is that some stories are not so true and, because of their agenda, they are not bringing the facts as they are [. . .] I think the army itself deals with most problems in a very, very good way. [Breaking the Silence] use terms like 'crimes against humanity'.[47] I hate this kind of thing. It's not right. I say this as an IDF officer for 25 years. It's not right. I know what it's like in the combat units and I see it and I know the problems. But I know the personalities of the officers in the IDF and I don't think there is any other army in the world that, in situations like we are, acts so sensitively and so . . . it's purity of arms, really . . . The way I want to see the IDF is just the way Breaking the Silence wants to see the IDF . . . Most of the members of Breaking the Silence were members of combat units, so they have to understand the complexity. I have a lot of examples of how sometimes the situation creates things that when you are looking at it from outside or you look at it from a sterile room you say 'how could he do it?' or 'how could he shout at the Arab?' But when you are under stress and the situation is not

---

[47] In fact, Breaking the Silence deliberately eschews legalistic language in favour of a discourse of morality. In months of observing the organisation, I do not recall an activist using this phrase in public.

simple, things happen and it's not good. But it's not 'crimes against humanity' or something like this.[48]

By arguing that he shares Breaking the Silence's view of how the IDF should be, David Nachman shows how easily a critique which is expressed in moral terms through testimony can lose its political content. In this framing, Nachman and Breaking the Silence share a common goal for a more moral IDF; they simply disagree about how to achieve it. Moreover, when properly contextualised, Nachman believes that Breaking the Silence can assist him in achieving this goal by showing certain 'points of truth' through testimony.

At Nachshon Academy, I spoke with another teacher who contextualised the lecture by Breaking the Silence in the same way:

... every year we meet Breaking the Silence, for a talk with the kids ... and I remember one year someone came who was in the Naḥal and he talked about . . . I mean, horrendous things that happened in Hebron when he was there as a soldier . . . And I gave him a lift in the car to a bus stop in the evening, it was quite late. So we had a chance for a chat. And whilst chatting I remembered, I realised that he was in the Naḥal in a certain company, the company he was talking about, where the company commander was someone I knew, who had worked in this *mekhina* in Nachshon in the past. A really excellent guy and I said to him, you know, 'wait a second do you know, do you know Kuti?' – that's his name. And he said, 'yeah of course, Kuti is amazing . . . he was an amazing officer, an amazing company commander'. And I said to him, 'wait a second, you know, are you trying to say that the things you just told us about in the lesson happened in Kuti's company?' And he said, 'no, no, these things would never happen in Kuti's company'. And I remember the day after speaking to my students and telling them this, telling them this story. And why was it so important for me to tell this to my kids? And what I would say is that I'm not sure about, you know, what exactly happened in the stories that he was telling about atrocities that had happened in Hebron. But, first of all, in the lesson with the kids he didn't even mention the fact that when the company commander was doing a good job . . . these things didn't happen. And that is such an important thing to pass on to the kids. You know, the commanders and officers have

---

such an important job in dictating the values and the behaviour of the soldiers and the atmosphere and the way they do the missions and so on.[49]

The final example of this attitude in pre-military academies comes from the director of the Jerusalemite Academy. She explicitly referred to the fact that Ayal, who commonly lectured for Breaking the Silence in *mekhinot*, still serves in the IDF as important evidence that it remains important to work inside the army to improve its conduct:

I know he serves in the army and does reserves. It's very, very important that he comes and says 'this is very bad but I'm part of it' . . . and the moment you are part of it you can first of all understand how you can be part of it and still be critical, and the other thing is to know how you can make changes from inside. And I really think that people who choose not to go to the army or do reserves, I can say that I have many difficulties in having a conversation with them because they don't do the first obligation of being a part.[50]

In the view of Ilan, the former educational director of Breaking the Silence, the growing presence in the organisation of soldiers who still perform reserve service is a crucial factor in undermining the political message of the campaign:

When you stand in front of a group of high school kids and at the end of every talk they ask the same question, 'do you serve or do you refuse?' and you say, 'I serve', that's it. The message is completely blurred in that second. And it doesn't matter if he makes omelettes in the military: he serves. His message is lost.[51]

It also allows for beliefs such as those expressed by pre-military academy staff above to focus attention on moral improvement within the IDF, an aim which is fully in keeping with the pattern of militarism at *mekhinot*. As Ilan argued:

we went too far . . . We had to stop at a certain point and check . . . the outcome. And we were framed. We were seen as the worm in the apple. We

---

[49] Author interview with Daniel Berkeley.
[50] Author interview with Yael Domb.
[51] Author interview with Ilan Fathi.

were seen as what should be isolated from the general public. 'Look, these guys went wrong. They weren't ethical enough. They were rotten apples. Let's cut the rotten piece out and you guys will be the great shiny apple, you will serve there, you will have your values, you will be *erkiyim* [ethical]. You will stand in the checkpoint, be polite, know a few words in Arabic, blah, blah, blah . . .' And we didn't know where to stop. We didn't know or we didn't have the guts to stop and find new ways to deliver our message. We just continued. And now Breaking the Silence talks to pretty much all the *mekhinot* in Israel, in the West Bank as well by the way. And Breaking the Silence is being framed again and again as: look, you came to the *mekhina*, this is what you shouldn't become, be aware. And I think this is terrible . . . This is not what we started Breaking the Silence for.[52]

Conclusion: Militarism as 'Incitement to Discourse'

Breaking the Silence was founded on the belief that Israeli society does not talk about the occupation and that, by talking about the occupation, Israeli society could be encouraged to end it. This is based on a strongly liberal and democratic assumption about the way in which public discourse brings about political change, which holds that the free exchange of ideas will produce a consensus reflecting the best way forward. Such is the strength of its conviction in the power of soldiers' testimonies to reveal the immorality of the occupation that Breaking the Silence is prepared to present them to whomever will listen, often without regard to their ulterior motives. As Avichai Stollar explained to me:

We believe in discourse. Basically, the reason that we don't say a lot more than just giving out our materials is because we believe, you know, that the sun is the best steriliser, that . . . having those testimonies out there, no matter how they're being used, just . . . their sheer existence in the political, in the social sphere, has immense importance by itself.[53]

I have sought to show the limitations of this view of political activism in a situation of societal militarism. A critique couched in moral terms can be easily stripped of its political content and turned into a feature of ethical pedagogy in support of militarism. The transition from guilt to anxiety which Breaking the Silence seeks to effect is often

---

[52] Author interview.
[53] Author interview with Avichai Stollar.

unsuccessful. Moreover, this failed transition can also be captured and exploited by a militarist apparatus. This challenges the view that the political benefits gained from this kind of activism outweigh the costs of participating in the militarist discourse of soldiers' testimony which is steeped in masculinism and the perpetuation of social and racial hierarchies in Israeli society. It is therefore apt to reconsider the fundamental assumptions implicit in the Breaking the Silence project. Specifically, it seems important to ask, firstly, whether in fact Israeli society is quite as 'silent' as the organisation maintains and, secondly, whether 'breaking' that silence by participating in public discourse in Israel is really the most effective kind of activism.

In his celebrated history of European sexuality, Foucault describes the 'incitement to discourse' brought about by the discursive regimes constructed around sexuality (1998a: 1–50). He attacks the 'repressive hypothesis' as a chimera, arguing instead that it was obsessive, perverse speech and not silence which characterised the nineteenth-century attitude to sexuality. He maintains that it is this image of 'silencing' which maintains the illusory hope in emancipation through sexual freedom and free speech about sex. When one successfully claims to be breaking a silence, the object of one's discourse acquires a privileged status. What all these discourses on sexuality share therefore – whether they belong to Victorian sexologists or the sexual liberation movement – is a belief that sexuality speaks a privileged truth about the subject who participates in it.

It should not be too difficult to imagine how, in a militarist society such as Israel, military participation could also become the object of such a 'regime of truth'. Foucault himself gives a clear analysis of the importance of discourse about war for modern regimes of power in his *Society Must Be Defended* lectures (2004: 41–62, 239–63). Indeed, throughout this book, I have been documenting a wide range of practices of speech and testimony associated with military service in Israel. What this evidence suggests is not that Israeli society is silent about the occupation but rather that it speaks about it in code, its details parsed through very careful practices of testimony and self-examination. I have argued that these practices are an important feature of militarism, in that they produce an ethical subject for whom performance in warfare becomes a crucial test of the self. Despite its critical perspective, Breaking the Silence does not depart significantly from these trends. If anything, it contributes to them by invoking the idea of societal silence and thus privileging discourse about war as a measure of the moral character of the Israeli public.

Yet it would be fair to ask what the alternative to discourse about war could possibly be if the aim of a political organisation is to end the occupation. Even if the silence being broken is a partial illusion, it is harder to imagine a political strategy that would reject speech altogether. This is because, as Berlant has argued, the contemporary 'desire for the political' has increasingly taken on a form in which a listening public relies on speech and sound for the affective rewards of political participation, often at the expense of more thorough-going process of contestation and struggle: '. . . the social circulation of *noise*, of affective binding, converts the world to a space of moral action that seems juxtapolitical – proximate to, without being compromised by, the instrumentalities of power that govern social life' (Berlant, 2011: 224). This emphasis on speech generates the impression that 'there is already a better sensorial world that exists right here, right now, more intimate and secure and just as real' (2011: 224).

Indeed, in Ilan's view, Breaking the Silence increasingly works to facilitate this feeling of intimacy and experience of a better world, rather than directing attention towards genuine political change. Referring to the organisation's work with youth movements, high schools, and *mekhinot*, he reflected:

We created a situation where those groups in the society think that they are actually talking about [the occupation]. They think that they are really discussing it. But they are as wrong as they can be. They are having a nice comfortable discourse around it. They are not touching the real issue. They are talking about how to make it nicer . . . You can say very hard things. But within the right political frame of discourse, those things will be conveyed as very soft messages.[54]

For Berlant this very emphasis on speech can be a form of 'cruel optimism', in which relations of affective attachment formed through spoken exchange can obstruct a more radical political opening. She includes testimony as an ethical form in this:

---

[54] Author interview with Ilan Fathi.

There are vigils; there is witnessing, testimony, and yelling. But there is not yet a consensual rubric that would shape these matters into an event. The affective structure of the *situation* is therefore anxious and the political emotions attached to it veer wildly from recognition of the enigma that is clearly there toward explanations that make sense, the kind of satisfying sense that enables enduring. (Berlant, 2011: 225, emphasis in original)

It is notable that Berlant speaks of the affect of anxiety in this passage. As I have emphasised, it is in the production of such anxiety that Breaking the Silence comes closest to achieving its political goals. Yet, by filling the gap opened up by such anxiety with more speech and moral discourse, the organisation undoes its own work, producing a listening public which is more content to focus on moral improvement than political change. Berlant argues that, in these conditions, silent protest may offer a more effective paradigm for political activism. She sees promise in the moment when 'people enter the public sphere in order to withhold from it the very material – speech oriented toward opinion – that animates its world-making and world-building effectivity' (Berlant, 2009). In the regime of militaristic 'incitement to the discourse' that I have been describing, it may well be that a performative refusal to speak, rather than breaking the silence, would serve as a more radical gesture.

Conclusion: Towards an Anti-militarist Ethics

This book has been concerned with showing the conditions under which ethics can become a militarist practice. I have argued that the key process which allows this to happen is subject formation: simply put, both ethics and militarism make and remake subjects, and this allows them to encourage one another in certain conditions. Often ethical activities which are undertaken with critical, even political, intent can in fact reinforce this dynamic. In this Conclusion, I would like to explore some of the broader ramifications of this argument in connection with debates concerning the ethics of war. Specifically, I will discuss how the findings of this book might reshape our understanding of the role and purpose of military ethics as it is currently conceived and our use of ethics as a form of critical scholarly and political engagement in contexts such as Israel/Palestine. I will argue for a need to foreground militarism in debates concerning the ethics of war and, correspondingly, for a need to develop an anti-militarist politics as a precondition for effective ethical engagement.

From Military Ethics to Militarist Ethics

A major aim of this book has been to show how the practices and discourses of military ethics, which are often presented as a benign aspect of soldierly professionalism, can in fact serve to entrench patterns of militarism. The proper name for such practices and discourses would therefore be *militarist ethics*, not military ethics. My argument has been that Israel represents a paradigmatic case of militarist ethics, the dangerous consequences of which have been demonstrated in a number of ways throughout this book. In my view this reveals a broader potential, perhaps even a tendency, for military ethics to perpetuate and stabilise militarism rather than confront it. Rather than remaining sanguine about the recent 'ethical turn' in warfare, therefore, we should be highly suspicious of the political implications of this development.

In Israel, military ethical discourse, rather than providing for a critical enquiry into the legitimacy and necessity of military violence, has instead been subsumed into a neoliberal project for making the military more attractive to recruits, subordinated to counterinsurgency doctrine, and deployed for the legitimation of violence, the formation of soldierly identities, and the disciplining of dissent. Indeed, the expansion of interest in military ethics in Israel has had little to do with a virtuous project to restrain military violence or with the supposedly moral traditions of the IDF. Instead, this enhanced role for military ethics is firmly rooted in the need to reorganise and strengthen militarism in response to changing social and political realities. A brief review of the key findings of the book helps to bear out this overall conclusion, and brings together the conclusions from the closing sections of each chapter.

Although the IDF has maintained an image of itself as a moral army since its creation, its interest in military ethics was not fully regularised until the 1990s. This coincided with a period of rapid social and organisational change within the military, as well as with wider social transformations. The traditional model of recruitment through mandatory conscription began to be supplemented with aspects of professionalisation, individual incentivisation, and labour market competition for recruits. The social basis of IDF manpower also expanded to include new and peripheral groups beyond the traditional Ashkenazi secular elite, whose participation was declining as proportion of the military. The IDF's interest in military ethics, as manifested most prominently in the development of its ethical code, was profoundly shaped by this context. Ethical education was conceived as a way to enhance the professionalism of the soldier and to link military participation with individual projects of self-improvement and with a wider range of private moral communities. In this sense, the regularisation of military ethics should be thought of as a thoroughly neoliberal development in the governmental rationality of the IDF which provided a 'New Spirit' for the legitimation of militarism.

Following these developments, the IDF also faced a number of challenges after the 1990s which it sought to address in part through an enhanced emphasis on ethics. The renewed intensity of Palestinian resistance after 2000 prompted the implementation of a counterinsurgency strategy which would apply intensified violence to occupied civilian areas. The relatively decentralised structure of military organisation in counterinsurgency focused attention on the conduct and mentality of the individual soldier and his ethical capacities. Indeed, the neoliberal framing of ethics that had emerged in the 1990s proved extremely useful for this purpose. Ethical doctrines were developed which foregrounded the free judgement and rationality of the soldier in adapting to varying circumstances. The soldier was framed as a biopolitical subject who would be made responsible for managing risk, carefully preserving the lives of some while eliminating the lives of others. Ethical decisions were therefore examined as decontextualised moments of individual reasoning isolated from a wider pattern of escalating violence, occupation, and colonialism. Indeed, this emphasis on ethics would become particularly pronounced during the repeated and intensifying assaults on the Gaza Strip after the Second Intifada.

It is hardly surprising that the growth of the IDF's interest in military ethics has coincided with the mounting violence of occupation. This is because, against this backdrop of escalating counterinsurgency, ethics has also provided resources for the ideological legitimation of violence in the response to growing criticism, declining combat motivation, and increased casualty aversion. Pedagogical strategies have become a particularly important part of this ideological project. Programmes have been developed for teaching military ethics in major military colleges and officer schools, often with the assistance of philosophers and academics working in Israeli universities. Meanwhile, a reorganisation of pedagogical activities across the IDF under the rubric of developing 'Identity and Purpose' has produced a renewed focus on soldiers' moral, civic, and religious values. The IDF has achieved this through a variety of new external collaborations with educational foundations and charities, and through the augmentation and expansion of existing programmes such as pre-military academies. A variety of techniques have characterised these different pedagogical initiatives. Some have included more traditional lectures or group discussions, whereas others (particularly those focused on the lower ranks) have adopted visual media, computer technology, and interactive theatre. However, a key component of all these activities has been the importance of mobilising the practice of soldiers' testimony for pedagogical purposes, leading to a situation in which militarism has become synonymous with an ethical 'incitement to discourse'.

Ethics performs three key ideological operations to legitimate violence in these pedagogical activities. First, ethical pedagogy extends the emphasis on self-cultivation by embedding the desire to become a more moral soldier in the militarist unconscious. Not only is military participation in general framed as an opportunity for individual self-flourishing: moral reflection and moral behaviour in violent situations is framed as a 'test of the self', a demonstration of self-worth and good character. Second, ethical pedagogy works to produce unconscious fantasies to mask the structural violence of occupation. These 'sublime objects' of militarist ideology focus on aspects of ethical activity which could survive even the most compromised circumstances. Key examples include the effort to 'keep a human image' in inhuman circumstances or the pursuit of 'purity of arms' against a background of everyday violence. Crucially, the pursuit of these fantasies is divorced from any meaningful change in behaviour or accountability. Instead, these activities work to produce the maximum sense of personal moral worth for the soldier from the minimum degree of behavioural change. 'Purity of arms' and 'keeping a human image' mean politeness at checkpoints, cleaning occupied houses, and *post facto* reflection, rather than criminal investigation, fewer casualties, or an end to occupation or colonisation. Third, ethical pedagogy constantly focuses on the behaviour of the individual rather than structural factors in explaining violence. This produces an emphasis on affects of guilt, which locate moral blame in the subject, rather than anxiety, which focuses on lack in the Other. This closes off the possibility for projects of wider structural and political transformation of the violent *status quo* and hence limits ethics to what Berlant has called 'cruel optimism'.

Ethics has also become bound up with the reproduction of militarist identities in Israel. The formation of ethical soldier-subjects has clearly gendered dynamics, in which the consolidation of military masculinities becomes linked to the formation of a sense of moral character. This gendering process goes beyond the externally imposed bodily discipline of military training. It is generated from ascetic techniques of subjectivation which soldiers practise on themselves. Furthermore, the military masculinity produced by the ethics of Israeli militarism is not a straightforward pursuit of machismo. Particularly insofar as Israeli military ethics is attuned to the requirements of counterinsurgency, it demands deliberate modification of masculinity, incorporating dispositions such as 'empathy' and 'sensitivity' which are often explicitly (and problematically) identified as more feminine. Rather than subverting gendered hierarchies, however, this process in fact entails a restaging rather than a dismantling of hegemonic military masculinities (cf. Duncanson,

2015). Indeed, it often works to entrench women's subordinate role as the imagined bearers of ethical virtue and insight – true 'handmaids' indeed of the masculine 'profession of arms', to paraphrase the *Journal of Military Ethics* (Cook and Syse, 2010: 121).

Military ethics in Israel is also infused with the consolidation of religious and ethnic identities into militarism. For national-religious troops, new entrants into the ranks of the Israeli military, ethics has become a crucial means through which religious identity and observance have been reimagined as military pursuits. The revision of the ethical code to include 'Jewish' components, the establishment of the 'Identity and Purpose' programme, and the growth of pre-military academies are all evidence of the growing importance of ethics to the expansion of IDF manpower in new directions, as well as of the attempt to manage and negotiate the complexities of recruiting from an increasingly diverse population. At the same time, it should be made clear that this process has hardly been harmonious or egalitarian, as the racial dynamics of military ethical subject formation clearly attest. Racially stigmatised 'peripheral' groups are often problematised as the source of moral transgressions, turning military ethical pedagogy into a simultaneous project of moral and racial ordering which implicitly holds up dominant Ashkenazi identity as a source for moral inspiration and emulation. This stigmatisation of the behaviour of particular groups is certainly another strategy for distracting from the structural violence of occupation, but it also serves to bind militarist ethics to deeply held notions of whiteness.

There are therefore a great number of ways in which ethics clearly serves militarist purposes in Israel, whether by presenting war as an opportunity for self-realisation, by legitimating violence, by disciplining and reappropriating political criticism of war, by integrating war-fighting and war-preparation into the consolidation of social structures or identities, or by obscuring the structural violence of particular kinds of war-fighting (especially counterinsurgency). The Israeli case clearly illustrates the potential for military ethics, particularly as it is currently constituted, to reinforce patterns of militarism rather than undermine them.

Ethics and the Critique of War

This evidence should also prompt wider reflection on the usefulness of ethics as a component of critical scholarly and political interventions in militarised contexts such as Israel/Palestine. Debates surrounding

Israel's military engagements are often couched in fiercely moralising terms, in which the actions of both sides are variously framed as good or evil. Attempting to prove that Israel fights immorally is often thought of as an effective tactic in this public relations battle. Indeed, such attempts have been made time and again during Israel's most recent high-profile assaults on Gaza and Lebanon. The findings of this book, however, suggest that, rather than posing a threat, such discussions can be quite comfortable terrain for the Israeli military. Even the most eloquent of Israel's moral critics can find their campaigns neutralised and co-opted by the wider militarisation of ethics. This should cast doubt on the effectiveness of a purely moral critique of war, militaries, and militarism.

The experience of Breaking the Silence has been the primary focus of my exploration of the limits of the ethical critique of war. In the first place, I have raised questions about the effectiveness of soldiers' testimony as a mode of ethical critique. The use of soldiers' testimony by Breaking the Silence is often cited as a clear example of *parrhesia*, the practice of courageously telling truth to power which Foucault valorised in his final lectures. However, I have sought to show that the political *parrhesia* of Breaking the Silence shares its genealogy with the use of testimony in Israeli military ethical pedagogy. Both these practices build on a cultural and literary tradition of soldier's testimony; they both emerged as responses to intensifying counterinsurgency; they both oppose themselves to 'silence', either in the public sphere or within military units; above all, they are both manifestations of a form of militarism in which the conduct of the individual soldier has become an important object of scrutiny and discourse.

Understood from this perspective, institutions and individuals which appear at first glance to be operating in fierce opposition to each other in this moral debate are also working, often unwittingly, to produce different features of the same underlying structure. The very fact that the IDF is itself involved in eliciting testimonies from its soldiers about the most violent and troubling features of the occupation confounds the impression one receives from the publicity war being waged over its conduct. The IDF may prefer to speak about harassment at checkpoints in closed settings through discussion groups and drama workshops; Breaking the Silence may prefer to expose this information to the world. But it is possible for *both* these practices to draw on and reinforce militarism. In fact, viewed more closely, this is not a battle between silence and truth but a struggle between competing forms of militaristic truth-telling.

This problem is particularly acute given the narrow focus of the critique voiced by Breaking the Silence. The organisation has very deliberately limited its purview to the question of whether the occupation of the West Bank and Gaza can be moral. This is a carefully calibrated approach designed to attack prevailing Israeli discourse about the occupation in a way which is couched in the idioms of Zionism and militarism, principally the desire for a 'moral army' which demonstrates Israeli exceptionalism. The calculation of Breaking the Silence is that this gives their message a greater chance of gaining currency than an emphasis on, say, legal accountability or a more straightforwardly political critique of occupation or colonialism. However, this strategy instead has the effect of valorising rather than problematising the desire for a moral army, thereby reinforcing the connection between ethics and military participation which helps to underpin Israeli militarism.

In addition, by drawing on this militaristic impulse, the ethical response prompted by Breaking the Silence testimony tends to reproduce the affects of guilt characteristic of Israeli military ethics rather than the more destabilising affect of anxiety. Moral critique voiced through soldiers' testimony is liable to drift towards a focus on individual behaviour rather than structural factors, despite the best and shrewdest intentions of activists. Indeed, this is most evident when the testimonies produced by Breaking the Silence become material for the pedagogical institutions of Israeli military ethics, as in pre-military academies, where the disruptive potential of this moral critique is easily neutralised and appropriated. In this sense, ethical pedagogy in the IDF and soldiers' testimony in civil society not only cross-pollinate each other but also arise from and participate in an underlying structure of subjectivity which privileges a depoliticised ethics working in support of militarism.

The work of Breaking the Silence also excludes or marginalises a wide range of issues which must be engaged with in order to challenge to military violence effectively. Its encounter with issues of race and gender are perhaps the clearest examples of this. As I have shown, militarist ethics in Israel rest on an implicit hierarchy in which moral character is associated with dominant racial identities, especially Ashkenazi whiteness, and moral failures are associated with stigmatised racial identities, such as those of Mizrahim or Ethiopians. Likewise, moral military behaviour is linked to a hegemonic notion of military masculinity. These gendered and racial hierarchies help to underpin a militarist ethical imaginary in which the character of individuals, rather than structural factors, is held responsible for excessive violence. A proper challenge to Israeli military violence which is focused on its systemic nature, as Breaking the Silence aims to articulate, would therefore need to challenge these hierarchies.

However, Breaking the Silence has notably struggled to achieve this. Both women and non-Ashkenazim are under-represented among its activists and testifiers. In addition, the reliance on the authority of the moral soldier also draws and depends upon an image of militarist masculinity. The organisation has also largely ignored the issue of racism in its campaigning and testimonies, since it lies beyond the narrow remit of challenging the occupation of the West Bank and Gaza. Several Mizrahi activists indicated to me their perception that the organisation needed to do more to engage with this issue. Admittedly, the organisation has made more significant attempts to engage with the issue of gender and women in the military, including publishing a booklet of testimonies from women and contributing to the film *To See If I'm Smiling*. These testimonies include discussion of how the performance of military masculinity breeds violence, oppresses women, and rarely conforms to masculinist ideals of ethical self-control. However, the organisation as a whole has not developed these points into a political agenda challenging military masculinity. Moreover, while the critique voiced in women's testimony does seek to link military masculinity with violence, it still fails to challenge the valorisation of moral military behaviour as masculine. Instead, moral transgressions can be portrayed as failures of masculinity or as evidence of 'childish' and unmanly immaturity (cf. Sasson-Levy et al., 2011: 753), thus re-establishing moral behaviour as the preferred marker of masculinity. Indeed, by invoking their military service as authority for their moral critique, these testimonies, even though they come from women, still serve to 'accept and reaffirm the male-dominated republican ethos that grants political superiority and power to male warriors' (Sasson-Levy et al., 2011: 757). A more fundamental critique of military masculinity would be required to challenge militarism and, crucially, to break the link between ethical activity and the reproduction of gender hierarchies.

Breaking the Silence under Attack

While the manuscript for this book was being completed, Breaking the Silence entered a new period of political turmoil. In December 2015, the then Defence Minister Moshe Ya'alon banned the organisation from speaking to groups of soldiers, making the example which opened this book a future impossibility (Newman, 2015). He was followed swiftly by the Education Minister, Naftali Bennett, who indicated he would do the same in the Israeli education system (Kashti, 2015). At more or less the same time, the right-wing NGO Im Tirtzu released a video attacking four activists from the Israeli Left for being 'foreign agents' or 'plants' undermining the State of Israel from within (Im Tirtzu, 2015). The video insinuated that they supported stabbing attacks against Israeli civilians. One of the four was Avner Gvaryahu, a Breaking the Silence activist who features in this book. Then, in January 2016, the state attorney filed a legal petition to force Breaking the Silence to reveal the identity of soldiers who testified to the organisation concerning 'Operation Protective Edge' in Gaza, about which the organisation had published an extensive report the previous year (Harel and Cohen, 2016). Breaking the Silence announced that, if upheld, the application would amount to a 'lethal blow' (Breaking the Silence, 2016a).

After the elections of March 2016, in which Netanyahu emerged victorious and far right parties were newly ascendant, this hostile atmosphere intensified further. Ya'alon publicly described Breaking the Silence as 'traitors' for allegedly sharing state secrets (Shpigel, 2016). Meanwhile, the new Justice Minister, Ayelet Shaked, put forward sweeping legislation to restrict the activities of NGOs like Breaking the Silence which receive funding from foreign governments (Lis, 2016). The law proposed forcing them to declare their foreign funding on all pages of their public materials and even forcing their representatives to wear special badges indicating this (this latter proposal was later dropped). In the summer of 2016, the President of Ben-Gurion University intervened to prevent its Middle East Studies department from awarding the 'Berenson Prize' to Breaking the Silence in honour of their work, even though the award had already been announced (Kashti, 2016). All these events, combined with an atmosphere of rising animosity in civil society and the media, prompted Breaking the Silence to declare that it was 'the target of well-funded, organized, political and violent attacks, whose purpose has been to incite the public against us, to frighten and deter our activists and ultimately, to destroy the organization' (Breaking the Silence, 2016a).

This undoubtedly vicious and targeted wave of attacks on the organisation raises the possibility that Breaking the Silence is becoming more of a serious threat to the Israeli State than in the past. One commonly advanced explanation for this latest round of attacks is that the increasing circulation of Breaking the Silence materials abroad has begun to worry the Israeli political establishment. In the intensified struggle for international legitimacy of recent years and especially in the context of the recent Palestinian application to join the International Criminal Court, this line of thinking suggests that the evidence Breaking the Silence has gathered is particularly incriminating. While I would not want to downplay the severity of the recent attacks on the organisation, I do not share this interpretation. In the first instance, the evidence gathered by Breaking the Silence is highly unlikely to form the basis of any international criminal prosecution against the IDF. Such a prosecution is itself only a remote possibility at present, but even if it were to happen almost all of the evidence collected and released by Breaking the Silence is corroborated by other available sources and is therefore unlikely to be crucial. Moreover, there is strong reason to believe that the public relations impact of Breaking the Silence outside the state is just as ambiguous as its record inside Israel. In response to common accusations of 'de-legitimising' Israel abroad, I frequently heard the organisation defend itself by referring to the praise they have received from liberal Zionists in America and Europe for restoring faith in the Israeli conscience.

It is also striking that the attacks on Breaking the Silence have not come from the military itself, but rather from the political echelon – and in particular from politicians attempting to raise their profiles in the Knesset in the context of a rightward surge in Israeli politics. The attacks appear to be timed in relation to a much broader right-wing offensive spearheaded by a number of far right NGOs (Shulman, 2016). In this context, it is more accurate to think of Breaking the Silence as a scapegoat than as a genuine threat to the State. Moreover, they are not the only target: the aim is to foment a much more general hostility to the Israeli Left, of which Breaking the Silence are only a part. It is indeed telling that far worse attacks have been suffered by activists in organisations involving Palestinians, whose work is seen as far more of an obstruction. For example, in January 2016, at the same time that the attacks on Breaking the Silence were unfolding, a television report for the popular Israeli news programme *Uvda* featured undercover reporting conducted by the right-wing group *Ad Kan* into the organisation *Ta'ayush*, a group which works to defend Palestinian land from confiscation. The report spuriously accused members of the organisation of incitement to violence, and three of them were subsequently arrested by the police (including one Palestinian who was also *rearrested* even after a court ordered him released) (Shulman, 2016). In the Israeli media, however, far less attention was paid to these incidents than to the attacks on Breaking the Silence, who received a full-throated defence from liberal commentators.

Indeed, the nature of the support which Breaking the Silence has received since the attacks on it began is instructive. Although a few pre-military academies did decide to stop inviting Breaking the Silence, over 500 academy graduates subsequently wrote and signed a letter condemning incitement against the organisation (Stop the Incitement Against the President and Human Rights Organisations, 2015). Following media coverage of the disinvitations, the Joint Council of *Mekhinot* was also forced to issue a statement confirming that it had not banned the organisation and that the decision would be left to individual academies (Joint Council of Mekhinot, 2016). Breaking the Silence continued to publicise their work with pre-military academies after this point. Furthermore, the promised ban from the education system did not materialise. One year later, after Breaking the Silence continued to boast of their visits to high schools, Naftali Bennett conceded that principals had ignored his guidance and that his ban was not legally binding (though he promised to propose legislation to that effect) (Wootliff, 2016). Most tellingly of all, after the withdrawal of the Berenson Prize by Ben-Gurion University, the New Israel Fund (one of the longstanding international donors to Breaking the Silence) stepped in to offer it an alternative award (Curiel, 2016). They also quadrupled the original prize money to $20,000. The organisation received the award in a much-publicised ceremony in November 2016. A speech of appreciation was given by none other than Amos Oz, the famous Israeli author who years earlier had played such a crucial role in the careful editing of *Siaḥ Loḥamim*, the classic text of the 'shooting and crying' genre.

At the same event, the executive director of Breaking the Silence gave a speech in which she announced the organisation was 'proud to be outside the consensus' of Israeli society (Novak, 2016). It is true that Breaking the Silence is outside the consensus in Israeli society regarding the continuation of the occupation of the West Bank and Gaza. The growing acknowledgement of this marginality may augur a more radical future for the organisation if it is no longer allowed access to a mainstream Israeli audience. However, for the time being, while that audience remains accessible and often receptive, it should also be made clear that the organisation remains firmly within the militarist and Zionist consensus which I have been describing in this book. Until it develops a more confrontational political stance against *this* consensus, Breaking the Silence will remain dependent upon rather than corrosive of the ethics of Israeli militarism.

The Challenge of Anti-militarist Ethics

What has consistently emerged in this study is that it precisely such political questions which are often be obscured by the ethics of militarism. The colonial origins of counterinsurgency, the fundamentally settler–colonial and racist structures underpinning the Israeli occupation, the patriarchal nature of the military, the fundamental militarism of Israeli society – all of these are regularly effaced in the examples discussed in this book. This is true even when ethics becomes a terrain of contestation, as the experience of Breaking the Silence shows. When the political field is so circumscribed, even a Foucauldian recourse to *parrhesia* or a Lacanian ethics of anxiety do not seem sufficient on their own. What is more, they often seem effective in strengthening the edifice of militarism, which deploys its own ethical techniques to capture and discipline this criticism.

Given this, how might we then begin to reconstitute ethics on an anti-militarist footing? In my view, *contra* military ethics as it is commonly practised, it is an emphasis on the centrality of the politics of war and violence which grounds the possibility of an anti-militarist ethics. An anti-militarist ethics should work to restore attention to the political realities underpinning the use of military violence, pointing out the ways in which these realities can promote militarism. It should seek to investigate how war becomes bound up with projects of class, gender, and racial domination, and with colonialism, nation-building, education, and subject formation in all its guises. It should also explore how war can exert its own pull on these social practices, giving them new dynamics and making it harder to extricate violence from them. It should highlight the dangers of entering a situation in which the original rationale for violence is elided and violence is instead pursued simply because it is desired and normalised for its own sake – in other words, a situation of militarism. In short, anti-militarist ethics should seek to make explicit the political rationale for the use of violence, to evaluate it on these terms, and then to highlight the risks posed by militarism with the aim of either confronting and minimising them or of deciding that they cannot be countenanced.

The nature of war undoubtedly makes this a difficult task. There can be no clean act of violence which does not in some way transform and begin to overwhelm those making use of it for their political objectives. But there may be ways and traditions of acting ethically which help to reduce this risk, even if they cannot eliminate it. One part of my objective in this book has been to help locate such modes of ethics by highlighting the shortcomings of those that certainly do not offer this promise. As I have shown, military ethics as practised in Israel is very poorly suited to the task of anti-militarism. In fact, it pursues precisely the opposite of an anti-militarist approach by working to obscure political discussions about the rationality, effectiveness, and social consequences of military violence and by constantly returning to the task of producing a better soldier-subject. Beyond this, however, I have also shown that even approaches which attempt to mobilise ethics from a critical standpoint are also inadequate if they do not grapple with the political realities of militarism, as the example of Breaking the Silence demonstrates.

By contrast, of the alternative ethical traditions available, feminism and anti-colonialism stand out as strands of thought which have the resources to steadfastly refuse this bracketing of political issues and instead to incorporate them into ethical judgements about war. This is because these traditions emerge from an engagement with the concrete political realities of gender oppression and colonialism, both of which are literally shot through with violence, and from which it is impossible for scholars working in these traditions to fully abstract their thinking. For example, Kimberley Hutchings, inspired by both traditions, has argued that ethical judgements about violence must consider the constantly changing political realities which make both war and ethical judgements about it possible. Noting the absence of violent repertoires or ethical registers which do not tend to reinforce gender hierarchies, she argues that it becomes necessary 'to justify the trade-off being proposed between the gendered implications of violence and the feminist ethical goals that it is being said to serve' (Hutchings, 2007a: 102). This is a task, she acknowledges, which is fraught with difficulties and ambiguities and which cannot be resolved in the abstract or determined in advance. Instead, it requires an engagement with 'the extraordinary ideological and institutional investment required to sustain violence as a mode of lived subjectivity, the potential for corruption of ends by means, and our lack of control over the outcomes of our actions' (Hutchings, 2007b: 128). Such an awareness is crucial for the possibility of an anti-militarist ethics, which constantly confronts the possibility that the purposes of violence may be subverted by the political realities of militarism. This demands not only extreme caution in ethical judgements about violence, but also a broader effort and commitment to reshape those realities such that this subversion becomes less likely.

What I have primarily insisted on above, then, is the importance of restoring politics to the ethics of war and violence in order to rescue it from militarist reappropriation. An ethics which seeks merely to restrain the excesses of military violence, or which seeks merely to develop procedures, standards, or dispositions which are averse to those excesses, cannot alter the political realities which make militarism possible. At a certain point, these realities must be confronted and resisted on their own terms. While this alternative unquestionably entails tremendous difficulties and risks, my final conclusion is that this is the only way that ethics can reliably break with militarism.

List of Interviews

Name	Role	Date	Location
Anonymous	Founding member of Breaking the Silence	29 January 2013	Jerusalem
Idan Barir	Testifier to Breaking the Silence	12 December 2012	Tel Aviv
Yishai Beer	Major General (reserves) in the IDF; former Judge Advocate General; member of committee to redraft IDF ethical code; teacher of ethics in the IDF	15 March 2013	Jerusalem
Yokhanan Ben-Ya'akov	Education Ministry official responsible for pre-military academies	30 April 2013	Jerusalem
Daniel Berkeley	Teacher at Nachshon Academy	11 March 2013	Sde Yoav
Nadav Bigelman	Activist in Breaking the Silence	25 November 2012	Jerusalem
Ya'akov Castel	Former education director of the IDF; member of committee to redraft IDF ethical code; convenor of Maḥzabim and Lev Aharon programmes	13 March 2013	Jerusalem
Noam Chayut	Activist in Breaking the Silence	7 February 2013	Haifa

Name	Role	Date	Location
Hillel Cohen	*Activist in Breaking the Silence*	*15 January 2013*	*Beer Sheva*
Michael Cohen	*Teacher at Keshet Yehuda Pre-military Academy*	*23 April 2013*	*Keshet*
Atar Dagan	*Colonel in the IDF*	*3 May 2013*	*Telephone conversation*
Yael Domba	*Head of Jerusalemite Pre-military Academy*	*21 November 2012*	*Jerusalem*
Eran Efrati	*Former activist and testimony collector in Breaking the Silence*	*25 February 2013*	*Jerusalem*
Ilan Fathi	*Former education director of Breaking the Silence*	*4 December 2012*	*Beer Sheva*
Michal Feuras	*Convenor of soldiers' drama workshops at Beit Morasha*	*7 March 2013, 9 April 2013*	*Tel Aviv*
Dana Golan	*Former executive director of Breaking the Silence*	*10 December 2012*	*Tel Aviv*
Ben Tzion Gruber	*Colonel in the IDF; teacher of ethics in the IDF*	*1 May 2013*	*Tel Aviv*
Moshe Halbertal	*Professor of Philosophy at the Hebrew University of Jerusalem; member of committee to redraft IDF ethical code; teacher of ethics in the IDF*	*7 April 2013*	*Jerusalem*
Ilana Hammerman	*Editor of two anthologies of soldiers' testimonies*	*5 May 2013*	*Jerusalem*
Amos Harel	*Defence Correspondent, Ha'aretz*	*1 May 2013*	*Tel Aviv*

Name	Role	Date	Location
Shai Herskowitz	*Convenor of Identity and Purpose Programme at* Beit Morasha	*7 May 2013*	*Latrun*
Gil Hillel	*Activist in Breaking the Silence*	*15 March 2013*	*Tel Aviv*
Guy Immerman	*Teacher at Telem Pre-military Academy*	*7 March 2013*	*Tel Aviv*
Ayal Kantz	*Former education director at Breaking the Silence*	*1 May 2013*	*Tel Aviv*
Asa Kasher	*Professor of Philosophy at Tel Aviv University; principal author of IDF ethical code; teacher of ethics in the IDF*	*28 April 2013*	*Ramat Gan*
Micha Kurz	*Former (founding) member of Breaking the Silence*	*14 January 2013*	*Jerusalem*
Reuven Mass	*Teacher at Karmei Ḥayil Pre-military Academy*	*22 April 2013*	*Beit Rimon*
Avi Mograbi	*Director; member of Breaking the Silence board of trustees*	*1 April 2013*	*Tel Aviv*
David Nachman	*Director of Ein Prat Pre-military Academy*	*28 January 2013*	*Kfar Adumim*
Avi Sagi	*Professor of Philosophy at Bar Ilan University; member of committee to redraft IDF ethical code; teacher of ethics in the IDF*	*3 April 2013*	*Jerusalem*
Micha Shalvi	*Teacher at several pre-military academies*	*18 April 2013; 5 May 2013*	*Jerusalem; telephone conversation*

Name	Role	Date	Location
Ohad Shamama	*Teacher at Lakhish Pre-military Academy*	*20 January 2013*	*Beit Guvrin*
Itamar Shapira	*Former activist in Breaking the Silence*	*21 January 2013*	*Jerusalem*
Daniel Statman	*Professor of Philosophy at Haifa University; member of committee to redraft IDF ethical code; teacher of ethics in the IDF*	*28 February 2013*	*Jerusalem*
Avichai Stollar	*Head of testimonies project at Breaking the Silence*	*13 March 2013*	*Jerusalem*
Roni Sulimani	*Former education director of IDF*	*4 April 2013*	*Latrun*
Shachar Tzemach	*Activist in Breaking the Silence*	*3 March 2013*	*Beer Sheva*
Nadav Weiman	*Activist in Breaking the Silence*	*5 December 2012*	*Tel Aviv*
Shuki Yoshav	*Former member of Soldiers Against Silence*	*28 November 2012*	*Jerusalem*
Dani Zamir	*Director of Rabin Pre-military Academy; Chair of the Joint Council of Pre-military Academies*	*30 November 2012*	*Tiv'on*

Appendix A: 'The Spirit of the IDF', First Version, 1994

Preface[1]

1. The Spirit of the Israel Defence Forces (IDF) is the moral and normative identity card of the IDF as an organisation, which stands as the foundation for all actions carried out by all men and women soldiers in the framework of the IDF.

2. The Spirit of the IDF includes eleven IDF values, presenting the essence of each one of them, and detailing its definition and parameters. The Spirit of the IDF also contains basic principles that express these values.

3. The Spirit of the IDF draws its values and basic principles from three traditions:
   a. The traditions of the Jewish people throughout the generations.
   b. The traditions of the State of Israel, as expressed in its democratic principles, its laws and its institutions.
   c. The traditions of the IDF and its battle heritage as the defence forces of Israel.

4. The Spirit of the IDF is the code of ethics according to which all the IDF's soldiers, officers, units and forces will comport themselves, and it will serve in molding their patterns of action. They will educate and critique themselves and their fellows in accordance with the Spirit of the IDF.

5. The complex nature of military activity in general, and of combat in particular, is liable to produce conflicts among the values and basic principles of the Spirit of the IDF, and to raise problems in judgement and decision-making regarding the balance required among them in practice. The obligation to execute the mission and to win in the war will be the compass in every effort to arrive at

---

[1] Translation adapted with modifications from Hauser (1997: 64–72) and Kasher (1996: 230–7).

a proper balance within the system of values and basic principles of the Spirit of the IDF. The effort to attain the proper balance in light of this compass will permit the preservation of the IDF as a principled and high-quality organisation, which properly executes all its obligations and missions.

The Values

Pursuit of the Mission

The soldier will fight and otherwise act with the utmost bravery, notwithstanding any and all dangers and obstacles in his path. He will move forward and be tenacious and brave in the pursuit of his mission, persistently and intelligently, and will not flinch from risking his life.

The pursuit of the mission of IDF soldiers means their ability and readiness to fight bravely, even in the face of danger and in the most arduous of situations, carrying on and pushing ahead to reach their objective, in accordance with the circumstances, fully and efficiently, with thoughtfulness and without haste, despite any difficulty, pressure or suffering, or even danger to their lives.

Responsibility

The soldier will see himself as an active partner in the security of the country and its citizens, carrying out his duties decisively and quickly within the bounds of his authority.

The responsibility of IDF soldiers means their effective partnership and readiness to fully utilise their maximum ability to defend the country and its sovereignty and the life and safety of its citizens, within the bounds of their authority. They will demonstrate complete and rapid implementation of their functions, with continual involvement, initiative and perseverance, and with absolute readiness to take part in every endeavour.

Integrity

The soldier will aspire, in all his actions, to fulfil his orders in the proper fashion, with the highest professional standard, from meticulous and painstaking preparations for the mission up through accurate, honest, complete and exact reporting of its results.

The integrity of IDF troops means that they carry out all military operations to the fullest possible extent, on the basis of their expertise, with a belief and awareness that they are acting in the proper professional manner, with unflagging eagerness to be scrupulous in planning, implementation and accurate reporting, exhaustively and meticulously, bravely, frankly and fairly.

Personal Example

The soldier will behave according to what is expected of him, and will act in the way that he himself demands of others, with sympathy and intelligence, aware of his ability and responsibility to be a shining beacon for all those around him.

The personal example of IDF soldiers means acting according to the highest standard in whatever is demanded of them, from them and by them, with genuine and unshakable readiness to serve as an example to all those around them, in their actions and their behaviour; to produce, perpetuate and expand mutual understanding and joint responsibility for implementation of assignments and attainment of objectives in the proper manner, in all areas of military endeavour.

Human Life

The soldier will do his utmost to preserve human life, with an awareness of its supreme importance, and will endanger himself and his colleagues only to the extent necessary for implementation of the mission.

The sanctity of life in the eyes of IDF troops will be manifest in all of their actions, in thoughtful and precise planning, in astute and safely conducted exercises and in proper implementation, in accordance with the mission, with the appropriate level of risk and caution, and with continual effort to restrict the loss of human life to the extent required by the mission.

Purity of Arms

The soldier will use his weapon and his power to vanquish the enemy only to the degree required, and will exercise self-restraint in order to prevent unnecessary harm to human life, body, honour and property.

Purity of arms among IDF troops means the restrained use they make of their weapons and their power in the implementation of missions, only to the extent necessary for their attainment, without unnecessary harm to human life, body, honour and property, whether to troops or civilians (especially the defenceless), during war and security operations as well as during times of peace and tranquillity.

Professionalism

The soldier will aspire to be aware of and understand the expertise involved in his military role, and will be competent in all skills connected with the performance of his duties.

The professionalism of IDF soldiers means their ability to carry out their military function properly, with an effort to attain excellence and continual upgrading of their accomplishments and those of their units, through broadening of knowledge and sharpening of skills, taking into account the cumulative lessons of experience and research, while continually broadening and deepening their military know-how.

Discipline

The soldier will strive towards complete and successful implementation of all that is demanded of him according to his orders and their spirit, in the framework of the law.

The discipline of IDF troops means their readiness to act with all their faculties to carry out what is demanded of them, fully and successfully, according to their understanding of the orders and in keeping with their spirit, with the continual aspiration to understand and internalise, while taking care to give lawful orders and repudiate those that are manifestly illegal.

Loyalty

The soldier will act with utter devotion to the defence of the State of Israel and all its citizens, in accordance with IDF orders, within the framework of the laws of the state and the principles of democracy.

The loyalty of IDF soldiers lies in their devotion, in all their deeds, to their homeland the State of Israel, to all its citizens, and to its army, and in their continual readiness to fight, to devote all their strength, and even to sacrifice their lives in defence of the lives of its residents and their well-being, and in defence of the sovereign State of Israel, in accordance with the values of the IDF and its orders, and while upholding the laws of the state and its democratic principles.

Representation

The soldier will see himself always as the representative and agent of the IDF, acting only within the bounds of his authority and orders.

Representation of IDF soldiers means the awareness, manifest in all of their actions, that the military power in their hands and the right to use it are given to them only by virtue of their belonging to the IDF, in their capacity as responsible agents carrying out their functions in its service, within its authorities, according to orders and decisions made by the IDF, the army of the State of Israel, acting according to its laws, and subject to the authority of its government.

Camaraderie

The soldier will always come to the aid of his comrades when they are in need or dependent upon him, notwithstanding any danger or difficulty, even to the point of self-sacrifice.

The camaraderie of IDF soldiers means *esprit de corps*, everlasting devotion to one another, readiness to extend deserved help, even to endanger their lives for their comrades in arms. They will act to preserve and bolster the cohesiveness of their unit, with full cooperation among different units, maintaining uniformity of aims throughout the IDF.

Guiding Principles

Values

1. The soldier, in all of his actions and deeds, will incorporate the basic values of the IDF: pursuit of the mission, responsibility, integrity, personal example, human life, purity of arms, professionalism, discipline, loyalty, representation and camaraderie, in accordance with their definition and with the circumstances encountered.

2. The soldier will take into account, in all his activities during his military service, that he bears responsibility not only for the results of his actions and omissions, but also for the patterns of behaviour that he helps to produce, through his orders or his personal example, explicitly or implicitly, directly or indirectly, intentionally or unintentionally.

In Military Service

3. The soldier will see himself, in all his various actions, as bearing full and pivotal responsibility for the lives of the troops and all others who are dependent on his actions and decisions.
4. The soldier will be prepared to endanger his life when encountering the enemy, and to save human life (to the extent necessary), but will do everything possible to preserve his life and that of his comrades in any other military activity.
5. The soldier will take into account, in all relevant contexts, not only proper concern for human life, but also the influence his actions have on the spiritual and physical integrity of the individual, and on his honour.
6. The soldier will endeavour to utilise all of his faculties to the maximum degree possible, in line with the demands made of him and with the preference given by the IDF to combat and command roles.
7. The soldier, in all his deeds, will scrupulously protect the honour of the country, its institutions, sites and symbols, including the IDF's honour and symbols.
8. The soldier will show particular reverence for his fallen comrades. He will act respectfully at cemeteries, memorial displays and remembrance ceremonies, and will treat the bereaved families with deference.
9. The soldier will preserve the IDF tradition of honouring disabled and wounded IDF veterans.
10. The soldier will preserve the IDF tradition of learning IDF battle lore and of helping to boost the spirit of his unit.
11. The soldier will not express his personal opinions on issues beyond his area of responsibility, authority and professional skill, and certainly not his personal opinions on political, social or ideological topics subject to public debate.

12. The soldier will use his power and his military, command or professional status only for the good of the IDF, never using them illegitimately in order to advance a personal interest or any other objective that is beyond the boundaries of his authority and responsibility, whether by the letter or spirit of the law, within or without the IDF.

13. The soldier will see himself as responsible for the results of actions taken under his orders, and will stand behind anyone acting in line with them or in an otherwise proper fashion. The soldier will see himself as responsible for behavioural patterns that he has instilled.

14. The soldier will stand by his unit and its commanders in every effort necessary to fulfil the unit's missions, and in building, developing and utilising military force. The soldier will obey his superiors as required by law and will respect his superiors, colleagues and subordinates.

15. The soldier will not conceal any infraction or mishap and will dismiss any suggestion to be a partner in such enterprise. In the face of an infraction or mishap, the soldier will act intelligently and do whatever is needed to remedy the misdeed.

16. The soldier participating in a discussion or argument connected with IDF activity, before, during or after implementation, will take a stand and express his opinion in line with his knowledge and professional belief, honestly, bravely and fairly.

17. The soldier will use the force at his disposal towards another person only in a fair, restrained, intelligent and professional fashion, showing the proper respect for the privacy of the body and life of the other.

18. The soldier will see his appearance in IDF uniform as a symbol of his loyalty to the principles and basic guidelines of the IDF.

Encountering the Enemy

19. In every encounter with the enemy, the soldier will use the force at his disposal bravely and wisely, while demonstrating tenacity, and with on-going readiness to fulfill all his duties, notwithstanding danger to his life or any other obstacle.

20. The soldier will be prepared to do whatever is necessary, even risk his life, in order to rush to the aid of his comrades and not to abandon wounded troops on the battlefield.

21. The soldier will act, in every encounter with the enemy, in accordance with the letter and spirit of the laws of war, preserving the purity of arms and ethics of warfare.

22. The soldier will treat enemy soldiers and civilians, in areas controlled by the IDF, in accordance with the letter and spirit of the laws of war, and only within the bounds of his duties.

23. The soldier will act fairly, restrained to the extent necessary, wisely and professionally, within the bounds of his duties, in every contact with civilians residing or otherwise present in areas controlled by the IDF, whether during combat or thereafter. The soldier will respect, as much as possible, the beliefs, values, and holy and historical sites of these civilians, according to the principles and basic guidelines of the IDF, and to military necessity under the given circumstances.

24. The soldier will fight and strive up to the limit of his endurance, even when his life is threatened, in order to avoid surrendering to the enemy; on the contrary, the enemy must be overcome. The soldier will not surrender to the enemy as long as he has a chance to carry out his mission. Even barring this circumstance, the soldier will not surrender as long as he is in communication with his commander or is able to evacuate.

25. The soldier who, despite everything, falls captive, will act in accordance with IDF directives, responsibly, thoughtfully and honourably.

With Regard to Civilian Bodies

26. The soldier will give preference to the aims of the IDF, in keeping with its directives, orders, principles and basic guidelines, over the advancement of any civilian organisation, in any case of conflict between the aims of the IDF and those of the organisation.

27. The soldier will conduct all official contacts with civilian bodies in a professional manner and without impairing the principles, basic guidelines and honour of the IDF.

28. The soldier may be connected with a commercial or civilian body only in accordance with existing orders and practices, in their letter and spirit, and within the bounds of his duties.

29. The soldier will refuse personal favours derived from his role, rank, status or actions. The soldier will not request and will not agree to receive favours of any kind from any source, within or

without the IDF, directly or indirectly, whether for himself or for someone else, except in line with existing orders and practices.

30. The soldier will take care, in any public appearance (especially in the media), to secure prior approval, to express absolute and unflinching loyalty to the principles and basic guidelines of the IDF, to represent the policies and decisions of the IDF, and to contribute to the public's faith in the IDF.

31. The soldier will be certain that his behaviour in private circumstances cannot be interpreted as detrimental to the IDF's principles and basic guidelines, nor harmful to the public's faith in the IDF, nor contributing to the creation of behavioural patterns liable to impair the realisation of the IDF's principles and basic guidelines.

In Reserves and Retirement

32. The soldier will act, during his reserve duty, according to the same IDF principles and basic guidelines that apply to the soldier in regular service.

33. The discharged soldier may use privileged or sensitive information coming into his possession during his military service only with appropriate permission to use this information for commercial, media or other purpose outside the framework of IDF service, to advance a personal or other aim.

34. The discharged soldier will make use of his military status, including his reserve or retirement rank, or will give others permission to do so, after finishing his tour of active duty, only in civilian contexts in which there is no harm to the IDF's principles, basic guidelines, honour or trust placed in it by the public.

Appendix B: 'The Spirit of the IDF', Updated Version, 2001

Preface[1]

The Israel Defence Forces (IDF) are the State of Israel's military force. The IDF is subordinate to the directions of the democratic civilian authorities and the laws of the state. The goal of the IDF is to protect the existence of the State of Israel and her independence, and to thwart all enemy efforts to disrupt the normal way of life in Israel. IDF soldiers are obligated to fight, to dedicate all their strength and even sacrifice their lives in order to protect the State of Israel, her citizens and residents. IDF soldiers will operate according to the IDF values and orders, while adhering to the laws of the state and norms of human dignity, and honouring the values of the State of Israel as a Jewish and democratic state.

'The Spirit of the IDF' – Definition and Origins

The Spirit of the IDF is the identity card of the IDF values, which it is appropriate that should stand as the foundation of all of the activities of every IDF soldier, on regular or reserve duty. The Spirit of the IDF and the guidelines of operation resulting from it are the ethical code of the IDF. The Spirit of the IDF will be applied by the IDF, its soldiers, its officers, its units and corps to shape their mode of action. They will behave, educate and evaluate themselves and others according to the Spirit of the IDF.

The Spirit of the IDF draws on four sources:

- The tradition of the IDF and its military heritage as the Israel Defence Forces.
- The tradition of the State of Israel, its democratic principles, laws and institutions.

[1] Translation adapted with modifications from: www.aka.idf.il/SIP_STORAGE/FILES/4/47634.pdf [accessed 16 June 2015].

259

- The tradition of the Jewish People throughout their history.
- Universal moral values based on the value and dignity of human life.

Fundamental Values

Defence of the State, its Citizens and its Residents – The IDF's goal is to defend the existence of the State of Israel, its independence and the security of the citizens and residents of the state.

Love of Homeland and Loyalty to the State – At the core of service in the IDF stand the love of the homeland and the commitment and devotion to the State of Israel – a democratic state that serves as a national home for the Jewish People – to its citizens and to its residents.

Human Dignity – The IDF and its soldiers are obligated to protect human dignity. Every human being is of value regardless of his or her origin, religion, nationality, gender, status or position.

Values

Pursuit of the Mission and Drive to Victory – IDF servicemen and women will fight and conduct themselves with courage in the face of all dangers and obstacles. They will persevere in their missions resolutely and thoughtfully even to the point of endangering their lives.

Responsibility – The IDF serviceman or woman will see themselves as active participants in the defence of the state, its citizens and residents. They will carry out their duties at all times with initiative, involvement, and diligence with common sense and within the framework of their authority, while prepared to bear responsibility for their conduct.

Honesty – The IDF servicemen and women shall present things objectively, completely, and precisely, in planning, performing, and reporting. They will act in such a manner that their peers and commanders can rely upon them in performing their tasks.

Personal Example – The IDF servicemen and women will comport themselves as required of them, and will demand of themselves as they demand of others, out of recognition of their ability and responsibility within the military and without to serve as a deserving role model.

Human Life – The IDF servicemen and women will act in a judicious and safe manner in all they do, out of recognition of the
supreme value of human life. During combat they will endanger themselves and their comrades only to the extent required to
carry out their mission.

Purity of Arms – The IDF servicemen and women will use their
weapons and force only for the purpose of their mission, only
to the necessary extent and will maintain his human image even
during combat. IDF soldiers will not use their weapons and force
to harm human beings who are not combatants or prisoners of
war, and will do all in their power to avoid causing harm to their
lives, bodies, dignity and property.

Professionalism – The IDF servicemen and women will acquire the
professional knowledge and skills required to perform their tasks,
and will implement them while striving continuously to perfect
their personal and collective achievements.

Discipline – The IDF servicemen and women will strive to the best of
their ability to fully and successfully complete all that is required
of them according to orders and their spirit. IDF soldiers will be
meticulous in giving only lawful orders, and shall refrain from
obeying manifestly illegal orders.

Camaraderie – The IDF servicemen and women will act out of fra-
ternity and devotion to their comrades, and will always go to their
assistance when they need their help or depend on them, despite
any danger or difficulty, even to the point of risking their lives.

Representation – The IDF soldiers view their service in the IDF as
a mission. They will be ready to give their all in order to defend
the state, its citizens and residents. This is due to the fact that
they are representatives of the IDF who act on the basis and in
the framework of the authority given to them in accordance with
IDF orders.

Bibliography

Adler H. (2007) Teaching the Law of War in the Israel Defence Forces. *IDF Law Review* 3: 34–48.

Agamben G. (1998) *Homo Sacer: Sovereign Power and Bare Life*. Stanford, CA: Stanford Univeristy Press.

Al-Khalidi M. (2010) 'The Most Moral Army in the World': The New Ethical Code of the Israeli Military and the War on Gaza. *Journal of Palestine Studies* 39(3): 6–23.

Alternate Focus (2006) Burning Conscience [video interview with Noam Chayut and Avichai Sharon]. Available from: www.youtube.com/watch?v=37MFa7ZKQWo (accessed 16 July 2014).

Althusser L. (1971) Ideology and Ideological State Apparatuses. In: *Lenin and Philosophy and Other Essays*, New York: Monthly Review Press.

Amnesty International (2014) *Nothing Is Immune: Israel's Destruction of Landmark Buildings in Gaza*. Available from: www.amnesty.org/en/documents/mde15/0029/2014/en/.

(2015) 'Black Friday': Carnage in Rafah during 2014 Israel/Gaza Conflict. Available from: https://blackfriday.amnesty.org/.

Aran G. (1991) Jewish Zionist Fundamentalism: The Bloc of the Faithful in Israel (Gush Emunim). In: Marty M. and Appleby S. (eds), *Fundamentalisms Observed*, Chicago, IL: University of Chicago Press.

Arutz Sheva (2004) 'Identity and Purpose', a Strategic Educational Revolution in the IDF. 1st March, Available from: www.inn.co.il/News/News.aspx/73052 (accessed 29 January 2014) [Hebrew].

Aviner S. (2012) He Who Is Not Joyful to Kill a Terrorist – Is He Gentle or Impervious? Available from: www.ateret.org.il/hebrew/torah/view.asp?id=1086 (accessed 20 May 2015) [Hebrew].

(2014) Short & Sweet – Text Message Q&A #263 – Shut Operation Protective Edge #3. Available from: www.ravaviner.com/2014/08/short-sweet-text-message-q-263-shut.html (accessed 8 September 2014).

(n.d.) Is It Permissible to Kill a Terrorist Who Takes Shelter Behind Ordinary People? Available from: www.ateretmedia.org/ra_sic/ra_sic_741421.mp3 (accessed 5 September 2014) [Hebrew].

Azoulay A. and Ophir A. (2012) *The One State Condition: Occupation and Democracy in Israel/Palestine*. Stanford, CA: Stanford Univeristy Press.

B'Tselem (2003) Soldier Testimony: 'IDF Soldiers Are Creating the Next Generation of Terrorists'. Available from: www.btselem.org/testimo nies/20030801_soldiers_testimonies_witness_d_h (accessed 24 April 2014).

(2009) *Guidelines for Israel's Investigations into Operation Cast Lead*. Available from: www.btselem.org/download/200902_operation_cast_ lead_position_paper_eng.pdf.

(2013) *Human Rights Violations during Operation Pillar of Defence*. Available from: www.btselem.org/download/201305_pillar_of_ defense_operation_eng.pdf.

(2015) *Black Flag: The Legal and Moral Implications of the Policy of Attacking Residential Buildings in the Gaza Strip, Summer 2014*. Available from: www.btselem.org/download/201501_black_flag_eng.pdf.

(2016) Financial Statements as of December 31st 2015. Available from: http://documents.guidestar.org.il/PDF/newfiles/fin/2014/117-99-2015- 0162262.pdf (accessed 4 January 2017).

Badiou A. (2001) *Ethics: An Essay in the Understanding of Evil*. London: Verso.

(2009) *Theory of the Subject*. London: Continuum.

Barak O. and Sheffer G. (eds) (2010) *Militarism and Israeli Society*. Bloomington, IN: Indiana University Press.

Basham V. (2013) *War, Identity, and the Liberal State: Everyday Experiences of the Geopolitical in the Armed Forces*. Oxford: Routledge.

Beit Morasha (n.d.) Jewish Identity Programmes in the IDF. Available from: www.bmj.org.il/inner_en/30 (accessed 4 February 2014).

Ben-Ari E. (1999) Masks and Soldiering: The Israeli Army and the Palestinian Uprising. In: Ben-Ari E. and Lomsky-Feder E. (eds), *The Military and Militarism in Israeli Society*, Albany, NY: State University of New York Press.

Ben-Ari E. and Lomsky-Feder E. (eds) (1999) *The Military and Militarism in Israeli Society*. Albany, NY: State University of New York Press.

Ben-Eliezer U. (1998) *The Making of Israeli Militarism*. Bloomington, IN: Indiana University Press.

(2004) Post-modern Armies and the Question of Peace and War: The Israeli Defense Forces in the 'New Times'. *International Journal of Middle East Studies* 36(1): 49–70.

Benziman Y. (2010) Contradictory Representations of the IDF in Cultural Texts of the 1980s. In: Barak O. and Sheffer G. (eds), *Militarism and Israeli Society*, Bloomington, IN: Indiana University Press.

Berlant L. (2006) Cruel Optimism. *Differences: A Journal of Feminist Cultural Studies* 17(5): 20–36.

(2009) Affect, Noise, Silence, Protest: Ambient Citizenship. Transformations of the Public Sphere. Available from: http://publicsphere.ssrc.org/berlant-affect-noise-silence-protest-ambient-citizenship/ (accessed 22 June 2015).

(2011) *Cruel Optimism*. Durham: Duke University Press.

Blidstein G. (1996) The Treatment of Hostile Civilian Populations: The Contemporary Halakhic Discussion in Israel. *Israel Studies* 1(2): 27–45.

Bnei David Academy (2014) Bnei David – Protective Edge – Report on Channel 10. Available from: www.bneidavid.org/Web/He/VirtualTorah/Lessons/Default.aspx?subject=&rabi=&name=&rfs=&id=8212 (accessed 5 September 2014).

(n.d.) Mechina Kdam Tzva'it [syllabus outline]. Available from: www.bneidavid.org/Web/He/about/Routes/Preparatory/Default.aspx (accessed 2 September 2014) [Hebrew].

Boltanski L. and Chiapello E. (2005) *The New Spirit of Capitalism*. London: Verso.

Bosteels B. (2011) *Badiou and Politics*. Durham: Duke University Press.

Bourg J. (2007) *From Revolution to Ethics: May 1968 and Contemporary French Thought*. Montreal: McGill-Queen's University Press.

Breaking the Silence (2005) *Soldiers' Testimonies from Hebron, 2001–2004*. Available from: www.breakingthesilence.org.il/wp-content/uploads/2011/02/Soldiers_Testimonies_from_Hebron_2001_2004_Eng.pdf.

(2009) *Soldiers' Testimonies from Cast Lead, Gaza 2009*. Available from: www.breakingthesilence.org.il/wp-content/uploads/2011/02/Operation_Cast_Lead_Gaza_2009_Eng.pdf.

(2010) *Soldiers' Testimonies from Hebron, 2008–2010*. Available from: www.breakingthesilence.org.il/wp-content/uploads/2011/09/Soldiers_Testimonies_from_Hebron_2008_2010_Eng.pdf.

(2011a) Huwara Checkpoint. Available from: www.youtube.com/watch?v=dtTL32Gkb40&list=UUVHKNEtUu-DqZfHCA2NQ6rQ (accessed 30 September 2014).

(2011b) Tour in Hebron. Available from: www.youtube.com/watch?v=TGbV_rXmS1M (accessed 18 September 2014).

(2013) *Our Harsh Logic: Israeli Soldiers' Testimonies from the Occupied Territories, 2001–2010*. New York: Picador.

(2016a) An Urgent Message from Breaking the Silence's Executive Director, Yuli Novak. Available from: http://us8.campaign-archive2.com/?u=74133baa00bece6467cded211&id=a93f5d0714 (accessed 4 January 2017).

(2016b) Financial Statements as of December 31 2015. Available from: www.breakingthesilence.org.il/inside/wp-content/uploads/2016/05/%D7%93

%D7%95%D7%97-%D7%9B%D7%A1%D7%A4%D7%99-2015-
%D7%97%D7%AA%D7%95%D7%9D.pdf (accessed 4 January 2017).

Bronner E. (2009a) Israel Disputes Soldiers' Accounts of Gaza Abuses. *New York Times*, 27th March.

(2009b) Soldiers' Accounts of Gaza Killings Raise Furor in Israel. *New York Times*, 19th March.

Brown W. (1999) Resisting Left Melancholy. *Boundary 2* 26(3): 19–27.

Burchell G. (1995) Liberal Government and Techniques of the Self. In: Barry A., Osborne T., and Rose N. (eds), *Foucault and Political Reason: Liberalism, Neo-Liberalism, and Rationalities of Government*, Chicago, IL: University of Chicago Press.

Butler J. (1996) *The Psychic Life of Power: Theories in Subjection*. Stanford, CA: Stanford Univeristy Press.

Carrick D. (2008) The Future of Ethics Education in the Military: A Comparative Analysis. In: Robinson P., De Lee N., and Carrick D. (eds), *Ethics Education in the Military*, Aldershot: Ashgate.

Carrick D., Connelly J. and Robinson P. (eds) (2009) *Ethics Education for Irregular Warfare*. Farnham: Ashgate.

Castiel E. (n.d.) Purity and the Victory of the Army in War. B'nei David Academy, Available from: www.bneidavid.org/Web/He/VirtualTorah/Lessons/Default.aspx?subject=&rabi=&name=&rfs=&id=8168 (accessed 5 September 2014) [Hebrew].

Catignani S. (2009) *Israeli Counterinsurgency and the Intifadas: Dilemmas of a Conventional Army*. Oxford: Routledge.

Challans T. (2007) *Awakening Warrior: Revolution in the Ethics of Warfare*. Albany, NY: State University of New York Press.

Chamayou G. (2015) *Theory of the Drone*. New York: The New Press.

Chayut N. (2010) *Ganevet HaShoah Sheli*. Tel Aviv: Am Oved [Hebrew].

(2013) *The Girl Who Stole My Holocaust*. London: Verso.

Chiesa L. (2007) *Subjectivity and Otherness: A Philosophical Reading of Lacan*. Cambridge, MA: MIT Press.

Chouchane S. (2009) The Judicialization of Israeli Military Ethics. *Bulletin du Centre de recherche français à Jérusalem* 20: 1–17.

Cohen S. (1995) The Israel Defence Forces – From a 'People's Army' to a 'Professional Military' – Causes and Implications. *Armed Forces and Society* 21(2): 237–254.

(1997) *Between the Sword and the Scroll: Dilemmas of Religion and Military Service in Israel*. Amsterdam: Harwood.

(2007) The Quest for a Corpus of Jewish Military Ethics in Modern Israel. *Journal of Israeli History: Politics, Society, Culture* 26(1): 35–66.

(2008) *Israel and Its Army: From Cohesion to Confusion*. Oxford: Routledge.

(2013) *Divine Service? Judaism and Israel's Armed Forces*. Ashgate: Berghahn Books.

Coker C. (2001) *Humane Warfare*. London: Routledge.

(2008) *Ethics and War in the 21st Century*. Oxford: Routledge.

(2013) *Warrior Geeks: How 21st Century Technology Is Changing the Way We Fight and Think about War*. London: Hurst.

Collins J. (2012) *Global Palestine*. London: Hurst.

Conway D. (2012) *Masculinities, Militarisation, and the End Conscription Campaign: War Resistance in Apartheid South Africa*. Manchester: Manchester University Press.

Cook M. (2004) *The Moral Warrior: Ethics and Service in the U.S Military*. Albany, NY: State University of New York Press.

Cook M. and Syse H. (2010) What Should We Mean by 'Military Ethics'? *Journal of Military Ethics* 9(2): 119–22.

Cowen D. (2008) *Military Workfare: The Soldier and Social Citizenship in Canada*. Toronto: University of Toronto Press.

Curiel I. (2016) Amos Oz Presents Prize to Breaking the Silence. Ynet News, 7th November. Available from: www.ynetnews.com/articles/ 0,7340,L-4875815,00.html (accessed 4 January 2017).

Dalsheim J. (2011) *Unsettling Gaza: Secular Liberalism, Radical Religion, and the Israeli Settlement Project*. Oxford: Oxford University Press.

David A. (2013) Civil-Military Relations in Israel: The Debate and the Missing Link. *Theory and Criticism*, 41: 326–40 [Hebrew].

Davidi D. (2004) The Influence of the Tactical Command College on Officers and Training in the IDF. *Ma'arachot* 396: 32–5 [Hebrew].

Dean M. (2010) *Governmentality: Power and Rule in Modern Society*. Second edition. London: Sage.

Dean J. (2012) *The Communist Horizon*. London: Verso.

Der Derian J. (2009) *Virtuous War: Mapping the Military-Industrial-Entertainment Network*. Oxford: Routledge.

Dillon M. and Neal A. (2008) *Foucault on Politics, Security, and War*. London: Palgrave.

Douzinas C. (2003) Humanity, Military Humanism and the New Moral Order. *Economy and Society* 32(2): 159–83.

Duncanson C. (2009) Forces for Good? Narratives of Military Masculinity in Peacekeeping Operations. *International Feminist Journal of Politics* 11(1): 63–80.

(2015) Hegemonic Masculinity and the Possibility of Change in Gender Relations. *Men and Masculinities* 18(2): 231–48.

Edkins J. (1999) *Poststructuralism and International Relations: Bringing the Political Back In*. London: Lynne Rienner.

Education Ministry (2012) Mekhinot Kdam Tzva'iyot [on file with the author, Hebrew].

Elshtain J. (1995) *Women and War*. Second edition. Chicago, IL: University of Chicago Press.

Enloe C. (1993) *The Morning After: Sexual Politics at the End of the Cold War*. Oakland, CA: University of California Press.

    (2000) *Maneuvres: The International Politics of Militarising Women's Lives*. Berkeley, CA: University of California Press.

    (2007) *Globalization and Militarism: Feminists Make the Link*. Lanham, MD: Rowman and Littlefield.

Erlanger S. (2011) By His Own Reckoning, One Man Made Libya a French Cause. *New York Times*, 1st April. Available from: www.nytimes.com/2011/04/02/world/africa/02levy.html.

Evans B. (2010) Foucault's Legacy: Security, War, and Violence in the 21st century. *Security Dialogue* 41(4): 413–33.

Evenshpenger N. (2011) The Mekhinot under Examination. *Ma'arachot* 336 [Hebrew]: 62–9.

Even-Tzur E. (2011) *Truth, Guilt and Responsibility in Testimony: Psychological and Ethical Aspects of Giving Witness Accounts of Immoral Acts Performed by Israeli Soldiers during Military Service in the Occupied Territories*. MA Thesis, Jerusalem: Hebrew University of Jerusalem [Hebrew].

Fanon F. (2001) *The Wretched of the Earth*. London: Penguin.

Fassin D. (2011) *Humanitarian Reason: A Moral History of the Present Times*. Oakland, CA: University of California Press.

    (ed.) (2012) *A Companion to Moral Anthropology*. Oxford: Blackwell.

    (2014) The Ethical Turn in Anthropology: Promises and Uncertainties. *Journal of Ethnographic Theory* 4(1): 429–35.

Faubion J. (2012) *An Anthropology of Ethics*. Cambridge: Cambridge University Press.

Fink B. (1996) *The Lacanian Subject: Between Language and Jouissance*. Princeton, NJ: Princeton University Press.

Foucault M. (1998a) *The History of Sexuality, Volume I: The Will to Know*. London: Penguin.

    (1998b) *The History of Sexuality, Volume II: The Use of Pleasure*. London: Penguin.

    (2000a) On the Genealogy of Ethics: An Overview of Work in Progress. In Rabinow P. (ed.), *Essential Works of Foucault, 1954–1984, Volume 1: Ethics*, London: Penguin.

(2000b) Self Writing. In Rabinow P. (ed.), *Essential Works of Foucault, 1954–1984, Volume 1: Ethics*, London: Penguin.

(2000c) Technologies of the Self. In Rabinow P. (ed.), *Essential Works of Foucault, 1954–1984, Volume 1: Ethics*, London: Penguin.

(2000d) The Ethics of the Concern for the Self as a Practice of Freedom. In Rabinow P. (ed.), *Essential Works of Foucault, 1954–1984, Volume 1: Ethics*, London: Penguin.

(2002a) The Political Technology of Individuals. In: Faubion J. (ed.), *Essential Works of Michel Foucault, 1954–1984, Volume 3: Power*, London: Penguin.

(2002b) The Subject and Power. In: Faubion J. (ed.), *Essential Works of Michel Foucault, 1954–1984, Volume 3: Power*, London: Penguin.

(2004) *Society Must Be Defended*. London: Penguin.

(2005) *The Hermeneutics of the Subject: Lectures at the College de France, 1981–1982*. London: Picador.

(2008a) *Security, Territory, Population: Lectures at the College de France, 1977–1978*. London: Palgrave.

(2008b) *The Birth of Biopolitics: Lectures at the College de France, 1978–79*. London: Palgrave.

(2010) *The Government of Self and Others: Lectures at the College de France, 1982–1983*. London: Palgrave.

(2012) *The Courage of Truth: Lectures at the College de France, 1983–1984*. London: Palgrave.

(2014) *Wrong-Doing, Truth-Telling: The Function of Avowal in Justice*. Chicago, IL: University of Chicago Press.

Freud S. (2001) Mourning and Melancholia. In Strachey J. (ed. and trans.), *The Standard Edition of the Complete Psychological Works of Sigmund Freud*, Volume XIV, London: Vintage.

Friends of the IDF (2012) Friends of the IDF – Identity and Purpose. Available from: www.youtube.com/watch?v=fY3GhARHo24 (accessed 5 March 2014).

Gonzáles R. (2007) Towards Mercenary Anthropology? The New US Army Counterinsurgency Manual FM 3–24 and the Military-Anthropology Complex. *Anthropology Today* 23(3): 14–19.

Gordon N. (2008) *Israel's Occupation*. Berkeley, CA: University of California Press.

(2010) Israel's Emergence as a Homeland Security Capital. In: Zureik E. (ed.), *Surveillance and Control in Israel/Palestine: Population, Territory, and Power*, New York: Routledge.

Graham S. (2010a) *Cities under Siege: The New Military Urbanism*. London: Verso.

(2010b) Laboratories of War: Surveillance and US-Israeli Collaboration in War and Security. In: Zureik E., Lyon D., and Abu-Laban Y. (eds), *Surveillance and Control in Israel/Palestine: Population, Territory, and Power*, London: Routledge.

Grassiani E. (2013) *Solidering under Occupation: Processes of Numbing among Israel Soldiers in the Al-Aqsa Intifada*. Oxford: Berghahn Books.

Greenberg H. (2009) Military: Case on Soldiers' Testimonies Closed. *Ynet News*, 30th March. Available from: www.ynetnews.com/articles/0,7340,L-3694616,00.html (accessed 29 April 2014).

Gregory D. (2004) *The Colonial Present: Afghanistan, Palestine, Iraq*. Oxford: Blackwell.

(2008) The Rush to the Intimate: Counterinsurgency and the Cultural Turn. *Radical Philosophy* 150: 8–23.

Guiora A. (2006) Teaching Morality in Armed Conflict: The Israel Defence Forces Model. *Jewish Political Studies Review* 18(1–2).

Ha'aretz (2009) The Legend of Ambushed Palmach Squad '35'. 27th April. Available from: www.haaretz.com/the-legend-of-ambushed-palmach-squad-35-1.274876.

(2015) Israeli Soldiers May Have Killed Comrade to Prevent His Abduction During Gaza War. 8th July. Available from: www.haaretz.com/israel-news/.premium-1.665021.

Hajjar L. (2006) International Humanitarian Law and 'Wars on Terror': A Comparative Analysis of Israeli and American Doctrines and Policies. *Journal of Palestine Studies* 36(1): 21–42.

Halbertal M. (2009) The Goldstone Illusion. *The New Republic*, 6th November.

(2013) Moral Challenges in Asymmetric Warfare. *Mishpat ve'asakim* [on file with the author, Hebrew].

Halper J. (2010) *The Second Battle of Gaza: Israel's Undermining of International Law*. Monthly Review Online, 26th February. Available from: https://mronline.org/2010/02/26/the-second-battle-of-gaza-israels-undermining-of-international-law/.

(2014) Globalising Gaza: How Israel Undermines International Law Through 'Lawfare'. *Counterpunch*, 18th August. Available from: https://www.counterpunch.org/2014/08/18/globalizing-gaza/.

(2015) *War Against the People: Israel, the Palestinians, and Global Pacification*. Chicago, IL: University of Chicago Press.

Hammerman I. and Rosen R. (eds) (2002) *Poets Will Not Write Poetry: In Uniform in the Land of Ishmael. Stories and Documents*. Tel Aviv: Am Oved [Hebrew].

Handelman D. and Shamgar-Handelman L. (1997) The Presence of Absence: The Memorialisation of National Death in Israel. In: Ben-Ari E. and Bilu Y. (eds), *Grasping Land: Space and Place in Contemporary Israeli Discourse and Experience*, Albany, NY: State University of New York Press.

Hanieh A. (2006) The Politics of Curfew in the Occupied Territories. In: Beinin J. and Stein R. (eds), *The Struggle for Sovereignty: Palestine and Israel, 1993–2005*, Stanford, CA: Stanford Univeristy Press.

Harel A. (2009a) Authors of IDF Ethics Code Demand Gaza War Probe. *Ha'aretz*, 9th November.

(2009b) IDF Killed Civilians in Gaza under Loose Rules of Engagement. *Ha'aretz*, 19th March.

(2009c) IDF Rabbinate Publication during Gaza War: We Will Show No Mercy on the Cruel. *Ha'aretz*, 26th January.

(2009d) The Philosopher Who Gave the IDF Moral Justification in Gaza. Ha'aretz, 6th February.

(2013) *Tada col im ivriya*. Kinneret: Zmora-Bitan Dvir [Hebrew].

Harel A. and Cohen G. (2016) Court to Decide if Israel Can Force Breaking the Silence to Reveal Its Sources. *Ha'aretz*, 18th May. Available from: www.haaretz.com/israel-news/.premium-1.720135 (accessed 4 January 2017).

Hauser T. (1997) The Spirit of the IDF. *Azure Magazine*.

Helman S. (1997) Militarism and the Construction of Community. *Journal of Political and Military Sociology* 25(2): 305–22.

Higate P. (2012) The Private Militarised and Security Contractor as Geocorporeal Actor. *International Political Sociology* 6(4): 355–72.

Hirschkind C. (2006) *The Ethical Soundscape: Cassette Sermons and Islamic Counterpublics*. New York: Columbia University Press.

Howell A. (2015) Resilience, War, and Austerity: The Ethics of Military Human Enhancement and the Politics of Data. *Secuirty Dialogue* 46(1): 15–31.

Human Rights Watch (2009a) *Precisely Wrong: Gaza Civilians Killed by Israeli Drone-Launched Missiles*. Available from: https://www.hrw.org/report/2009/06/30/precisely-wrong/gaza-civilians-killed-israeli-drone-launched-missiles

(2009b) *White Flag Deaths: Killings of Palestinian Civilians during Operation Cast Lead*. Available from: https://www.hrw.org/sites/default/files/reports/ioptwf0809webwcover_1.pdf

(2010) '*I Lost Everything': Israel's Unlawful Destruction of Property During Operation Cast Lead*. Available from: https://www.hrw.org/report/2010/05/13/i-lost-everything/israels-unlawful-destruction-property-during-operation-cast-lead

Hutchings K. (2007a) Feminist Ethics and Political Violence. *International Politics* 44: 90–106.

(2007b) Simone de Beauvoir and the Ambiguous Ethics of Political Violence. *Hypatia* 22(3): 111–32.

(2008) Making Sense of Masculinity and War. *Men and Masculinities* 10(4): 389–404.

(2010) *Global Ethics: An Introduction*. London: Polity.

Hyzagi J. (2015) Why Does Everyone Hate Bernard Henri-Lévy? *Observer*, 1st May. Available from: http://observer.com/2015/05/why-does-everyone-hate-bernard-henri-levy/.

Im Tirtzu (2015) The Foreign Agents – Revealed! Available from: www.youtube.com/watch?v=02u_J2C-Lso (accessed 4 January 2017).

International Committee of the Red Cross (1977) Protocol Additional to the Geneva Conventions of 12 August 1949, and Relating to the Protection of Victims of International Armed Conflicts (Protocol I). Available from: www.refworld.org/docid/3ae6b36b4.html (accessed 19 May 2015).

Israeli Ministry of Foreign Affairs (2014) PM Netanyahu Addresses the UN General Assembly. Available from: http://mfa.gov.il/MFA/PressRoom/2014/Pages/PM-Netanyahu-addresses-the-UN-General-Assembly-29-Sep-2014.aspx (accessed 5 January 2017).

Israeli State Comptroller (2011) 67th Annual Report [Hebrew]. Available from: http://www.mevaker.gov.il/he/Reports/Report_117/7c1440fc-4930-4bb6-a6f9-afe37e097ad5/7645.pdf

Jerusalem Post (2011) The Moralist. 22nd April. Available from: www.jpost.com/Opinion/Columnists/Editors-Notes-The-moralist.

(2013) Over 3000 High School Students to Begin Army Programmes. 29th October. Available from: www.jpost.com/National-News/Over-3000-high-school-graduates-to-begin-pre-army-programs-324707 (accessed 15 April 2014).

Joint Council of Mekhinot (n.d.) About the Joint Council of Mekhinot. Available from: http://mechinot.org.il/english/about/ (accessed 10 February 2016).

Joint Council of Mekhinot (2016) Newsletter 83. Available from: http://mechinot.org.il/%D7%93%D7%A3-%D7%A2%D7%93%D7%9B%D7%95%D7%9F-83-14-12-16-%D7%91-%D7%91%D7%98%D7%91%D7%AA-%D7%AA%D7%A9%D7%A2%D7%95-%D7%A9%D7%91%D7%95%D7%A2-%D7%98%D7%95%D7%91/ (accessed 4 January 2017).

Jones C. (2015) Frames of Law: Targeting Advice and Operational Law in the Israeli military. *Environment and Planning D: Society and Space* 33: 676–96.

Joronen M. (2015) 'Death Comes Knocking on the Roof': Thanatopolitics of Ethical Killing during Operation Protective Edge in Gaza. *Antipode* 48(2): 336–54.

Kasher A. (1996) *Military Ethics*. Tel Aviv: HaUniversita HaMeshuderet, Israel Ministry of Defence [Hebrew].

(2002a) Between Obedience and Discipline: Between Law and Ethics. *Professional Ethics* 10(2-3-4): 97–122.

(2002b) The Spirit of the IDF and Love of the Land. *Ma'arachot* 382: 72–78 [Hebrew].

(2005) Professional Ethics and Collective Professional Autonomy: A Conceptual Analysis. *Ethical Perspectives: Journal of the European Ethics Network* 11(1): 67–98.

(2009) Operation Cast Lead and Just War Theory. *Azure Magazine*.

(2010) Reply to Daniel Statman. *Azure Magazine* [Hebrew].

(2014) The Ethics of Protective Edge. *Jewish Review of Books*.

Kasher A. and Yadlin A. (2005) Military Ethics of Fighting Terror: An Israeli Perspective. *Journal of Military Ethics* 4(1): 3–32.

(2009) Israel and the Rules of War: An Exchange. *New York Review of Books*, 11th June.

Kashti O. (2015) Education Minister Bennett Bars Breaking the Silence from Schools. *Ha'aretz*, 15th December. Available from: www.haaretz.com/israel-news/.premium-1.692042 (accessed 4 January 2017).

(2016) Ben-Gurion University Slammed for Nixing Breaking the Silence's Prize. *Ha'aretz*, 5th July. Available from: www.haaretz.com/israel-news/.premium-1.729110 (accessed 4 January 2017).

Katriel T. (1986) *Talking Straight: Dugri Speech in Israeli Sabra Culture.* Cambridge: Cambridge University Press.

Kaufman A. (2010) Forgetting the Lebanon War? On Silence, Denial and the Selective Remembrance of the 'First' Lebanon War. In: Ben-Ze'ev E., Ginio R., and Winter J. (eds), *Shadows of War: A Social History of Silence in the Twentieth Century*, Cambridge: Cambridge University Press.

Khalili L. (2007) *Heroes and Martyrs of Palestine: The Politics of National Commemoration.* Cambridge: Cambridge University Press.

(2010) The Location of Palestine in Global Counterinsurgencies. *International Journal of Middle East Studies* 42(3): 413–33.

(2011) Gendered Practices of Counterinsurgency. *Review of International Studies* 37(4): 1471–91.

(2013) *Time in the Shadows: Confinement in Counterinsurgencies.* Stanford, CA: Stanford Univeristy Press.

(2014) The Uses of Happiness in Counterinsurgencies. *Social Text* 32(1): 23–43.

Kimmerling B. (1993) Patterns of Militarism in Israel. *European Journal of Sociology* 34(2): 196–223.

(2005) *The Invention and Decline of Israeliness: State, Society, and the Military.* Berkeley, CA: University of California Press.

Kinsella H. (2011) *The Image before the Weapon: A Critical History of the Distinction between Combatant and Civilian.* Ithaca, NY: Cornell University Press.

Knesset (2008) The Law for Pre-military Academies. Available from: http://mechinot.org.il//wp-content/uploads/2014/10/mechinot_law.pdf.

Lacan J. (2004) *Seminar XI: The Four Fundamental Concepts of Psychoanalysis.* London: Karnac.

(2007a) *Ecrits: The First Complete Edition in English*. New York: W. W. Norton.

(2007b) *The Ethics of Psychoanalysis*. London: Routledge.

Laidlaw J. (2013) *The Subject of Virtue: An Anthropology of Ethics and Freedom*. Cambridge: Cambridge University Press.

Landy D. (2008) Authenticity and Political Agency on Study Trips to Palestine. In: Lentin R. (ed.), *Thinking Palestine*, London: Zed Books.

Lebel U. (2013) Post-modern or Conservative? Competing Communities over Military Doctrine. Israeli National-Religious Soldiers as (Counter) Strategic Agents. In: Karakatsanis N. and Swarz J. (eds), *Political and Military Sociology: An Annual Review*, Volume 40, Oxford: Routledge.

Levy Y. (2007) *Israel's Materialist Militarism*. Lanham, MD: Lexington Books.

(2009) The Second Lebanon War: Coping with the 'Gap of Legitimacies' Syndrome. *Israel Studies Forum* 24(1): 3–24.

(2012) *Israel's Death Hierarchy: Casualty Aversion in a Militarised Democracy*. New York: New York University Press.

(2014) The Theocratisation of the Israeli Military: A Structural Analysis. *Armed Forces and Society* 40(2): 269–94.

Levy Y., Lomsky-Feder E. and Harel N. (2007) From 'Obligatory Militarism' to 'Contractual Militarism' – Competing Models of Citizenship'. *Israel Studies* 12(1): 127–48.

Libel T. (2010) Teaching Citizens to Be Professional Soldiers: IDF Responses and Their Implications. In: Cohen S. (ed.), *The New Citizen Armies: Israel's Armed Forces in Comparative Perspective*, Oxford: Routledge.

(2013) From the People's Army to the Jewish People's Army: The IDF's Force Structure between Professionalisation and Militarisation. *Defence and Security Analysis* 29(4): 280–92.

(2014) Constructing the Ideal Officer: Israeli Society and the IDF Officer School. In: Rosman-Stollman E. and Kampinsky A. (eds), *Civil-Military Relations in Israel: Essays in Honor of Stuart A. Cohen*, Lanham, MD: Lexington Books.

Linn R. (1991) Holocaust Metaphors and Symbols in the Moral Dilemmas of Contemporary Israeli Soldiers. *Methaphor and Symbolic Activity* 6(2): 61–86.

Lis J. (2016) Despite Global Criticism, Israel Approves Contentious 'NGO Law'. *Ha'aretz*, 11th July. Available from: www.haaretz.com/israel-news/1.730324 (accessed 4 January 2017).

Lisle D. (2000) Consuming Danger: Re-Imagining the War/Tourism Divide. *Alternatives: Global, Local, Political* 25(1): 91–116.

Luzzatto M.H. (1966) *The Path of the Upright*. Philadelphia, PA: The Jewish Publication Society of America.

Mahmood S. (2005) *The Politics of Piety: The Islamic Revival and the Feminist Subject.* Princeton, NJ: Princeton University Press.

Makor Rishon Dyokan Magazine (2006) Building Jewish Identity: Prof. Benjamin Ish-Shalom and Former Chief of Staff Moshe Ya'alon Join Forces to Combat Israel's Identity Crisis. Available from: www.bmj .org.il/userfiles/articles/Building%20Jewish%20Identity%20-%20 Yaalon%20&%20Ish-Shalom.pdf (accessed 30 January 2014).

Maman D., Ben-Ari E. and Rosenhek Z. (eds) (2001) *Military, State and Society in Israel: Theoretical and Comparative Perspectives.* New Brunswick: Transaction Publishers.

Mann M. (1987) The Roots and Contradictions of Modern Militarism. *New Left Review* 162: 35–50.

Mao Z. (2000) On Guerilla Warfare. www.marxists.org.

Marteu E. (2009) *Civil Organisations and Protest Movements in Israel: Mobilisation Around the Israeli-Palesinian Conflict.* Oxford: Routledge.

Matar A. (2006) What Makes Asa Kasher Possible? *Mitaam: A Review of Literature and Radical Thought*, 3: 1–16 [Hebrew].

McSorley K. (2013) *War and the Body: Militarisation, Practice, and Experience.* Oxford: Routledge.

Mendelsohn-Maoz A. (2011) Hurled into the Heart of Darkness: Moral Luck and the Hebrew Literature of the Intifada. *Hebrew Studies* 52: 315–39.

Morag R. (2013) *Waltzing with Bashir: Perpetrator Trauma and Cinema.* London: IB Tauris.

Morris B. (2004) *The Birth of the Palestinian Refugee Problem Revisited.* Cambridge: Cambridge University Press.

Morton S. and Bygrave S. (eds) (2008) *Foucault in an Age of Terror: Essays on Biopolitics and the Defence of Society.* London: Palgrave.

Natanel K. (2016) *Sustaining Conflict: Apathy and Domination in Israel-Palestine.* Oakland: University of California Press.

Near H. (ed.) (1970) *The Seventh Day: Soldiers Talk about the Six Day War.* London: Penguin.

Newman M. (2015) Ya'alon Bans Breaking the Silence NGO from Engaging Soldiers. *Times of Israel*, 14th December. Available from: www.timesofisrael.com/yaalon-bans-breaking-the-silence-ngo-from-engaging-soldiers/ (accessed 4 January 2017).

Novak Y. (2014a) The Occupation Has Entered the Officers' School. *Walla! News*, 7th December [Hebrew].

(2014b) When I Served, the Israeli Military Was the Most Moral in the World. No More. *The Guardian*, 28th July. Available from: www .theguardian.com/commentisfree/2014/jul/28/israeli-military-most-moral-no-more-outrage-indifference (accessed 17 September 2014).

(2016) Proud to Be Outside the Consensus, until the Occupation Ends. *+972 Magazine*, 7th November. Available from: https://972mag.com/proud-to-be-outside-the-consensus-until-the-occupation-ends/123033/ (accessed 4 January 2017).

Ophir A., Givoni M. and Hanafi S. (eds) (2009) *The Power of Inclusive Exclusion: Anatomy of Israeli Rule in the Occupied Territories*. New York: Zone Books.

Owens P. (2003) Accidents Don't Just Happen: The Liberal Politics of High-Technology 'Humanitarian' War. *Millennium: Journal of International Studies* 32(3): 595–616.

(2010) The Ethics of War: Critical Alternatives. In: Bell D. (ed.), *Ethics and World Politics*, Oxford: Oxford University Press.

Peri Y. (1996a) Afterword. In: *The Rabin Memoirs*, Berkeley, CA: University of California Press.

(1996b) The Radical Social Scientists and Israeli Militarism. *Israel Studies* 1(2): 230–66.

Perugini N. and Gordon N. (2015) *The Human Right to Dominate*. Oxford: Oxford University Press.

Physicians for Human Rights (2015) *Gaza 2014: Findings of an Independent Medical Fact-Finding Mission*. Available from: http://cdn2.phr.org.il/wp-content/uploads/2017/02/PHRI_Report_Gaza-2014.pdf.

Piterberg G. (2007) *The Returns of Zionism: Myth, Politics, and Scholarship in Israel*. London: Verso.

Rabin Academy (2009) Protocols of the Siah Lohamim of Graduates of Rabin Academy Following Operation Cast Lead. Available from: www.news1.co.il/uploadFiles/384121119976044.pdf (accessed 28 April 2014) [Hebrew].

Rabin Y. (1994) Nobel Lecture. Available from: www.nobelprize.org/nobel_prizes/peace/laureates/1994/rabin-lecture.html (accessed 20 May 2015).

Rancière J. (2006) The Ethical Turn of Aesthetics and Politics. *Critical Horizons: A Journal of Philosophy and Social Theory* 7(1): 1–15.

Raviv A. (2004) The Educational Outlook on Military Ethics in IDF Colleges. *Ma'arachot* 396: 53–55 [Hebrew].

Reid J. (2006) *The Biopolitics of the War on Terror*. Manchester: Manchester University Press.

Reid J. and Dillon M. (2009) *The Liberal Way of War: Killing to Make Life Live*. Oxford: Routledge.

Robinson P., De Lee N. and Carrick D. (eds) (2008) *Ethics Education in the Military*. Aldershot: Ashgate.

Rodin D. (2006) The Ethics of War: State of the Art. *Journal of Applied Philosophy* 23(3): 241–246.

Ron J. (2003) *Frontiers and Ghettos: State Violence in Serbia and Israel*. Berkeley, CA: University of California Press.

Rose N. (1995) Governing Advanced Liberal Democracies. In: Barry A., Osborne T., and Rose N. (eds), *Foucault and Political Reason: Liberalism, Neo-Liberalism, and Rationalities of Government*, Chicago, IL: University of Chicago Press.

(1999) *Powers of Freedom: Reframing Political Thought*. Cambridge: Cambridge University Press.

Rosman-Stollman E. (2014) *For God and Country? Religious Student-Soldiers in the Israel Defence Forces*. Austin, TX: University of Texas Press.

Sagi A. (2011) The Spirit of the IDF Ethics Code and the Investigation of Operation Cast Lead. *Shalom Hartman Institute Blog*. Available from: http://hartman.org.il/Blogs_View.asp?Article_Id=401&Cat_Id=275&Cat_Type=Blogs.

Sasson-Levy O. (2002) Military, Masculinity, and Citizenship: Tensions and Contradictions in the Experience of Blue-Collar Soldiers. *Identities: Global Studies in Culture and Power* 10(3): 319–45.

(2003a) Constructing Identities at the Margins: Masculinities and Citizenship in the Israeli Army. *The Sociological Quarterly* 43(3): 357–83.

(2003b) Feminism and Military Gender Practices: Israeli Women Soldiers in 'Masculine' Roles. *Sociological Inquiry* 73(3): 440–65.

(2008) Individual Bodies, Collective State Interests: The Case of Israel Combat Soldiers. *Men and Masculinities* 10(3): 296–321.

Sasson-Levy O. and Levy G. (2008) Militarised Socialisation, Military Service, and Class Reproduction: The Experiences of Israeli Soldiers. *Sociological Perspectives* 51(2): 349–74.

Sasson-Levy O., Levy Y. and Lomsky-Feder E. (2011) Women Breaking the Silence: Military Service, Gender, and Anti-war Protest. *Gender and Society* 25(6): 740–763.

Scanlon T. (2008) The Proper Role of Intention in Military Decision Making. In: Wertheimer R. (ed.), *Empowering Our Military Conscience: Transforming Just War Theory and Military Moral Education*, Farnham: Ashgate.

Schwarz E. (2013) *The Biopolitical Condition: Re-Thinking the Ethics of Political Violence in Life-Politics*. PhD Thesis, London: London School of Economics and Political Science.

(2015) Prescription Drones: On the Techno-Biopolitics Regimes of Contemporary 'Ethical Killing'. *Security Dialogue* 47(1): 59–75.

Segal L. (2008) Gender, War and Militarism: Making and Questioning the Links. *Feminist Review* 88: 21–35.

Segev T. (1993) *The Seventh Million: Israel and the Holocaust*. New York: Owl Books.

Shalom Hartman Institute (2012) Lev Aharon Programme for Senior IDF Officers Brochure. Available from: http://hartman.org.il/Fck_Uploads/file/Lev%20Aharon%20brochure%20-%20for%20site.pdf (accessed 28 January 2014).

Shapira A. (ed.) (1968) *Siaḥ Loḥamim: Pirqei haqshavah ve-hitbonenut.* Tel Aviv: Haverim Tse'irim mehaTnuah haKibutsit [Hebrew].

Shavit N. and Katriel T. (2011) Between Moral Activism and Archival Memory: The Testimonial Project of 'Breaking the Silence'. In: Neiger M., Meyers O., and Zandberg E. (eds), *On Media Memory*, London: Palgrave Macmillan.

(2013) Speaking Out: Testimonial Rhetoric in Israeli Soldiers' Dissent. *Versus: Quaderni di Studi Semiotici* 116: 79–103.

Shaw M. (1991) *Post-military Society: Militarism, Demilitarisation, and War at the End of the Twentieth Century.* Philadelphia, PA: Temple University Press.

(2002) Risk-Transfer Militarism, Small Massacres, and the Historical Legitimacy of War. *International Relations* 16(3): 343–59.

(2013) Twenty-first Century Militarism: A Historical-Sociological Framework. In: Stavrianakis A. and Selby J. (eds), *Militarism and International Relations: Political Economy, Security, Theory*, Oxford: Routledge.

Sherman N. (2007) *Stoic Warriors: The Ancient Philosophers behind the Military Mind.* Oxford: Oxford University Press.

Shpigel N. (2016) Defense Minsiter Ya'alon: Breaking the Silence Is Gathering Military Secrets – That's Treason. *Ha'aretz*, 21st March. Available from: www.haaretz.com/israel-news/.premium-1.710073 (accessed 4 January 2017).

Shulman D. (2016) Israel: The Broken Silence. *New York Review of Books.* Available from: www.nybooks.com/articles/2016/04/07/israel-the-broken-silence/#fnr-1.

Sjoberg L. (2006) *Gender and the Wars in Iraq: A Feminist Re-Formulation of Just War Theory.* Lanham, MD: Rowman and Littlefield.

Sjoberg L. and Via S. (eds) (2010) *Gender, War, and Militarism: Feminist Perspectives.* Santa Barbara,CA: Praeger.

Statman D. (2010) The Morality of Warfare and Operation Cast Lead. *Azure Magazine* [Hebrew].

Stavrianakis A. (2006) Call to Arms: The University as a Site of Militarised Capitalism and a Site of Struggle. *Millennium: Journal of International Studies* 35(1): 139–54.

Stavrianakis A. and Selby J. (2013) Militarism and International Relations in the 21st Century. In: Stavrianakis A. and Selby J. (eds), *Militarism and International Relations: Political Economy, Security, Theory*, Oxford: Routledge.

Stern E. (2012) *Struggling over Israel's Soul: An IDF General Speaks of His Controversial Moral Decisions.* New York: Gefen.

Stop the Incitement Against the President and Human Rights Organisations (2015). Available from: www.atzuma.co.il/wwwshovrimshtik (accessed 4 January 2017).

Turkel Commission (2013) *Israel's Mechanisms for Examining and Investigating Complaints and Claims of Violations of the Laws of Armed Conflict According to International Law.*

UNHRC (2009) *Report of the United Nations Fact-Finding Mission on the Gaza Conflict.* Geneva: UNHRC.

(2015) *Report of the Detailed Findings of the Independent Commission of Inquiry Established Pursuant to Human Rights Council Resolution S-21/1.* Geneva: UNHRC.

Vagts A. (1959) *A History of Militarism: Civilian and Military.* Second edition. New York: Meridian Books.

Van Baarda T.A. and Verweij D.E.M. (2009) *The Moral Dimensions of Asymmetrical Warfare: Counter-Terrorism, Democratic Values, and Military Ethics.* Leiden: Brill.

Vásquez-Arroyo A. (2016) *Political Responsibility: Responding to Predicaments of Powers.* New York: Columbia University Press.

Vighi F. and Feldner H. (2007) Ideology Critique or Discourse Analysis? Žižek against Foucault. *European Journal of Political Theory* 6(2): 141–159.

Walla! News (2012) Soldiers Will Train in Ethical Dilemmas with the Help of Theatre. 17th December, Available from: http://news.walla.co.il-/?w=/2689/2597253 (accessed 28 February 2014) [Hebrew].

Walzer M. (1977) *Just and Unjust Wars.* New York: Basic Books.

Weiss M. (2002) *The Chosen Body: The Politics of the Body in Israeli Society.* Stanford, CA: Stanford Univeristy Press.

Weizman E. (2007) *Hollow Land: Israel's Architecture of Occupation.* London: Verso.

(2009) Thanato-Tactics. In: Ophir A., Givoni M., and Hanafi S. (eds), *The Power of Inclusive Exclusion: Anatomy of Israeli Rule in the Occupied Palestinian Territories,* New York: Zone Books.

(2010) Legislative Attack. *Theory, Culture, Society* 27(11): 11–32.

(2012) *The Least of All Possible Evils.* London: Verso.

Wertheimer R. (ed.) (2008) *Empowering Our Military Conscience: Transforming Just War Theory and Military Moral Education.* Farnham: Ashgate.

Wolfendale J. (2008) What Is the Point of Teaching Ethics in the Military? In: Robinson P., De Lee N., and Carrick D. (eds), *Ethics Education in the Military,* Aldershot: Ashgate.

Wootliff R. (2016) Bennett Seeks to Legally Bar Breaking the Silence from Schools. *Times of Israel,* 27th December. Available from: www.timesofisrael.com/bennett-seeks-to-legally-bar-breaking-the-silence-from-schools/ (accessed 4 December 2016).

Ya'alon M. (2006) The IDF and the Israeli Spirit. *Azure Magazine* 24.

Yehoshua Y. (2014) New Spirit at Bahad 1: Respecting Religious Cadets But Also Protecting Secular Identity. *Yediot Ahronot,* 24th November [Hebrew].

Yesh Din (2011) *Alleged Investigation: The Failure of Investigations into Offences Committed by IDF Soldiers against Palestinians*. Available from: https://s3-eu-west-1.amazonaws.com/files.yesh-din.org/%D7%9 7%D7%A7%D7%99%D7%A8%D7%94+%D7%9C%D7%9B%D 7%90%D7%95%D7%A8%D7%94/%D7%97%D7%A7%D7%99 %D7%A8%D7%94+%D7%9C%D7%9B%D7%90%D7%95%D7 %A8%D7%94+%D7%94%D7%93%D7%95%D7%97+%D7%94 %D7%9E%D7%9C%D7%90+EN.pdf

(2013) MPCID Investigations into the Circumstances Surrounding the Deaths of Palestinians: Convictions and Penalties. Available from: https://s3-eu-west-1.amazonaws.com/files.yesh-din.org/+%D7%90% D7%95%D7%92%D7%95%D7%A1%D7%98+2013+%D 7%93%D7%A3+%D7%A0%D7%AA%D7%95%D7%A0 %D7%99%D7%9D+%D7%9E%D7%A6%D7%97/ICAP+ Death+cases+investigations+and+indictments_July+2013_ENG.pdf

(2015) Financial Statements as of December 31st 2014. Available from: http://documents.guidestar.org.il/PDF/newfiles/fin/2014/117-99-2015-0094672.pdf (accessed 4 January 2017).

Yiftachel O. (2006) *Ethnocracy: Land and Identity Politics in Israel*. Philadelphia, PA: Penn Press.

Zehfuss M. (2011) Targeting: Precision and the Production of Ethics. *European Journal of International Relations* 17(3): 543–56.

(2012a) Contemporary Western War and the Idea of Humanity. *Environment and Planning D: Society and Space* 30(5): 861–76.

(2012b) Culturally Sensitive War? The Human Terrain System and the Seduction of Ethics, *Security Dialogue* 43(2): 175–90.

Zertal I. (2005) *Israel's Holocaust and the Politics of Nationhood*. Cambridge: Cambridge University Press.

Zerubavel Y. (2006) Patriotic Sacrifice and the Burden of Memory in Israeli Secular National Hebrew Culture. In: Makdisi U. and Silverstein P. (eds), *Memory and Violence in the Middle East and North Africa*, Bloomington, IN: Indiana University Press.

Žižek S. (1991) *Looking Awry: An Introduction to Jacques Lacan through Popular Culture*. Cambridge, MA: MIT Press.

(2000a) De Capo Senza Fine. In: Laclau E., Butler J., and Žižek S. (eds), *Contingency, Hegemony, Universality: Contemporary Dialogues on the Left*, London: Verso.

(2000b) Melancholy and the Act. *Critical Inquiry* 26(4): 657–81.

(2008a) *The Plague of Fantasies*. Second edition. London: Verso.

(2008b) *The Sublime Object of Ideology*. Second edition. London: Verso.

(2008c) *The Ticklish Subject: The Absent Centre of Political Ontology*. Second edition. London: Verso.

(ed.) (2012) *Mapping Ideology*. London: Verso.

Zupančič A. (2006) *Ethics of the Real: Kant and Lacan*. London: Verso.

Index